The
Complete Guide to
Internet
Security

The
Complete Guide to
Internet
Security

Mark S. Merkow, CCP
&
James Breithaupt

AMACOM
American Management Association
New York • Atlanta • Boston • Chicago • Kansas City • San Francisco • Washington, D. C.
Brussels • Mexico City • Tokyo • Toronto

Special discounts on bulk quantities of AMACOM books are
available to corporations, professional associations, and other
organizations. For details, contact Special Sales Department,
AMACOM, a division of American Management Association,
1601 Broadway, New York, NY 10019.
Tel.: 212-903-8316. Fax: 212-903-8083.
Web site: www.amanet.org

This publication is designed to provide accurate and authoritative
information in regard to the subject matter covered. It is sold with the
understanding that the publisher is not engaged in rendering legal, accounting, or other professional service. If legal advice or other expert assistance is required, the services of a competent professional person
should be sought.

Screen shots in this book have not been altered in any way by the
publisher or the author.

Library of Congress Cataloging-in-Publication Data

Merkow, Mark S.
    The complete guide to Internet security / Mark S. Merkow and James
Breithaupt.
       p.   cm.
    ISBN 0-8144-7070-X
    1. Internet (Computer network)—Security measures.   2. Computer
security.   I. Breithaupt, Jim.   II. Title.
TK5105.875.I57 M465   2000
005.8—dc21   00–026634

Printing number

10   9   8   7   6   5   4   3   2   1

Contents

Acknowledgments

FROM MARK MERKOW:

To begin, thanks goes to my co-author, James Briethaupt, for his dedication, hard work, and skillful writing, which has helped to make this book possible in the first place.

As daunting a task as book writing often becomes, being surrounded by highly skilled professionals and friends eased the burden significantly. To that end, I'd like to thank the following individuals for their help, support, patience, and reassurance, which has helped to bring this book into print: David Armes, Michael Barrett, Toby Barrick, Pete Bennett, Bill Blaney, Fred Bishop, Dr. James Dzierzanowski, Allen Forbes, Roger Fox, Stephen Gibbons, Michael Kibbe, Joe Lesko, Sally Meglathery, Harry Pearson, Mona Sana, Jerry Stumper, Isabelle Theisen, and Danny Yong.

To my son, Joshua, and my daughter, Jasmine: My sincere thanks for your courage and support in enduring the endless opportunity costs of living in a household with a writer.

My deepest gratitude goes to my new bride, Amy Merkow, for her tenacity and encouragement toward my writing this book in the wake of several positive life-altering events throughout the last few months.

A hearty thank you goes to Jacquie Flynn of AMACOM for her belief and support throughout this project as it slowly meandered to completion. Thanks are also in order for Mike Sivilli, Associate Editor at AMACOM, for the commitment to excellence that he demonstrated throughout the production process.

To Judy Lopatin, whose thorough proofreading of the work contributed greatly to the final product.

Special thanks goes to my agent, Carole McClendon at

Waterside Production, for her incredible ability to *get things done.*

Thanks also to a cast of countless others who have contributed time, material, and expertise into the production of this book: Tushar Padhiar, Bill Canning, and Kent Kiefer of Ernst & Young, Bruce Schneier of Counterpane Internet Security, 3Com (and the Computer Emergency Response Team for their insights and expertise on the Internet security issues and approaches discussed in Chapter 7), Cisco, Nortel Networks, VeriSign, Shiva Corporation, Intel Corporation, the U.S. National Institute of Standards and Technology (NIST), the U.S. National Security Agency (NSA), RSA Data Security, GTE Cyber Trust, Atalla Corporation, Cryptography Research, CyberCash Inc., Rainbow Technologies, Internet Engineering Task Force (IETF), and the World Wide Web Consortium (W3C).

Finally, I'd like to extend my gratitude to our readers, who are actively making the Internet a safer place to work, live, and play!

FROM JAMES BREITHAUPT:

First of all, I wish to thank my wife, Margaret, for her forbearance and support. I hate to write and I love to write, and she knows it, but she still keeps me around. I also want to acknowledge my children, Bo and Faye, who, along with my wife, Margaret, constitute my universe. My hat is also off to friend and co-author Mark Merkow, who has proven once again that he enjoys editing far, far more than I do, as he nimbly works his way through the intricacies of publishing. Finally, to the editors at AMACOM, who have shown nothing but enthusiasm for our words.

The
Complete Guide to
Internet
Security

1

Building a Foundation for Information Security

In cyberspace, no one hears your screams.

When talking about the incidents that befell them, victims of computer hacker attacks often use the same discourse and manners as the victims of violent crimes and natural disasters. Fear, shock, anger, disbelief, and helplessness are the common themes that are all too often repeated across the globe on an ever increasing frequency. "This is a game for these guys, but for us it was like a tornado came through the building and ripped our lives apart," claimed Eric Paul, vice president of Aye.net, describing an August 1998 security breach of his company's networks.

So what stands between your systems and those intent on causing you harm? Fundamental to all activities that lead to protecting computing resources is security awareness. Belief on your part that "it can never happen to me" is akin to suicide without the concrete plans for where, when, or how you'll carry it out. At least with Russian roulette, the participants are prepared, willing, and just waiting to pay the ultimate price.

Developing these fundamental skills of security awareness requires a sense of paranoia that may be foreign to you. Harnessing this paranoia effectively, however, helps you to recognize the threats you're up against before you expose your company to the world or make a fundamental mistake that you'll later regret. Maintaining a security consciousness places you at a distinct advantage over those who treat computer uses casually or take them for granted. Furthermore, this consciousness often spells the difference between success and disaster.

INFORMATION SECURITY IN CONTEXT

As the world's computers become more interconnected, and as more people and companies rely upon the Global Village to communicate and transact, the more exposed these systems become to break-in attempts and successes. Computer security cannot be guaranteed on any level. Even if a computer were to be buried on a distant planet with no source of power for it to be turned on, and with armed guards watching over the area at all times, someone would probably find a way to connect to that computer and break into its data.

Because disconnected and buried computers don't serve you or your business too well, everyone needs to bite the bullet when connecting his or her systems to the Internet. Understanding the risks of being connected is akin to launching an effective defense against a well-armed and well-prepared enemy. To defend yourself adequately, you need to prepare for anything the offense throws your way. This preparation begins with a comprehensive understanding of the information security umbrella, as illustrated in Figure 1-1.

As Figure 1-1 shows, information security (or infosec) is a discipline that's difficult to put your arms around—much like electronic commerce itself. Each topic within the umbrella can easily fill an entire book, necessitating an encyclopedia for completeness. (To aid you in gaining full understanding of these matters, consult the suggested readings found in Appendix D.) For the purposes here, we treat Internet security as a subset of infosec that provides you with a sufficient high-level understanding of the environment without bogging you down in technical or implementation details. When you've completed this book, you'll not only have the basis for a lifetime of security consciousness, but you'll also know how to focus your search for appropriate solutions to your security concerns.

Internet security draws upon the best practices and experiences from multiple domains within the infosec umbrella but always begins with the nontechnical, human aspects of a security posture, discussed in this chapter and

Figure 1-1. An umbrella of information security.

Chapter 2. Your security posture defines your tolerance for risk and outlines how you plan to protect information and resources within your charge. This posture is documented in standards, guidelines, and procedures that you must instill long before a single program is written or a computer is installed.

Often, the standards related to infosec are dictated by the nature of your business. Retail operators in the United States are governed by the Federal Trade Commission and Department of Commerce, among other groups. U.S. banks are regulated by federal banking standards, U.S. medical device manufacturers or suppliers fall under Federal Drug Administration guidelines, and so on. By selecting the most comprehensive or strict sets of relevant published standards, you're likely to meet the requirements outlined by any applicable sets of standards that are less stringent. For example, if a retailer chooses to adopt Department of Defense standards for controlled access to computer systems (the Orange Book or C2 Criteria), she also meets the requirements dictated by the Better Business Bureau as they apply to computer security.

Because U.S. government standards for infosec (Federal Information Processing Standards, or FIPS) address higher concerns than you're likely to face, these standards make for a great starting point when developing your own standards. You can find the current list of FIPS at *www.itl.nist.gov/fipspubs/*. FIPS are categorized using related groups of standards, shown below.

General Publications (GP)

- Hardware and Software Standards/ Guidelines (HS)
- Databases
- Electronic Data Interchange (EDI)
- Graphics
- Hardware Description Language
- Information Interchange
- Modeling Techniques
- Operating Systems

- Programming Languages
- Software Maintenance
- Validation, Verification, and Testing

Data Standards/Guidelines (DATA)

- Representations and Codes

Computer Security Standards/Guidelines (CS)

- Access Control
- Cryptography
- General Computer Security
- Risk Analysis and Contingency Planning
- Security Labels

Telecommunications Standards (TELECOM)

- Cables and Wiring
- Coding and Character Sets
- Facsimile Equipment
- Grounding and Bonding
- Integrated Services Digital Network
- Modems
- Performance Measurement
- Security
- Telecommunications Administration

Other sources of widely accepted standards for computer security include the International Standards Organization (ISO, at *www.iso.org*), the American National Standards Institute (ANSI, at *www.ansi.org*), and the Internet Engineering Task Force (IETF, at *www.ietf.org*).

Once you've found the infosec standards from which to draw, it's time to build your own policy that applies general principles and guidelines to specific ones that you adopt for running your business.

A SECURITY POLICY THAT SETS THE STAGE FOR SUCCESS

You're faced with many choices when deciding how to protect your computer assets. Some choices are based upon quantifiable trade-offs, but others involve conflicting trade-offs, questions of your organization's strategic directions, and other factors that don't easily lend themselves to quantitative analysis. The security policies you establish are used as the basis for protecting your information and technology resources and for guiding employee behavior regarding those resources. Familiarity with these types of policies will aid managers within your company to address computer security issues that are important to your organization as a whole. Effective policies ultimately result in the development and implementation of better computer security and better protection of your systems and information.

THE FOUR TYPES OF POLICIES

According to the Computer Systems Laboratory (CSL), there are four types of computer security policies:

1. *Program-level policies* are used for creating your computer security program. Management needs program-level policies to help establish such a security program, assign program management responsibilities, state its organizationwide computer security purpose and objectives, and provide a basis for policy compliance. Program-level policies are typically issued by the head of the organization or other senior officials, such as an organization's top management officers. A program-level policy might dictate that e-commerce sales presence is mandated by the board of directors.

2. *Program-framework policies* establish your overall approach to or framework for computer security. Program-framework policies provide an organizationwide direction on broad areas of program implementation. For example, these policies may be issued to assure that everyone addresses contingency planning or risk analysis. Program-framework policies are issued by managers or departments with sufficient authority to direct all organization components on computer security issues. This may be the organi-

zation's management official or the head of the computer security program. One such policy may dictate that all corporate PCs follow DoD guidelines for controlled access.

3. *Issue-specific policies* address specific issues of concern to the organization. Issue-specific policies identify and define the specific areas of concern and state the organization's position or posture. Depending upon the issue and its controversy—as well as its potential impact—issue-specific policies may come from the head of the organization, the top management official, the chief information officer (CIO), or the computer security program manager. One example here might be that all corporate PCs operate using current virus protection software.

4. *System-specific policies* focus on policy issues that management has focused upon for a specific system. System-specific policies state the security objectives of a specific system, define how the system should be operated to achieve the security objectives, and specify how the protections and features of the technology are to be used to support or enforce the security objectives. System-specific policies are normally issued by the manager or owner of the system (which could be a network or application), but they may originate from a high-level official, especially if all impacted departments don't agree with the new policy. An example of this type of policy might mandate that all NT server software be hardened, using a specific configuration.

Tools That Implement Policies: Standards, Guidelines, and Procedures

Because policies are written at a broad level, you also need to develop standards, guidelines, and procedures to provide users, managers, and others with a clear approach to implementing policies and meeting organizational goals. Standards and guidelines specify technologies and methodologies that are used to secure systems. Procedures are yet more detailed steps that must be followed to accomplish particular security-related tasks. Standards, guidelines, and procedures can be disseminated throughout an organization via handbooks, regulations, manuals, or an intranet.

Organizational standards specify the consistent use of specific technologies, parameters, or procedures when these uses will benefit an organization. Standardization of organizationwide identification badges is a typical example, providing ease of employee mobility and automation of entry/exit systems. Standards are normally compulsory within an organization. Meanwhile, guidelines assist users, systems personnel, and others in effectively securing their systems. The nature of guidelines recognizes that systems vary considerably and that imposing new standards is not always achievable, appropriate, or cost-effective. Guidelines are often used to help ensure that specific security measures are not overlooked, even though it's possible to implement standards in more than one way. As for procedures, they normally assist in complying with applicable security policies, standards, and guidelines. They are detailed steps that should be followed by users, system operations personnel, or others to accomplish a particular task (e.g., preparing new user accounts and assigning the appropriate privileges).

Some organizations issue overall computer security manuals, regulations, handbooks, or similar documents. These may mix policy, guidelines, standards, and procedures, since they are closely linked. While manuals and regulations can serve as important tools, they are most useful when they clearly distinguish between policy and its implementation (sometimes a tricky process). This promotes flexibility and cost-effectiveness by offering alternative implementation approaches to achieving policy goals.

Comparing your organization's computer security policies to the types described here can assist you in determining if your policies are comprehensive and appropriate. Let's look at the four types of policies in detail.

Program-Level Policies

Program-level policies establish the computer security program and its basic framework. This high-level policy defines the purpose of the program and its scope within the organization. It also assigns responsibilities for direct program implementation (to the computer security organization), assigns responsibilities to related offices, and addresses compliance issues. A program-level policy should include the components discussed below.

Purpose

This component clearly states the purpose of the program. This includes defining the goals of the computer security program as well as its management structure. Security-related needs, such as integrity, availability, and confidentiality, can form the basis of organizational goals established in the policy. For instance, in an organization responsible for maintaining large mission-critical databases, reduction in errors, data loss, or data corruption might be specifically stressed. In an organization responsible for maintaining confidential personal data (as in most e-commerce systems), the goals might emphasize stronger protection against unauthorized disclosure. A program management structure should be organized to best address the goals of the program and respond to the particular operating and risk environment of the organization. Important issues for the structure of the central computer security program include management and coordination of security-related resources, interaction with diverse communities, and the ability to relay issues of concern to upper management. The policy could also establish operational security offices for major systems, particularly those at high risk or most critical to organizational operations.

Scope

This component specifies which resources (including facilities, hardware, and software), information, and personnel the program covers. Often the program covers all systems and agency personnel, but this is not always the case. In some instances, a policy may name specific assets, such as major sites and large systems. Sometimes tough management decisions arise when defining the scope of a program, such as determining the extent to which the program applies to contractors and outside organizations utilizing or connected to the organization's systems.

Responsibilities

This component addresses the responsibilities of officials and offices throughout the organization, including the role of line managers, applications owners, users, and the information processing or IT (information technology) organization. The policy statement should distinguish between the responsibilities of computer services providers and the managers of applications utilizing the computer services. It can also serve as the basis for establishing employee accountability. Overall, the program-level assignment of responsibilities should cover those activities and personnel who are vital to the implementation and continuity of the computer security policy.

Compliance

This component authorizes and delineates the use of specified penalties and disciplinary actions for individuals who fail to comply with the organization's computer security policies. Since the security policy is a high-level document, penalties for various infractions are normally not detailed here. However, the policy may authorize the creation of compliance structures, which include violations and specific penalties. Infractions and associated penalties are usually defined in issue-specific and system-specific policies. When establishing compliance structures, consider that violations of policy can be unintentional on the part of employees. For example, nonconformance can be the result of a lack of knowledge or training.

Program-Framework Policies

Program-framework policies define the organization's security program elements that form the framework for the computer security program and reflect decisions about priorities for protection, resource allocation, and assignment of responsibilities. Criteria for the types of areas addressed as computer security program elements include:

- Areas for which there is an advantage to the organization by having the issue addressed in a common manner
- Areas that need to be addressed for the entire organization
- Areas for which organizationwide oversight is necessary
- Areas which, through organizationwide implementation, can yield significant economies of scale

The types of areas addressed by a program-framework policy vary within each organization, as does the way in which the policy is expressed. Some organizations issue policy directives, while others issue handbooks that combine policy, regulations, standards, and guidance. (See "Tools That Implement Policies: Standards, Guidelines, and Procedures" earlier in this chapter.) Many organizations issue policy on "key" areas of computer security, such as life-cycle management, contingency planning, and network security. If the policy (and associated standards and guidance) are too rigid, cost-effective implementations and innovation could be adversely impacted.

For an example of a program-framework policy, consider a typical organization policy on contingency planning. An organization may require that all contingency plans categorize criticality of processing according to a standard scale. This assists the organization in preparing a master plan (in the event your physical plant is destroyed) by supporting prioritization across departmental boundaries. Policies in these areas normally apply throughout the organization and are usually independent of technology and the system or application. Program-framework policies may consist of components similar to those contained in program-level policies, but they may be in different formats (organizational handbooks, etc.).

Issue-Specific Policies

Issue-specific policies focus on areas of current relevance and concern to your company. A program-level policy is usually broad enough that it requires little modification over time. Conversely, issue-specific policies require more frequent revision because of changes in technology and related factors. As new technologies develop, some issues diminish in importance while new ones appear. It may be appropriate, for example, to issue a policy on the proper use of a cutting-edge technology, the security vulnerabilities of which are still largely unknown. A useful structure for an issue-specific policy is to break the policy into its basic components:

- Statement of an issue
- Statement of the organization's position
- Statement of applicability
- Definition of roles and responsibilities
- Compliance
- Points of contact
- Other topic areas as needed

Statement of an Issue

This component defines a security issue along with any relevant terms, distinctions, and conditions. For example, an organization might want to develop an issue-specific policy on the use of Internet access, which may define what Internet activities it permits and does not permit. In addition, other distinctions and conditions may need inclusion—for instance, Internet access that's gained using a personal dial-up ISP (Internet service provider) connection from an employee's desktop PC that makes your internal network vulnerable to interlopers when the connection is alive.

Statement of the Organization's Position

This component clearly states an organization's position on the issue. To continue with the example of Internet access, the policy should state what types of sites are prohibited in all or some cases (e.g., porn sites or brokerage sites), whether or not there are further guidelines for approval and use, or whether case-by-case exceptions may be granted, and, if so, by whom and on what basis.

Statement of Applicability

This component clearly states where, how, when, to whom, and to what a particular policy applies. For example, the hypothetical policy on Internet access may apply only to the organization's own on-site resources and employees and not to contractor organizations with offices at other locations. In addition, the policy's applicability to employees traveling among different sites or working at home who require Internet access from multiple sites might require further clarification.

Definition of Roles and Responsibilities

This component assigns roles and responsibilities to the issue. Continuing with the Internet access example, if the policy permits private ISP access given the appropriate approvals, then the approving authority should be identified. The office or department(s) responsible for compliance should also be named.

Compliance

This component gives descriptions of the infractions that are unacceptable and states the corresponding penalties. Penalties must be consistent with organizational personnel policies and practices and need to be coordinated with appropriate officials, offices, and perhaps employee bargaining units.

Points of Contact and Supplementary Information

This component lists the names of the appropriate individuals to contact for further information and lists any applicable standards or guidelines. For some issues, the point of contact might be a line manager; for other issues, it might be a facility manager, technical support person, or system administrator. For yet other issues, the point of contact might be a security program representative. Using the Internet access example, employees need to know whether the point of contact for questions and procedural information would be the immediate superior, a system administrator, or a computer security official.

System-Specific Policies

Program-level policies and issue-specific policies both address policies from a broad level, usually involving the entire organization. System-specific policies, on the other hand, are much more focused since they address only one system. Many security policy decisions apply only at the system level. Examples include:

- Who is allowed to read or modify data in the system
- Under what conditions data can be read or modified
- Whether users are allowed to dial into the computer system from home or while traveling

To develop a comprehensive set of system security policies, use a management process that derives security rules from security goals. Consider using a three-level model for system security policy: (1) security objectives, (2) operational security, and (3) policy implementation.

Security Objectives

First, define your security objectives. While you may begin with an analysis of the need for integrity, availability, and confidentiality, you can't stop there. Security objectives must be more specific, concrete, and well-defined. They should be stated so that it is clear that the objective is achievable. The security objectives should consist of a series of statements to describe meaningful actions about specific resources. These objectives should be based on system functional or mission requirements but should state the security actions to support the requirements.

Operational Security

Next, define the operational policies that list the rules for operating a system. Using data integrity as an example, the operational policy would define authorized and unauthorized modification: who (by job category, by organization placement, or by name) can do what (modify, delete, etc.) to which data (specific fields or records), and under what conditions. Managers need to make decisions in developing this policy since it is unlikely that all security objectives will be fully met, since cost, operational, technical, and other constraints will intervene.

Consider the degree of *granularity* needed for operational security policies. Granularity indicates how specific the policy is with regard to resources or rules. The more granular the policy, the easier it is to enforce it and to detect violations. (This is important, since a policy violation may indicate a security problem.) In addition, the more granular the policy, the easier it is to automate policy enforcement.

Also consider the degree of *formality* you want in documenting the policy. Once again, the more formal the documentation, the easier it is to enforce it and to follow the policy. Formal policy should be published as a distinct policy document, less formal policy may be written in memos, and informal policy may not be written at all. Note that unwritten policy is extremely difficult to follow or enforce. On the other hand, very granular and formal policy at the system level can also be an administrative burden.

In general, good practice suggests a granular, formal statement of the access privileges for a system due to its complexity and importance. If you document access controls policy, the policy is substantially easier to follow and to enforce. Another area that normally requires a granular and formal statement is the assignment of security responsibilities. Other types of computer security documents—such as risk analyses, accreditation statements, or procedural manuals—may be recorded in less formal policy decisions. However, any controversial or uncommon policies may need formal policy statements. Uncommon policies include any areas where the system policy is different (either more or less stringent) from standard organization policy or from normal practice within the organization. They should also contain a statement explaining the reason for deviating from the organization's standard policy.

Policy Implementation

Determine the role technology plays in enforcing or supporting the policy. Security is normally enforced through a combination of technical and traditional management methods. This is especially true in the areas of Internet security, where security devices protect the perimeter of the company's information management systems. While technical means are likely to include the use of access control technology, there are other automated means of enforcing or supporting security policy. For example, technology can be used to block telephone systems users from calling certain numbers. Intrusion detection software can alert systems administrators to suspicious activity and enable them to take action to stop the activity. Personal computers can be configured to prevent booting from a floppy disk.

Automated security enforcement has both advantages and disadvantages. When properly designed, programmed, and installed, a computer system can consistently enforce policy, although no computer can force users to follow all procedures. In addition, deviations from the policy may sometimes be necessary and appropriate. This situation occurs frequently if the security policy is too rigid.

USEFUL HINTS FOR POLICY CREATION

Policies require high visibility to be effective. Visibility aids in the implementation of policy by helping to assure that knowledge of the policy is widely spread throughout the organization. Use management presentations, videos, panel discussions, guest speakers, question/answer forums, and newsletters, as resources permit, to make your policies visible. Also, the organization's computer security training and awareness program can effectively notify users of new policies. Introduce computer security policies in a manner that ensures that management's unqualified support is clear, especially in environments where employees feel inundated with policies, directives, guidelines, and procedures. The organization's policy is the vehicle for emphasizing management's commitment to computer security and making clear its expectations for employee performance, behavior, and accountability.

Computer security policy should also be integrated into and consistent with other organizational policies (such as personnel policies). One way to help ensure this is to thoroughly coordinate policies during development with other offices in the organization. Formulating viable computer security policies is a challenge and requires communication and understanding of the organizational goals and potential benefits that will be derived from the policies. Through a carefully structured approach to policy development, you can achieve a coherent set of policies. Without these, there's little hope for any successful information security system.

Appendix A is a sample Internet security policy to help you in developing your own.

AN EXECUTIVE'S GUIDE TO THE PROTECTION OF INFORMATION RESOURCES

The remainder of this chapter is adapted from a U.S. government guide to infosec, published by the National Institute of Standards and Technology (NIST), an agency of the U.S. Department of Commerce. NIST is responsible for developing standards, providing technical assistance, and conducting research for computers and related telecommunications systems. These activities provide technical support to government and industry in the effective, safe, and economic use of computers. With the passage of the Computer Security Act of 1987, NIST's activities also include the development of standards and guidelines needed to assure the cost-effective security and privacy of sensitive information in federal computer systems.

This material is intended to acclimate government agency leaders to the world of information security and is designed to help policy makers to address a host of questions regarding the protection and safety of computer systems and data processed within a government agency. As such, this section is included here to provide another view on the importance of security policies and enforcement. Contained here are information systems security concerns, management issues that must be addressed by agency policies and programs, and essential components of an effective implementation process. Use this information in the development of your own standards, policies, guidelines, and procedures. They're equally applicable in private industry as they are in the federal government.

In the past, executives have taken a hands-off approach in dealing with computing resources, essentially leaving the area to the computer technologist. Today, executives and managers are recognizing that computers and computer-related problems must be understood and managed the same as any other resource. The success of an information resources protection program depends on the policy generated and on the attitude of management toward securing information on automated systems. Policy makers must set the tone and the emphasis on how important a role information security has. Your primary responsibility is to set the information resource security policy for the organization with the objectives of reduced risk, compliance with laws and regulations, and assurance of operational continuity, information integrity, and confidentiality.

The Risks

The proliferation of personal computers, local area networks, and distributed processing has drastically changed the way we manage and control information resources. Internal controls and control points that were present in the past when we were dealing with manual or batch processes have not always been replaced with comparable controls in many of today's automated systems. Reliance upon inadequately controlled information systems can have serious consequences, including:

- Inability or impairment of the agency's ability to perform its mission
- Inability to provide needed services to the public
- Waste, loss, misuse, or misappropriation of funds
- Loss of credibility or embarrassment to an agency

To avoid these consequences, a broad set of information security issues must be addressed effectively and comprehensively. Toward this end, executives should take a traditional risk management approach, recognizing that risks are taken in the day-to-day management of an organization and that there are alternatives to consider in managing these risks. Risk is accepted as part of doing business or is reduced or eliminated by modifying operations or by employing control mechanisms.

Executive Responsibilities

Protecting information resources is an important goal for all organizations. This goal is met by establishing an information resource security program. This requires staff, funding, and positive incentives to motivate employees to participate in a program to protect these valuable assets. The information resource protection policy should state precisely:

- The value to the agency of data and information resources and the need to preserve their integrity, availability, and confidentiality
- The intent of the organization to protect the resources from accidental or deliberate unauthorized disclosure, modification, or destruction by employing cost-effective controls
- The assignment of responsibility for data security throughout the organization
- The requirement to provide computer security and awareness training to all employees having access to information resources
- The intent to hold employees personally accountable for information resources entrusted to them

- The requirement to monitor and assess data security via internal and external audit procedures
- The penalties for not adhering to the policy

Executive Goals

The policy established for securing information resources should meet the basic goals of reducing the risk to an acceptable level, assuring operational continuity, complying with applicable laws and regulations, and assuring integrity and confidentiality. This section briefly describes these objectives and how they can be met.

Reducing the Risk to an Acceptable Level

The dollars spent for security measures to control or contain losses should never be more than the projected dollar loss if something adverse happened to the information resource. Cost-effective security results when reduction in risk is balanced with the cost of implementing safeguards. The greater the value of information processed, or the more severe the consequences if something happens to it, the greater the need for control measures to protect it. It is important that these trade-offs of cost versus risk reduction be explicitly considered and that executives understand the degree of risk remaining after selected controls are implemented.

Assuring Operational Continuity

With ever-increasing demands for timely information and greater volumes of information being processed, availability of essential systems, networks, and data is a major protection issue. In some cases, service disruptions of just a few hours are unacceptable. Agency reliance on essential computer systems requires that advance planning be done to allow timely restoration of processing capabilities in the event of severe service disruption. The impact resulting from inability to process data should be assessed and action taken to assure availability of those systems considered essential to agency operation.

Complying with Applicable Laws and Regulations

As the pervasiveness of computer systems increases and the risks and vulnerabilities associated with information systems become better understood, the body of law and regulations compelling positive action to protect information resources grows. A circular from the Office of Management and Budget (Circular No. A-130, "Management of Federal Information Systems") and Public Law 100-235 (Computer Security Act of 1987) are two documents where the knowledge of these laws provide a baseline for an information resources security program.

Assuring Integrity and Confidentiality

An important objective of an information resource management program is to ensure that the information is accurate. Integrity of information means you can trust the data and the processes that manipulate it. A system has integrity when it provides sufficient accuracy and completeness to meet the needs of the user(s). It should be properly designed to automate all functional requirements, include appropriate accounting and integrity controls, and accommodate the full range of potential conditions that might be encountered in its operation.

Agency information should also be protected from intruders, as well as from employees with authorized computer access privileges who attempt to perform unauthorized actions. Assured confidentiality of sensitive data is often, but not always, a requirement of agency systems. Privacy requirements for personal information are generally dictated by statute, while protection requirements for other agency information are a function of the nature of that information. Determination of requirements in the latter case is made by the official responsible for that information. The impact of wrongful disclosure should be considered in understanding confidentiality requirements.

THE PROGRAM ELEMENTS OF INFORMATION PROTECTION

Successful execution of the responsibilities previously outlined requires establishing agency policies and practices regarding information protection. The security policy directive facilitates consistent protection of information resources. Supporting procedures are most effectively implemented with top management support, through a program focused on areas of highest risk. A compliance assessment process ensures ongoing effectiveness of the information protection program throughout the agency.

Scope

Although the protection of automated information resources is emphasized here, protection requirements usually extend to information on all forms of media. Agency programs should apply safeguards to all information requiring protection, regardless of its form or location. Comprehensive information resource protection procedures should address accountability for information, vulnerability assessment, data access, hardware/software control, systems development, and operational controls. Protection should be afforded throughout the life cycle of information, from creation through ultimate disposition.

Accountability for Information

An effective information resource protection program identifies the information used by the agency and assigns primary responsibility for information protection to the managers of the respective functional areas supported by the data. These managers know the importance of the data to the organization and are able to quantify the economic consequences of undesirable happenings. They are also able to detect deficiencies in data and know definitively who must have access to the data supporting their operations. A fundamental information protection issue is assignment of accountability. Information flows throughout the organization and can be shared by many individuals. This tends to blur accountability and disperse decision making regarding information protection. Accountability should be explicitly assigned for determining and monitoring security for appropriate agency information.

When security violations occur, management must be accountable for responding and investigating. Security violations should trigger a reevaluation of access authorizations, protection decisions, and control techniques. All apparent violations should be resolved; since absolute protection is never achieved, some losses are inevitable. It is important, however, that the degree of risk assumed be commensurate with the sensitivity or importance of the information resource to be protected.

Vulnerability Assessment

A risk assessment program ensures management that periodic reviews of information resources have considered the degree of vulnerability to threats causing destruction, modification, disclosure, and delay of information availability in making protection decisions and investments in safeguards. The official responsible for a specific information resource determines protection requirements. Less sensitive, less essential information requires minimal safeguards, while highly sensitive or critical information might merit strict protective measures. Assessment of vulnerability is essential in specifying cost-effective safeguards; overprotection can be needlessly costly and add unacceptable operational overhead.

Once cost-effective safeguards are selected, residual risk remains and is accepted by management. Risk status should be periodically reexamined to identify new threats, vulnerabilities, or other changes that affect the degree of risk that management has previously accepted.

Data Access

Access to information should be delegated according to the principles of need-to-know and least possible privilege. For a multiuser application system, only individuals with authorized need to view or use data are granted access authority, and they are allowed only the mininum privileges needed to carry out their duties. For personal computers with one operator, data should be protected from unauthorized viewing or use. It is the individual's responsibility to ensure that the data is secure.

Systems Development

All information systems software should be developed in a controlled and systematic manner according to agency standards. Agency policy should require that appropriate controls for accuracy, security, and availability are identified during system design, approved by the responsible official, and implemented. Users who design their own systems, whether on a personal computer or on a mainframe, must adhere to the systems development requirements.

Systems should be thoroughly tested according to accepted standards and moved into a secure production environment through a controlled process. Adequate documentation should be considered an integral part of the information system and should be completed before the system can be considered ready for use.

Hardware/Software Configuration Control

Protection of hardware and resources of computer systems and networks greatly contributes to the overall level of control and protection of information. The information protection policies should provide substantial direction concerning the management and control of computer hardware and software.

Agency information should be protected from the potentially destructive impact of unauthorized hardware and software. For example, software viruses have been inserted into computers through games and apparently useful software that was acquired via public-access bulletin boards; viruses can spread from system to system before being detected. Also, unauthorized hardware additions to personal computers can introduce unknown dial-in access paths. Accurate records of hardware/software inventory, configurations, and locations should be maintained, and control mechanisms should provide assurance that unauthorized changes have not occurred.

To avoid legal liability, no unauthorized copying of software should be permitted. Agencies should also address the issue of personal use of federal computer systems, giving employees specific direction about allowable use and providing consistent enforcement.

Operational Controls

Agency standards should clearly communicate minimum expected controls to be present in all computer facilities, computer operations, input/output handling, network management, technical support, and user liaison. More stringent controls would apply to those areas that process very sensitive or critical information. Protection of these areas would include:

- Security management
- Physical security
- Security of system/application software and data
- Network security
- Contingency planning

IMPLEMENTATION OF THE INFORMATION PROTECTION PROGRAM

In most cases, agency executive management is not directly involved in the details of achieving a controlled information processing environment. Instead, executive action should focus on effective planning and implementation and an ongoing review structure. Usually, an explicit group or organization is assigned specific responsibility for providing day-to-day guidance and direction of this process. Within this group, an information security manager (ISM) should be identified as a permanent focal point for information protection issues within the agency.

The ISM must be thoroughly familiar with the agency mission, organization, and operation. The manager should have sufficient authority to influence the organization and have access to agency executives when issues require escalation.

Independence

In determining the reporting relationship of the ISM, independence of functional areas within the agency is desirable. Plans and budget for the ISM function should be approved by agency management, rather than being part of any functional area budget. This approach avoids conflicts of interest and facilitates development and maintenance of a comprehensive and consistent protection program that serves the needs of agency management.

Degree of Centralization

The desirability of centralized versus decentralized security is heavily debated and largely depends on size, organizational structure, and management approach at the individual agency. A centralized approach to security has the advantages of being directly responsive to executive direction and specifically accountable for progress and status. A decentralized approach to security has the advantages of being close to the functional area involved. In the long term, decentralization may provide better integration of security with other entity functions.

An effective combined approach also offers advantages. A small dedicated resource at the agency level can direct the information protection program, while additional resources are utilized at the functional area level to implement the program in each area.

Dedicated Staff

The common practice of assigning responsibility for information security to existing staff with other major responsibilities is often unsuccessful. At least one dedicated staff member is recommended at the program management level. The need for additional full-time resources depends on the agency's computer environment. The resources needed may be affected by the number of information systems, their technical complexity, the degree of networking, the importance of information processed, the adequacy of existing controls, and the extent of agency dependence on information systems.

Implementation Stages

Development of a comprehensive information protection program that is practiced and observed widely throughout a federal agency occurs in stages and requires ongoing monitoring and maintenance to remain viable.

First, organizational requirements for information protection are identified. Different agencies have varying levels of need for security, and the information protection program should be structured to most effectively meet those needs. Next, organizational policies are developed that provide a security architecture for agency operations, taking into consideration the information protection program elements discussed above. The policies undergo normal review procedures, then are approved by agency management for implementation. Last, activities are then initiated to bring the agency into compliance with the policies. Depending on the degree of centralization, this might require development of further plans and budgets within functional entities of the agency to implement the necessary logical and physical controls.

Training

Training is a major activity in the implementation process. Security violations are the result of human action, and people can usually identify problems in their earliest stages. Developing and maintaining personnel awareness of information security issues can yield large benefits in prevention and early detection of problems and losses.

Target audiences for this training are executives and policy makers, program and functional managers, IRM (information resource management) security and audit personnel, computer management and operations, and end users. Training can be delivered through existing policy and procedues manuals, written materials, presentations and classes, and audiovisual training programs. The training provided should create an awareness of risks and the importance of safeguards, underscoring the specific responsibilities of each of the individuals being trained.

Monitoring and Enforcement

An ongoing monitoring and enforcement program assures continued effectiveness of information protection measures. Compliance can be measured in a number of ways, including audits, management reviews or self-assessments, surveys, and other informal indicators. A combination of monitoring mechanisms provides greater reliability of results.

Variances from policy requirements should be accepted only in cases where the responsible official has evaluated, documented, and accepted the risk of noncompliance. Enforcement of agency policies and practices is important to the overall success of an information protection program. Inconsistent or lax enforcement quickly results in deterioration of internal controls over information resources.

A positive benefit of an effective monitoring and enforcement process is an increased understanding of the degree of information-related risk in agency operations. Without such a feedback process, management unknowingly accepts too much risk. An effective information protection program allows the agency to continue to rely upon and expand the use of information technology while maintaining an acceptable level of risk.

Maintenance

As agency initiatives and operations change, and as the computer environment evolves, some elements of the information protection program require change as well. Information protection cannot be viewed as a project with a distinct end. Rather, it is a process that should be maintained to be realistic and useful to the agency. Procedures for review and update of policies and other program elements should be developed and followed.

SUMMARY

Security policy is an imperative element of a complete information security plan that touches every part of the organization where data is created, modified, stored, or processed. Internet security demands the presence of policies that dictate how security products and devices are to be used to protect your assets. In Chapter 2, we begin drilling down into the details and uses of information system policies related to the special cases of Internet-attached networks and e-commerce systems.

2

The Fundamental Elements of Security

In Chapter 1, you began to build a foundation for an information security plan by looking at the different types of policies needed and the principles behind them. In Chapter 2, you will learn more of the principles for implementing an effective e-commerce information security plan and how to roll your own (develop) security policies.

NO SINGLE SOLUTION BUT PLANNING

One of the paradoxes of the e-commerce success story is that the Internet both enables that success and serves as a potential gateway for the unscrupulous activities of intruders, hackers, and the disaffected. The open architecture of the Internet makes it possible for anyone from a mom and pop storefront to an industrial conglomerate to transact business globally. However, it is that same open architecture that exposes a company to fraud and financial loss. A company must be open to business partners and customers while at the same time close its doors to internal and external threats. This technological high-wire act requires the cultivation of a security culture within an organization that combines the best policies, procedures, and education with rigorous but flexible system administration techniques.

As you're beginning to see, planning and developing a security strategy as part of the standard system methodology pays big dividends in the end. As tempting as a "single source" solution might be, it cannot begin to address the complexities of system exposure and the wiliness, ingenuity, and persistence of the hacker who finds a weakness in a system if it exists. In addition, while new security tools arrive on the scene daily, these tools are only as good as the security policies and procedures behind them.

Any discussion about security must begin with the basic principles, which often have nothing to do with the security products or services you ultimately purchase or build. Common sense tells you to protect those things you value. You'd no more leave the front doors to your business wide open when no one is around than you'd leave your computer systems wide open to attack. Thus, one basic principle of security states that you should protect your assets just a little better than your neighbors protect theirs. Consider The Club, which is used to deter car theft. Given a long line of parked cars, a thief will opt to steal the one that's easiest to steal—presumably, the one that doesn't have the Club. The thief's goal is to maximize damage while minimizing the time it takes to carry out the misdeed. The same holds true for information protection: The more you deter thefts, the lower the likelihood that you'll be victimized.

Another basic principle states that different types of information call for different types of protection. Think about your information assets and the promises you've made to your customers to protect their private, sensitive, and confidential data. To keep your customers coming back for more, you must instill—and maintain—the highest possible levels of confidence and trust. Therefore, your customers' information calls for a high level of protection.

To help in classifying data appropriately, you need to ascertain its value, to both you and your customers. Establish a rank order system to help you determine your security needs. Start with information that you deem public, needing few controls (brochureware, marketing material, etc.), and end with the data that you consider mission-critical or that could wreak the most havoc if it fell into the wrong hands.

Once you've labeled your data, then begin looking at the omnipresent risks:

- *Integrity risk* looks at the consequences of data loss, modification outside normal processing, and theft that could lead to access breaches or place you at a competitive disadvantage.

- *Confidentiality risk* weighs the consequences if private, sensitive, or confidential information is stolen. What might occur if the wrong people gain access to your systems and are exposed to a treasure trove of information that threatens your promises of trust to your customers?

- *Availability risk* considers what might happen if your system is suddenly taken over, denying you, your users, and your customers access. How would you respond to such a denial of service attack on your e-commerce system?

Now you can begin to map data classes to risks based on your knowledge of your systems. Treat it as a mental exercise, and put yourself in the place of those hell-bent on causing you harm. Once you've completed the exercise, common sense will begin to tell you where to concentrate your efforts and point you to the controls you need to safeguard your systems most appropriately.

The best approach to security that you can take is a practical and realistic one. First, realize that there is no such thing as absolute security. With this in mind, conduct a thorough inventory of your system's data and formulate clear and consistent policies regarding its use. In addition, realize that security policies must be reviewed regularly and updated when needed. Just as your business changes in response to demands, so too does the world of security. In the rapidly accelerating game of electronic commerce, nothing stands still for very long.

Therefore, proper security planning requires a dual mind-set: (1) What steps should you take to prevent unwarranted system intrusions, and (2) what process should you follow after your system inevitably experiences its first attack? The idea here is to define the former in detail to prevent the latter, but reality dictates that your site *will* be attacked at some point. Undoubtedly, it already has been, whether you realize it or not.

THE NEW NEED FOR SECURITY

To many, security is a priority. Homeowners shell out thousands for it. Car owners won't park in their own garages, let alone public garages, without it. Parents buy it to protect their children's futures. Everyone, it appears, takes security seriously, buying insurance policies, alarms, and home protection devices—everyone, that is, except many IT (information technology) system administrators. Why is it that for so many companies (regardless of their size or purpose), security is an afterthought, rather than an integral part of every system design?

The most obvious reason is that until the arrival of the Internet's open architecture, the opportunities for cracking a system were significantly fewer and the intruders easier to detect. The perpetrator, most likely a disgruntled employee, had to have physical access to the computer. Remote attacks rarely occurred because networks were closed to outsiders. Thus, security remained low on the priority list of system managers. Installing RACF or ACF2 (two popular data security systems) on an IBM mainframe and devising a simple strategy for data set and transaction protection filled the bill (see Figure 2-1). In the standard IBM model, the user submits system requests using the user interface system, TSO(E). The request passes through the RACF security system, which determines whether or not the user has the authority he requests to perform the transaction.

Those old system policies and procedures now pose little more than a slight inconvenience to a truly determined hacker. Companies now must include security as a major component of system development.

PRINCIPLES FOR BUILDING A SECURITY CULTURE

A few basic principles go a long way toward building a security culture within an organization that will make the physical and logical security considerations discussed in the following chapters more effective.

Figure 2-1. An early example of adequate system security.

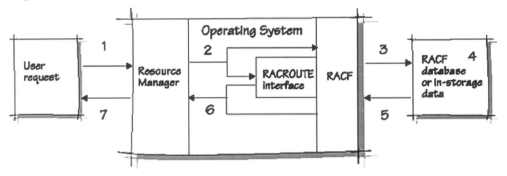

1. A user requests access to a resource using a resource manager (for example, TSO/E).
2. The resource manager issues a RACF request to see if the user can access the resource.
3. RACF refers to the RACF database or in-storage data and . . .
4. . . . checks the appropriate resource profile.
5. Based on the information in the profile . . .
6. RACF passes the status of the request to the resource manager.
7. The resource manager grants (or denies) the request.

Creating a Security Policy Team

Assemble a security policy team with participation from all interested parties—not just IT. The individuals involved in this group are those who have the most at stake, namely the owners of business data and processes such as the finance and human resources groups. But before you can build your security team, you need to take inventory of your corporate data and applications, rank them in order of how critical they are to your operation, determine the impact to your business should a particular database or system be compromised or lost, and determine what steps to take should the unforeseen occur.

Your security policy team should do more than create snappy slogans and define policies that they don't or can't enforce. The group should be visible and its purpose known to the organization. But most important, its role should be defined in real and verifiable actions that make your assets safer.

To help publicize the security policy team, and to emphasize the importance of security, hold security fairs and awareness weeks and conduct classes for your employees. Security to the average employee should cover everything from protecting passwords and not sharing accounts to taking company intrusion alerts seriously. Companies serious about their security policies have gone so far as to include them as part of their employees' development plans.

Clearly Defining Security Roles

Develop a system of policy cross-checking by separating the roles of security administrators, system administrators, and system installers. This activity is well known to quality assurance groups that understand the importance of peer review. No matter how capable a system administrator might be, she might be too busy to enforce security policies consistently. For example, a system installer could install a program that doesn't properly perform boundary checking, resulting in a buffer overflow situation that a studied hacker can exploit. If the system administrator alone has responsibility for checking such gaping holes in the network but she is overwhelmed by other duties, such a program could slip by her unnoticed. Having more than one individual responsible for such tasks as code review helps to avoid similar situations.

Routinely Auditing Security Policies

Make sure that you include security as a major deliverable in your project plan, and raise the security concern at the end of each phase. Security should not be a postimplementation activity! Unfortunately, security concerns are viewed by some IT managers as unnecessary overhead that slows the project down and adds little value.

You should also conduct routine audits of newly installed software systems as well as audits of existing applications. The individual or individuals conducting the review should be knowledgeable of current security trends and tools and should stay abreast of the latest news of hacker attacks.

Creating a Business Contingency Plan

Create a business contingency plan (BCP) even if it contains only the most rudimentary elements of disaster recovery. This plan should go beyond the standard disaster recovery plan that most companies already have in place to deal primarily with natural disasters or, less likely, acts of terrorism or sabotage.

Documenting Your Architecture

Document your systems starting at the physical layer, and locate the places where logical networks such as protocols and services overlap, looking for obscure links between networks. (This topic is discussed at greater length in Chapters 8 and 9.) Remember that your review of network topology should consider internal as well as external systems linked into the corporate network.

Simplifying Your System Design

Keep your system design simple, employing common directory services to limit the number of accounts. Also, minimize the number of passwords a user must remember. Manage perimeter authentication across the heterogeneous systems using Radius (Remote Authentication Dial-In User Service, which first appeared in 1992) or one of the TACACS (terminal access controller access system, a centralized token card system) variants for the Cisco environment.

Reducing Your Exposure

Minimize your losses by reducing your exposure, turning off or eliminating services that you don't use. In general, the more complex your system is, the more difficult it is for you or any group of people to understand it, let alone maintain it. You should deploy only those services that you use, decommissioning applications, accounts, etc., that are no longer valid. In particular, you shouldn't advertise network services to locations that don't need to know them. Not only will you reduce network traffic, you'll also give the hacker one less service to exploit. Finally, segregate internal from external DNS (Domain Name Service) servers, and closely examine your corporate directory service for security weaknesses. Consider mandating the use of the Network Address Translator (NAT) to hide internal network addresses from the outside world.

Keeping It Simple

Avoid human intervention by keeping security as simple and transparent to the user as possible, enforcing policies on ActiveX and Java at the point where they enter your network. Screen viruses here, as well as on the servers, and routinely perform virus scans on desktops. In general, automate as much of your security checking as possible. Reminding your employees of security threats is one thing: Counting on them to act on them is quite another.

Restricting Application Accounts

Restrict application process accounts when possible. For example, use of NetWare Loadable Modules (NLMs), a weakness in NetWare 4.X, should be restricted. Never run Web server processes under the UNIX "root" account, and never permit logins to the NT Administrator account. Rather, assign the appropriate privileges to individual system administrator accounts to keep them accountable for all the work that they perform while logged-in.

Communicating Security Threats

Quietly and quickly inform your users of open security threats you can't close or control, such as spurious executables, "zipped files," or ActiveX components that are received by e-mail from unknown sources.

In June 1999, a virus called Worm.ExploreZip propagated itself into some of the largest companies in the United States. Like the Melissa virus, Worm.ExploreZip used the e-mail addresses in the Microsoft Outlook address book and did one better than Melissa, automatically replying to the incoming e-mail of MS Exchange or MS Outlook users. Unlike the Melissa virus, Worm.ExploreZip actually deleted certain files and modified others at companies such as Boeing, GTE, and General Electric. The point here is that companies must quickly warn their users when such an attack occurs and give them specific instructions to follow to stem it.

Monitoring Organizational Changes

User account management should keep up with organizational changes. Delete old IDs and passwords when employees leave the company, and assign new IDs when they change departments. This is easier said than done in larger corporations, especially where a large percentage of the IT staff are transient contractors or consultants. You need to coordinate user account administration with the activities of human resources and outside contracting departments.

Locking Down Your Servers

Restrict physical access to your servers and critical network devices. NetWare and Windows NT servers, for example, may be safe when a user accesses them remotely, but they could potentially be compromised by someone at the system console.

Not Sharing

Users should not share account IDs and passwords, especially when using privileged accounts. A system administrator must forbid this. When users share accounts and a system leak occurs, it is far more difficult to figure out who did what.

Developing Internal Security Expertise

The question here is how much and how often you should rely on outside consulting companies to define your security policy for you, as opposed to cultivating the talent from within. Both options are expensive, and developing and depending on internal expertise may not necessarily be cheaper, at least in the short run. A prudent organization should strike a balance between having knowledgeable security experts in-house, who intimately know the network architecture of the organization, and bringing in security experts periodically for a review of policies and procedures. As Stuart McClure and Joel Scambray, security experts for Ernst & Young, put it, "Relying solely on your employees' security assessment is suicide."

Obviously, you should check the references of any external organization before bringing them in-house and opening your system to them. Much has been written in the trade press about big consulting companies that scare their clients by pointing out numerous holes in their networks and then overselling network penetration services, some of which may be useless. You want to know at the outset that you can trust the consultants you bring in.

Another alternative, sometimes referred to as White Hat hacking, is the use of internal and controlled hackers whose job is to break into the company's network. This has its pitfalls. For example, if a thorough background check has not been performed on a White Hat hacker, and he is given access to the company's network, he may use that access for unscrupulous activities. (However, White Hat hacking is generally considered to be an ethical and legitimate form of hacking.)

At a minimum, an IT organization should have one person who keeps up with the tools, tips, and techniques that make their way daily into the trade press. Such a person may be a luxury that smaller companies cannot afford. In that case, periodic reviews by an external consulting company may be the only solution.

ROLLING YOUR OWN POLICIES

As you saw in Chapter 1, policy creation is not the exclusive domain of technical experts. In fact, many of the policies you need should come as directives from management that clearly spell out which activities are tolerated and which are not. The policies you develop should cover as many of the following topics as possible.

Planning

Planning an e-commerce environment should include an evaluation of current work flows to determine how improve-

ments can come about through automation and investments in other technologies.

Desktop Standards

Desktop systems standards should be defined to provide
the framework needed to improve information sharing
among employees, external partners, vendors, and customers.

Systems Development Standards

Development standards define the processes governing the
design, development, and maintenance of software. E-commerce sites need software for profit making, and management uses software for decision making. The processes
used for this software development must be appropriately
established, controlled, and monitored.

Systems Support Functions

Reliability and availability should be assured for support
functions and should include plans for connecting to outside organizations as well as to the Internet.

Information Security

Policies regarding information security govern the access
to sensitive or critical data crucial to company operations.
The development of these types of standards is challenging,
since the lack of security features where they're needed
often restricts the ability to protect information properly.
Critical information must be secured regardless of where
it's stored and who accesses it.

Device Security

Portable computer use increases daily and will increase
more as there is greater reliance on laptops. Laptop and
portable computer theft is prevalent. Thieves steal them because they're small, expensive, and easily fenced. To help
minimize this threat, you need to protect these assets as

much as possible. Policies here include reporting thefts to company security personnel and basic training for employees regarding the protection of computing devices.

Work-at-Home Users

If you espouse telecommuting for your employees, you need guidelines to ensure that they use the equipment you send home with them in acceptable ways. You want to help ensure that the purposes for working at home are not being defeated through abuses. The same considerations for laptops apply to work-at-home equipment—perhaps even more so.

Inventory and Tracking

Asset inventory tracking policies should address the processing that accounts for hardware, software, licensing, financial records, reporting, and management.

Disaster Planning and Recovery

Disaster planning and recovery defines the procedures that protect the organization from losing valuable data by maintaining the reliability and availability of data systems. It also includes disaster recovery processes for data and critical systems that day-to-day operations depend upon. Plans in this category include backup schedules, off-site storage of backups, and immediate replacement of PCs and servers that fail. Plans may also specify remote computing facilities where the organization's work can continue in the event of a building fire or other casualties.

Policy Compliance

Compliance refers to the usage and monitoring of the policies and standards. You may decide to require each employee to sign a form (called Acceptable Use Policies or something similar) that states his or her intent to comply and spells out the consequences of noncompliance. Periodic auditing can indicate whether policy compliance is at an acceptable level. Realize that you can't develop policies in a vacuum. Formulation must include those who are expected to abide by the policies. Once these policies are developed, you must also disseminate them. You can publish the policies rapidly and efficiently with your intranet.

Continual Improvement

Policies developed, approved, and put into action must be revisited regularly. Things change—especially activities based on digital technology—and the policies that govern them must change too. To help aid in continual improvement, it's important for people to know that their opinion counts for something.

AN OUNCE OF PREVENTION IS WORTH A POUND OF SECURITY

As most industry experts agree, security is not about tools but about risk assessment and management. Without understanding what is at stake, a company that jumps headlong into the security tool frenzy may throw thousands of dollars at tools that either don't work together or simply do not live up to their billing. Fortunately, an international movement is working on defining the Common Criteria (CC), commonly known as ISO 15408, which is a common language and structure to express IT security requirements (as you'll see in Chapter 6). But until the day arrives when an IT organization truly understands what it is buying, sound security policies and practices can help to shore up defenses and thwart inadvertent or hostile attacks on its network.

3

Vulnerabilities to Internet-Attached Networks

The Internet is growing faster than any telecommunications system in history, including the telephone system. Often, however, users of the Internet fail to realize that Internet-attached corporate and back office networks are at risk to threats from intruders who use the Internet as a means for attacking systems and causing various forms of computer security incidents. Consequently, new Internet sites are often prime targets for malicious activity, including break-ins, file tampering, vandalism, and service disruptions. Such activity is often difficult to discover and correct, is usually highly embarrassing to the organization, and is typically costly in terms of lost productivity, damage to data, and damage to company reputation and customer goodwill.

Internet users are far better off being aware of the high potential for computer security incidents from the Internet and the steps that can be taken to secure their sites and their privacy. In later chapters, you'll discover several tools and techniques that provide sites with higher levels of security assurance and protection. Before we begin to examine the tools and technologies that help to foster protection, it's important to understand the nature of Internet communications. We'll start out by looking at some history of the Internet Protocol (IP) and some of the characteristics of packet-switched networks, like the Internet. But first, let's define some recurring networking terms and principles of operation.

Packet-Switched Networking Terms and Concepts

- *Protocol.* The "rules of the road" for network traffic. Protocols define network segments, how the network operates, and how the network uses frames and packets.

- *Layered Protocol.* A layered protocol isolates operations and functions into well-defined layers that offer services to the layers above it. The lowest layer contains the intelligence to physically attach to a network (adapters, wiring, etc.). As you move up the layers, more intelligence is added. For example, the data-link layer knows how to format, package, and unpackage messages for transit and receipt. The higher layers contain the intelligence regarding which services are intended for these messages and how to route the messages appropriately.

- *Topology.* This describes the network configuration (layout). Common network topologies include hierarchical (tree structures), horizontal (bus), star patterns, ring patterns, and meshes. Ethernet, for example, uses a central bus under a horizontal topology.

- *Frames.* These are the basic units of information that are transmitted over a network. Frames usually contain control bits, error checking bits, user data, addressing bits, and synchronization bits.

- *Packets.* These are used to describe Protocol Data Units (PDUs). Packets contain user data segments wrapped up with the network rules. Packets are turned into frames prior to being broadcast over the network.

- *IEEE.* The Institute of Electrical and Electronic Engineeers is a group that has been instrumental in defining standards for local area networks. As a well-known professional society, it influences the standards development efforts throughout the world and works with the standards-setting bodies (e.g., the International Telegraph and Telephone Consultative Committee, the International Standards Organization, and the American National Standards Institute).

A BRIEF HISTORY OF THE INTERNET

Today's Internet solves many of the problems faced by earlier users of computers, especially when trying to force communications between computers from different manufacturers. The days of open computing were long in coming. Many early computer systems relied upon unique and proprietary methods of communication that worked only when you bought all your equipment from the same manufacturer. If you wanted your Digital Equipment minicomputer to talk to your Wang computer, you were out of luck unless you were willing to write your own conversion and translation software.

When the Defense Advanced Research Projects Agency (DARPA) of the U.S. Department of Defense commissioned the construction of a network of networks (known today as the Internet) that could withstand a nuclear attack, academia responded with solutions that eventually were adopted as worldwide open standards for computer communications. Manufacturers of computers soon began to realize that if their equipment wouldn't work with these open standards, they wouldn't be selling many more units.

As the Internet moved out of research and academic circles and took on commercial and private traffic, many private organizations jumped at the opportunity to establish their own presence. Ethernet and TCP/IP (see below) offered a mother lode of technology already seasoned in the breeding ground of the Internet. And, best of all, the technology was available free.

Dawn of a New LAN

Robert Metcalfe and David Boggs of Xerox's Palo Alto Research Center invented Ethernet and made it public in a 1976 article entitled "Ethernet: Distributed Packet Switching for Local Computer Networks." (Ethernet, at a high level, is a specification for a type of network cabling and signaling.) Xerox, Intel, and Digital Equipment developed the first Ethernet standard Version 1 in September 1980.

They intended to end the problems people experienced with "sneaker nets" that involved putting data or programs on floppy diskettes to copy them into other computers. (This entailed walking across the room between computers and wearing out their sneakers.) Ethernet is fast, simple, and reliable. It became the primary way to connect different computers together within a local area. Since then, various companies and researchers have refined and expanded Ethernet so that today it achieves transfer rates up to 100 megabits per second, and researchers are still working to improve it.

Over time, the sharing of information and resources across individual LANs (local area networks) was beginning to cause problems. Ethernet ensures that any computer can physically connect to a network, but it does not ensure that connected machines can communicate appropriately. Early vendor implementations of Ethernet came alongside proprietary network communications techniques that were often incompatible with techniques from other vendors. System administrators soon realized that services such as e-mail and file transferring across outside networks require standardized approaches. They saw these incompatibilities as limiting factors to collaborative work with colleagues at other institutions.

TCP/IP Answers the Call

Dr. Vinton Cerf and Dr. Robert E. Kahn codeveloped the Transmission Control Protocol/Internet Protocol (TCP/IP) specifications to address these problems. The effort was such a significant contribution that Cerf is known today as the Father of the Internet. TCP/IP, a layered network protocol, follows the concepts used in the development of the Open Systems Interconnection (OSI) protocol by the International Standards Organization (ISO). The ISO-OSI model is implemented as X.25 and is used predominantly in Europe. The TCP/IP protocol stack is illustrated in Figure 3-1.

As Figure 3-1 shows, the principle behind layered protocols is to isolate operations and functions into well-defined segments that offer services to the layers above.

Figure 3-1. The TCP/IP protocol stack.

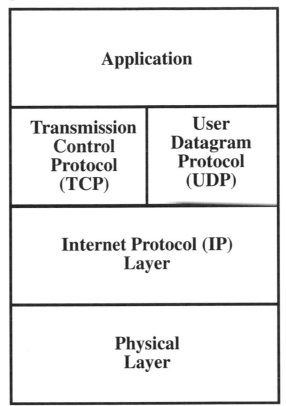

The lowest layer of the protocol stack contains the intelligence of how to attach physically to a network. As you move up the layers, you see more intelligence added. For instance, the data-link layer knows how to format, package, and unpackage messages meant for transit and receipt. The higher layers contain the intelligence to know which service(s) to use for these messages and how to route the messages appropriately.

By isolating these processes into layers, developers can develop software more efficiently, and network technology matures more rapidly: It's unnecessary to reinvent a service that already works well. Since the rules to implement these functions and processes are well known by virtue of being accepted standards, anyone who wishes to develop systems, software, or network hardware can do so with confidence that the products will work with products from other manufacturers.

TCP/IP is important because:

- It can be used on all networks alone or in conjunction with other network protocols.
- It is cross-platform and operating system–independent.
- It can be scaled infinitely larger.

A Network of Networks

Internetworks (internets) are formed from independent local area networks through the use of TCP/IP. The term *subnetwork* does not imply that fewer functions are available, but rather that when combined with other subnetworks, they together comprise an entire internetwork or internet that passes data through gateways or router devices. Of course, the largest internetwork is the Internet, and internal corporate internetworks today that use TCP/IP are called intranets.

What Makes TCP/IP Tick?

As you work your way up the layers of the TCP/IP protocol stack, the IP layer performs what's called connectionless services. The IP layer enables two host computers to communicate without a prior set-up process. It transfers data packets using a mechanism called datagrams. IP datagrams pass over Ethernet as frames through as many gateways as necessary until they reach the destination host computer. This is referred to as an unreliable delivery system and makes a best-effort-only attempt at delivery. It is connectionless because it may route each datagram differently along the path between computers. IP makes its services available to the transport layer of the stack above it. IP offers its service through two major means: (1) User Datagram Protocol (UDP), and (2) Transmission Control Protocol (TCP). Application programs use one of these two methods to conduct network communications.

- *UDP.* User Datagram Protocol works like the post office. When you mail a letter, you have no way of knowing or deciding the route it will take to reach your recipient, nor will the post office tell you if or when it arrives.

- *TCP.* Transmission Control Protocol, on the other hand, does offer a guarantee of service. It is a connection-oriented protocol that maintains status and states information about its activity. It provides reliable end-to-end transmission of data across the network. It works by creating what's called a virtual circuit that predetermines the path that all packet-switched traffic will follow prior to conducting the transmitting and receiving processes. Think of TCP in contrast to UDP. Where UDP works like the post office, TCP works like a telephone call that's dedicated from the time the call is connected to the time the call is terminated.

- *ICMP.* Another feature of TCP/IP is called the Internet Control Message Protocol (ICMP), which is used to report errors in the processing of datagrams and provides for administration and status messages from networked devices. ICMP is also a connectionless protocol with no error reporting or error-correcting mechanisms on ICMP traffic. Examples of a common use of ICMP datagrams is the ping (or "packet internet groper," a request that determines if a host computer is available "online") function that's pervasive in all versions of TCP/IP.

The application layer services built into most network operating systems use either TCP or UDP to perform their jobs, although network management utilities use ICMP packets. Some communication is well suited for connectionless operation (e.g., e-mail reader software), while other communications, such as Telnet and File Transfer Protocol (FTP), require a dedicated predictable circuit.

The application layer of the TCP/IP protocol stack is itself a series of layers, and its features and functions build upon one another to provide enhanced services. You find the most interesting development at the application layer of the TCP/IP protocol. As the UNIX operating system developed and matured in academic and research circles, Ethernet and TCP/IP became integral components of UNIX and are found in most commercial versions available today. For example, Gopher is a single application service that combines both the Telnet service, to establish and maintain remote terminal communications, and the FTP service, for bulk file transfers. It's important to understand that you can stack a potentially infinite number of layers both between and within each layer of the protocol.

TCP/IP services at the application layer use a scheme called listener applications that are assigned to specific port numbers on the network. TCP/IP supports up to 65,000 ports, and you can find the mapping of a UNIX server's specific ports to services in the /etc/services (pronounced et-c). Figure 3-2 shows an excerpt from the /etc/ services file of a UNIX host computer, listing some common applications, protocols used, and port assignments.

Supported services on UNIX host computers are im-

Figure 3-2. An excerpt of the /etc/ services file from a UNIX host computer.

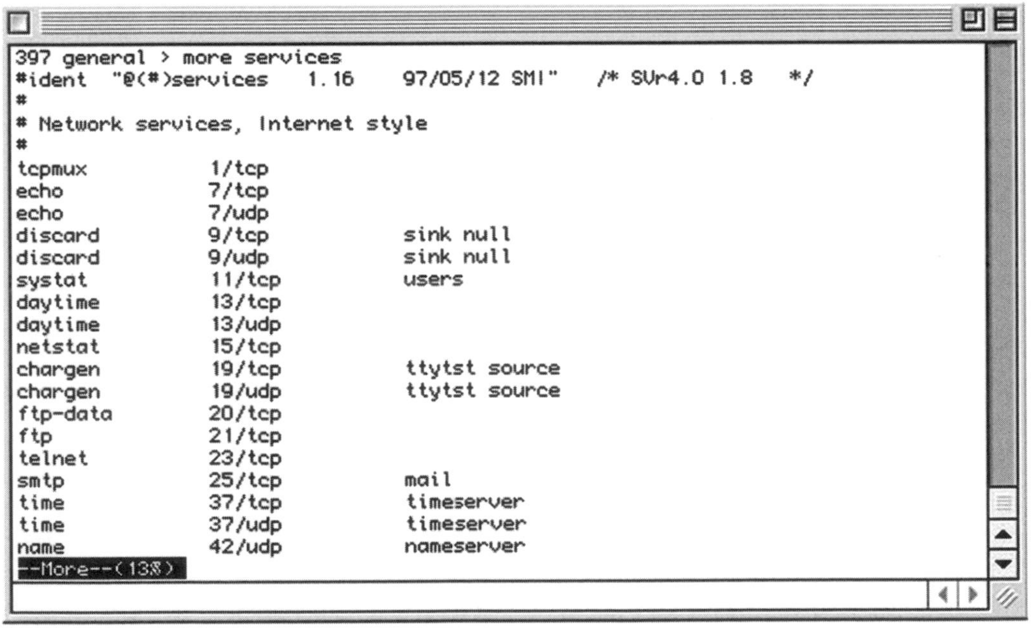

```
397 general > more services
#ident   "@(#)services   1.16    97/05/12 SMI"   /* SVr4.0 1.8   */
#
# Network services, Internet style
#
tcpmux            1/tcp
echo              7/tcp
echo              7/udp
discard           9/tcp           sink null
discard           9/udp           sink null
systat            11/tcp          users
daytime           13/tcp
daytime           13/udp
netstat           15/tcp
chargen           19/tcp          ttytst source
chargen           19/udp          ttytst source
ftp-data          20/tcp
ftp               21/tcp
telnet            23/tcp
smtp              25/tcp          mail
time              37/tcp          timeserver
time              37/udp          timeserver
name              42/udp          nameserver
--More--(13%)
```

plemented using an application called a daemon, which is a mythical little helper that waits around to service requests for help. Daemons listen to network traffic that bears their signal to activate. Messages to these daemons activate them from both sides of the network—users invoking them directly on a host computer and on the network side from remote users. When a request comes to a service from the network, the TCP/IP protocol stack unwraps it appropriately and routes it to the daemon (if available) to service the request. A few examples of common services and their associated daemons are listed in Table 3-1.

To summarize, think of Ethernet as a pipeline that delivers and receives TCP/IP-encoded messages. The job of Ethernet is to move messages along, and the job of TCP/IP is to make sense of them. TCP/IP's primary reason for existence is network reliability and survivability—not network security.

Table 3-1. Some common TCP/IP network services and their associated daemons.

Service	Daemon
Telnet	telnetd
File Transfer Protocol (FTP)	ftpd
HyperText Transport Protocol (HTTP, a World Wide Web protocol)	httpd
Sendmail	smtpd

THE VULNERABILITIES OF COMMUNICATIONS

Because standards make platform-independent communications possible, they also make communications vulnerable. Anyone can freely pick up the materials to help him understand and deconstruct frames and packets, even as they traverse the network. Because of its virtual routing features, the sender of a message never knows the route it takes for delivery until such time that it arrives, and only if it's traced from point to point. You also never know if someone stole a copy of a packet you sent and stored it somewhere for later deconstruction. Devices called *packet sniffers* do exactly that: They absorb the contents of packets streaming over a network connection and store them for analysis purposes, most commonly to diagnose network problems. Collection and analysis of frames and packets also reveals the data portion, where confidential or sensitive information may reside. While most people aren't predisposed to this type of activity, it's the unscrupulous few who wreak havoc for everyone else.

Without any specific forms of protection on the user data portions of packetized data, all of it should be considered vulnerable and at risk. As packet-sniffing technologies mature and improve, the simpler it becomes to breach—and even change—the contents of electronic communications. Worst of all, network breaches are often undetectable and leave no traces. You never know if someone eavesdropped on your communications until long after the fact, once the damage is done and the perpetrator is long gone.

Packet sniffing is time-consuming and often fruitless work since network traffic is virtually routed. The task in finding a complete credit card number, for example, can be hit-or-miss, and only the most tenacious find the patience. But other simpler and more productive ways to glean private or sensitive data are commonly found on the Internet, and often for free.

As users flock to the Internet, security problems using the network have become painfully apparent. Newspapers carry stories of high-profile hacker attacks via the Internet against governments, businesses, and academic sites. Hackers often roam the Internet with impunity, covering their tracks by moving from system to system or disguising the true source of an attack by "spoofing" the network-addressing mechanisms upon which the Internet relies. Intruders use Internet-connected systems illegally to exchange copyrighted software, to obtain sensitive information and trade secrets, to smear company reputations, to lock out legitimate users of a system or service, or simply to cause mischief and grief—often just for the fun of it.

System administrators are sometimes unaware of system break-ins or unauthorized users until they learn by accident when it's already too late. Several factors contribute to this state of affairs, described below.

Complexity of Configuration

Many companies and individuals connect systems to the Internet with little thought to the complexity of system administration and the increased potential for abuse from the Internet. New systems often arrive "out of the box" with network access controls preconfigured for maximum functional efficiency, usually with minimal or completely nonexistent secure access controls. Secure access controls are usually complex to configure, test, and monitor. As a result, controls that are accidentally misconfigured or left in a default state can result in unauthorized access.

Ease of Spying and Spoofing

The vast majority of Internet traffic is unencrypted and therefore easily readable. As a result, e-mail, passwords, and file transfers can be monitored and captured using readily available software. Intruders have been known to monitor connections to well-known Internet sites for the purpose of gaining information that would allow them to crack security or to steal valuable information. This information sometimes permits intruders to spoof legitimate connections and trick operating system security mechanisms into permitting normally disallowed network connections and commands.

Inherent Problems with TCP/IP Protocols

The TCP/IP protocol suite, as implemented in the Internet and described earlier, does not contain provisions for inherent network security. A number of the TCP/IP services, including remote login (rlogin) and remote shell (rsh), rely on mutually trusting systems and are intrinsically vulnerable to misuse and spoofing. Ironically, some of the other TCP/IP services, including Network Information Service (NIS) and Network File System (NFS), are widely used to coordinate local area network security and to distribute system resources among other local systems. If the vulnerabilities in these services are exploited, security on any trusting local area network segment may become compromised.

Wide-Open Network Policies

Many sites are configured unintentionally for wide-open Internet access without regard to the potential for abuse from the Internet. Some systems still employ passwordless guest accounts or anonymous FTP accounts that permit the placement of files, programs, or data on the host without restriction. Other sites store sensitive information on network-accessible systems, where it can be easily read and sometimes easily modified. The vast majority of sites permit more TCP/IP services than are required for their operations and make few (if any) attempts to limit access to information about their computers that could prove valuable to intruders.

Other High-Risk TCP/IP Services

Here are a few other TCP/IP services that are considered risky to run on Internet-accessible host computers:

- Web service (HTTP, or HyperText Transfer Protocol) is perhaps the most notorious of the protocols, but it is needed for World Wide Web access.
- Domain Name Service (DNS) zone transfers leak the names of internal systems to outsiders, making it easier for them to map out your network and build a strategy to attack it.
- Trivial File Transfer Protocol (TFTP) allows anonymous access to your file system, permitting an intruder to steal a copy of your password file and perform a brute-force attack on it (trying all possible combinations) to discover legitimate user ID/password pairs for direct access to your hosts.
- Remote Procedure Calls (RPCs), including NIS and NFS, can be exploited, enabling intruders to read or write files to your host file systems or databases.

- X window, Open Window, and other UNIX Graphical User Interface (GUI) desktop systems can permit intruders to use the network to monitor or hijack other users' terminal sessions to a host computer.
- Telnet, FTP, and SMTP (Simple Message Transport Protocol, part of the mail backbone) can be abused, so access to these services should be restricted to selected systems and selected users or groups.

EARLY RECOMMENDATIONS FOR NEW AND EXISTING INTERNET CONNECTIONS

Without getting into too much detail at this point on mitigating Internet risks, it's imperative to understand that you need to take strong and specific measures to improve computer security. These measures include creating TCP/IP service access policies, using strong authentication, and using secure Internet gateways, routers, and proxies that can implement network access policies.

Network Service Policy

One of your first steps toward a secure Internet site is to establish the policies that detail what types of connectivity are and are not permitted. If, for example, e-mail is the only service you need, then other forms of access, such as Telnet and FTP, should be restricted, thus reducing your overall risks. Eliminating those TCP/IP services that are not needed helps to provide a simpler, more manageable network environment. You'll never hear the final word on the need for strong security policies!

Strong User Authentication

Systems that can be accessed from the Internet or via modems require strong authentication such as that provided by SmartCards and authentication tokens (discussed in Chapters 7, 8, and 15). Some of these systems use onetime passwords that cannot be spoofed, even if traffic is sniffed and user IDs and passwords are monitored.

Secure Gateways

Secure gateways—often called firewalls or proxy servers—are highly effective in improving site network security, but they cannot provide you with all the network security you need. A secure gateway is a collection of dedicated computer systems and routers, placed at a site's central connection to a network, whose main purpose is to restrict access to internal systems. A secure gateway forces all network connections to pass through the gateway, where they can be examined and evaluated. The secure gateway may then restrict access to or from selected systems, block certain TCP/IP services, or provide other security features, as dictated by the security policy that you load into its rule sets. A simple network usage policy that can be implemented by a secure gateway is to provide access from internal to external systems, but little or no access from external to internal systems (except perhaps for e-mail).

Some secure gateways implement proxy services that require that all HTTP, FTP, or Telnet connections are first authenticated at the gateway before being allowed to continue. This feature is implemented using what are called Access Control Lists (ACLs) through the proxy server software. The basic authentication form that's displayed requesting an authorized user's ID and password is shown in Figure 3-3.

Typical corporate networks that offer Internet access to users on their local area networks use a proxy server to control abuses of Net surfing. The proxy permits you to establish "hot lists" of forbidden Uniform Resource Locators (URLs), refuse the request, and log any attempts to access them. Without secure gateways, your site's security depends entirely on the collective security of its individual systems. As you increase the number of systems on your network, it becomes more difficult to ensure that network security policies are enforced. Errors and simple mistakes in one system's configuration can easily cause problems for other interconnected systems.

Securing Modem Pools

Unrestricted incoming and outgoing modem pools (including Private Branch Exchange, or PBX, systems) can create

Figure 3-3. The basic authentication form, displayed to authenticate the user's identity.

back doors that permit intruders to scoot around the access controls of the secure gateways attached to the public network. Modem pools must be configured to deny access to unauthorized users.

Systems that can be accessed from modem pools require strong authentication, such as onetime passwords or two-factor authentication. Modem pools should not be configured to permit outgoing connections unless you're able to control carefully who's using them and which remote resources are being accessed.

Securing Public Access Systems

Public access systems, such as anonymous FTP archives, are often prime targets for abuse. Such systems, if misconfigured to allow writing or placement of files, can permit intruders to destroy or alter data or software and use your systems to distribute their illegally obtained software (warez). The existence of a secure gateway alone does not negate any need for stronger system security measures. Many programs are available for system administrators to enhance system security and provide additional audit capability. Such tools can check for strong passwords, log connection information, detect changes in system files, and provide other features that help administrators to detect signs of intruders and break-ins.

Keeping Up-to-Date

Web- and Internet-site managers need to be aware of other resources and information that permit them to update site security as new vulnerabilities are discovered and as new tools and techniques to improve security become available. In particular, site managers need to know who to contact when trouble arises.

So far, you've seen how problems at the network alone are sufficient to cause restless nights, but worse problems may be found in business-specific application software, like those used for e-commerce purposes. By relying on insecure networks to protect mission-critical software and applications, you may be setting yourself up for impending doom. In Chapter 4, you'll see some of these additional vulnerabilities, along with the internal threats from those people you trust the most to keep you in business—your employees!

4

Hacking Isn't beyond the Corporate Perimeter

In one of many reported instances of intrusions into corporate networks, a disgruntled employee at Omega Engineering, a private corporation in Stamford, Connecticut, planted a timed virus known as a Logic Bomb in the system. A few days after the employee was escorted out the door, the bomb detonated, wiping out all of Omega's R&D and production code. The estimated loss to Omega: approximately $10 million.

In some ways, the threat of disgruntled employees wrecking havoc upon their employers as a last desperate act of revenge is nothing new. Long before the advent of e-commerce and the accompanying explosion in the number of corporate intranets and extranets, companies found themselves the victims of employees who stole anything from office supplies to equipment, mailing lists to electronic files. The banking industry has for years mandated that each employee take at least seven consecutive days of vacation a year so that the companies can perform internal audits of employee activity to prevent the "covering of tracks" when employees engage in illicit practices. In some companies, employees are trained to look over the shoulders of fellow employees and question their every move.

So why the fuss about security in today's workplace? Electronic commerce hasn't necessarily changed the nature of the game, but it certainly has raised the stakes—and frighteningly so. Forrester Research estimated that e-commerce business-to-consumer revenue would top $18 billion in 1999, up from almost $8 billion the previous year, and that business-to-business revenue would increase from a little more than $43 billion in 1998 to a staggering

$109 billion in 1999. Given these numbers, a spring 1999 PricewaterhouseCoopers survey showing that e-commerce sites are three times more likely to lose data or trade secrets than the traditional mail order/telephone order businesses is particularly alarming.

There are two looming questions: How much of this revenue will disappear into the accounts of computer hackers? And who are these perpetrators?

UNCERTAINTY: THE WORST OF THE PROBLEMS

Omega's losses are but a small fraction of the estimated billions of dollars that companies will lose each year to intrusions of their computer systems. No one really knows exactly how large this figure might be. One reason is that companies often do not realize that hackers have compromised their systems—at least not until it is far too late for them to do anything about it. This is particularly true of small businesses that are just beginning to establish an e-commerce presence but cannot afford sophisticated intrusion detection systems, let alone a staff of security experts to establish policies, procedures, and countermeasures. According to Bruce Murphy, a managing director at PricewaterhouseCoopers and a consultant on information security issues, almost half of the companies surveyed aren't even sure if intruders got into their systems or not in the past year. The PricewaterhouseCoopers survey of 1,600 informations systems professionals in 50 countries showed that the greatest threats to computer security comes from within: 58 percent reported authorized users and employees as the source of a security breach or corporate espionage act within the past year, while 35 percent said the sources of attack were unknown.

In a report released by the Computer Security Institute (CSI) and the Federal Bureau of Investigation, a survey of over 500 technical security specialists showed that 44 percent of network intrusions are insider jobs performed by unauthorized users and not outside hackers (see Figure 4-1). Consultants put the figure much higher, stating that

Figure 4-1. Likely sources of computer network intrusions.

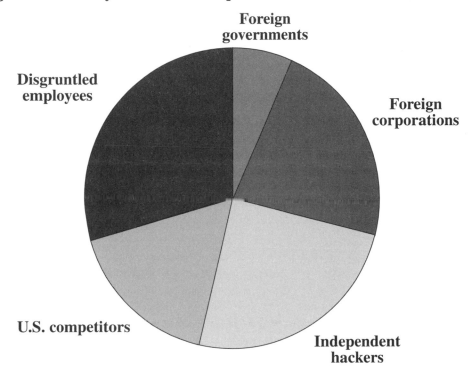

Source: Computer Security Institute (CSI) and Federal Bureau of Investigation (FBI) Computer Crime and Security Survey, March 1999.

between 70 and 80 percent of their clients' systems had been breached in some way by insiders (while allowing that some of the attacks undoubtedly are unintentional). In terms of sheer numbers, in 1996 the U.S. Department of Defense claimed there "may have been" 250,000 attacks on DoD networks in 1995, long before the Internet became what it is today. Of the 38,000 "friendly" attacks, 65 percent succeeded using only low-end hacker tools. Today these tools are far improved and far easier to obtain. Moreover, only 4 percent of the successful DoD attacks were noticed by network administrators, and only a small percentage of those detected were reported to authorities.

Companies are reluctant to disclose hacker attacks because of the associated bad press that the story of a compromised site necessarily entails. The banking industry is particularly guilty of keeping network break-ins under wraps. Traditionally, banks don't want to give the federal government any reason to question the integrity of their systems or practices (although some banks, such as First Union National Bank in Charlotte, North Carolina, make network security the first priority of any system it develops). Smaller businesses fear that if the public—or worse yet, other businesses with whom they trade—learn that their partner's sites are not secure, they will lose their hard-earned trust. And trust is what business is all about. The situation is analogous to the victims of violent crimes who are afraid of retaliation if they report the crime. Unfortunately, in too many cases the victim is perceived as a victimizer or as simply receiving his or her just deserts.

In a primer on computer crime and information warfare, the Computer Security Institute, based in San Francisco, reported that 75 percent of universities, financial institutions, and businesses experienced some type of computer crime, which included anything from the theft of laptops, to financial fraud, to the planting of Trojan horses and viruses. One goal of the hacker may be to disrupt a network or to shut it down completely (a denial of service attack). One such incident in February 2000 was considered by security and government officials as a "meltdown" of the Internet when eBay, Amazon.com, E*Trade, and other high-profile sites were hit with a distributed denial of service attack. In other cases, the objective is financial gain, such as the theft of customer data or corporate trade secrets.

THE ROLE OF LAZINESS AND INCOMPETENCE

You don't have to look far to realize how ubiquitous the frailty of network security really is. In early 1999, Joe Harris, a senior technical support professional at Blarg Online Services, an ISP (Internet service provider) in Bellevue, Washington, warned system administrators and Web developers about improperly configured e-commerce shopping cart software that created a world-readable log file of transaction data in a directory that was accessible via the public Internet—thus exposing confidential customer information. More than one hundred e-commerce businesses hosted by Blarg Online Services were unwittingly revealing customer credit card numbers, expiration dates, names, billing addresses, and other important information to Internet users. "This is like walking down the street and finding a black Hefty bag filled with 300 credit cards, all valid. Names, addresses, phone numbers, credit card numbers, e-mail addresses—it was all there. This is a nightmare," wrote Harris about the shopping cart vulnerabilities in his posting to the Bugtraq security online discussion list.

Harris found vulnerabilities in shopping cart systems in a variety of commercial products that people could purcharse, download for free, or use on a per-transaction basis. "All of these carts could have been secured by following the instructions that came with the CGI. The reason I found all of these is because the people did not follow those guidelines," said Harris. Web surfers could locate the data simply by using specific keywords while searching those sites. Most of the stores immediately rectified the problem. But how many other Web businesses are out there, inadvertently jeopardizing their existence by exposing themselves and their customers to theft and fraud?

Many experts feel that small businesses, rather than large corporations, run the greater risk of privacy breaches. They simply do not have the resources or know-how to protect their sites. Not that larger companies are not vulnerable—and important. "Smaller companies do cut corners, but the larger companies usually have large databases, and there's a lot more at stake," claims Ari Schwartz, policy analyst at the Center for Democracy and Technology in Washington, D.C. Schwartz recently cited an instance where Nissan North American Inc., in Carson, California, accidentally mailed the e-mail addresses of over 20,000 visitors who had registered on the company's Web site. Whether intentional or accidental, the financial losses for small and big business alike have made security a top priority for emerging and established businesses on the Internet.

BASIC THREATS

John Wylder, a senior vice president for information technology at SunTrust Service, one of the larger banks in Atlanta, has said, "The key to making sure you have the right security is not so much knowing the features of all the products. It's really just understanding what kind of Internet use creates what kinds of threats—and matching products to those threats."

Following his own advice, Wylder, along with other IT executives, developed a list of nine basic threats to Web sites as part of the Open User Recommended Solutions (OURS) Task Force, a Chicago-based committee of sixty corporate users and computer vendors. These are the threats that OURS has identified:

1. *Data Destruction.* The accidental or malicious loss of data on a Web site and the interception of data flowing from or to the Web site, whether this data is encrypted or not.

2. *Interference.* The derailing of a Web site by rerouting data intended for a site or overloading a site with data not intended for it, thus crippling the server.

3. *Modification.* The altering of incoming or outgoing data for a particular Web site, whether intentional or not. This is a particularly pernicious hazard since modification is difficult to detect in large transmissions.

4. *Misrepresentation.* The kind of electronic posturing that is the source of so many stories about bogus Web sites, where the perpetrator hands out false credentials, perhaps creating a counterfeit Web site to siphon off traffic intended for a legitimate destination.

5. *Repudiation.* The denial on the part of a consumer or customer that an online order was ever placed or the goods ever received.

6. *Accidental Use.* The inadvertent misuse of a Web site by a bona fide user.

7. *Unauthorized Altering or Downloading.* The inappropriate use of data, whether copying or updating, by someone without the proper security rights.
8. *Unauthorized Transactions.* Any use of a Web site by someone without approval.
9. *Unauthorized Disclosure.* The viewing of data without the appropriate permissions.

TYPES OF HACKERS

Who are these perpetrators, and what methods do they use to break into a network? The most popular view of the hacker is the antisocial late-night computer nerd with too much time on his hands and little better to do than try to break into computer networks from the outside. Hollywood has produced a glorified version of hackers as socially retarded, defiant, and angry teens and preteens. But the truth is that you may be living next door to a hacker. In fact, you may even find one in the next room, if you're thinking that your son or daughter is innocently chatting with friends on America Online.

The fact is that most studies show that the threats to computer network security may not come from external hackers but have an equally good chance of originating from inside an organization, where the trust of employees is often implicit. Furthermore, almost 90 percent of those responding to an American Society of Industrial Security (ASIS) report in March 1999 on the loss of intellectual property said their biggest worry was the disgruntled employee who had the access and ability to get even for what she feels was unjust treatment. Steve Dougherty, Senior Investigator–Electronic Operations for Pacific Bell, puts it this way: "The greatest exposure to any organization is what I call the knowledgeable insider—anybody from a janitor to a vendor or an active or ex-employee."

And then there is the Internet underground. As e-commerce has exploded, so has the growth of the underground, which is now more mainstream than ever before. The 1999 annual hacker convention known as DefCon in Las Vegas was the largest ever, and the secrecy that was once the by-word of the hacker community is now an obsolete concept. How many other criminal organizations hold open conventions and invite law enforcement personnel and the media?

There are three types of hackers:

1. Black Hat hackers
2. Gray Hat hackers
3. White Hat hackers

Black Hat Hackers

The Black Hats are the hackers who are most feared in the computer-reliant community. Their strength and motivation to wreak havoc is increasing, as are their numbers. Professional Black Hat hackers are also on the rise, and recruitment for their services is often found on the Internet underground. During the 1999 war over Kosovo, a world-wide concerted effort to attack U.S. government computer installations was orchestrated by Serbian rebels, and fears of intrusion and attack were heightened. Early in the year 2000, the U.S. government was beginning to organize strategically to ward off the greatest threat of an "Electronic Pearl Harbor."

Glory is perhaps the primary motivator for Black Hat hackers to perpetrate attacks. Being able to demonstrate their craft to their peers—especially after breaking a site that was thought to be secure—becomes a powerful motivator. Initiation into a Black Hat hacker group is similar to joining a street gang and may involve breaking the law, although in this community many believe that computers are fair game and that no one really owns the right to privacy or security.

Gray Hat Hackers

The Gray Hats are those people who want to perform a public service by sharing their knowledge of computer weaknesses but aren't particularly selective about who hears their warnings. Many of the Gray Hats are former Black Hats who have gotten caught or been frightened away from criminal activity but still yearn to explore computer vulnerabilities. Gray Hats are often found in the corporate world and are typically highly skilled programmers or system administrators. The U.S. Department of Defense, National Security Agency, and Central Intelligence Agency frequently call upon organized Gray Hats for help with security issues. The greatest threat from this community is not the act of hacking itself but the knowledge—in the form of published material—about how to perpetrate an attack. These published exploits on known systems and products are freely available to anyone who's interested.

White Hat Hackers

The White Hat hackers protect innocent computer users from the Black and Gray Hats—often at exorbitant costs. These hackers may be totally reformed criminals who've gone legitimate and are now working for commercial security consultants. Others are information security professionals who monitor or "play along" within the underground while remaining careful not to cross the line. Caution should be exercised in trying to convert a former Black Hat into a White Hat. It's possible to do—just be extra careful.

When dealing with any type of hacker, the best advice we can offer you rests in the old adage: Keep your friends close, but keep your enemies even closer!

A Hacker by Any Other Name . . .

There was a time when being called a hacker was one of the highest compliments you could pay a programmer. The hacker of yesteryear wrote program code that was elegant, compact, and impervious to flaws in its operation. Hackers usually worked without any formal specifications and used a code-and-fix approach to software development. Sometimes several programmers would compete on the same problem to see who could develop the most elegant solution. Many of the utilities and components of today's UNIX operating system variants were developed by these hackers.

Today's perjorative term *hacker* should more aptly be *cyberpunk*, a term popularized by Katie Hafner in her book *Cyberpunks: Outlaws and Hackers on the Computer Frontier.* Unfortunately, that term never stuck, and attempts to recoup the favor of the term *hacker* have failed miserably. Worse still, computer criminals prefer the term *hacker,* which leads to law enforcement searching for hackers, which in turn leads the media to report on hackers, and so forth.

Some of the other alternatives offered for the term *hacker* include:

- Cracker
- Ne'er-do-well
- Bad guy
- Adversary
- Malcontent
- Malicious user
- Script kiddie

TYPES OF HACKING

Security experts distinguish between two different kinds of computer hacking: (1) technical intrusion, where a hacker uses software and expertise to break into networks, and (2) nontechnical and less publicized intrusions, which are known as social engineering in hackerspeak. In both cases the hacker's objectives are the same: to gain access, disrupt service, or embarrass, or to steal confidential customer information, credit card numbers, program source code, trade secrets, or anything potentially valuable that's stored on an Internet-accessible server or database.

Often it's easy to find wide-open doors in the operating systems of the servers themselves. The UNIX operating system and TCP/IP (see Chapter 3) have over one hundred known vulnerabilities that are somewhere between patched and ignored. Information about these vulnerabilities travels rather quickly and spreads virulently throughout the world of would-be thieves. In fact, the Internet is a great tool to use to learn about the Internet—both its strengths and weaknesses. As Microsoft Windows NT Servers are becoming more pervasive, they're also becoming a larger target to those looking for new vulnerabilities that they'll inevitably find—creating a race between those installing new doors with locks and those trying to kick them down. Internal networks make an easy target to those wanting in. With the droves of auto-answer-enabled modems pervading modern desktop computers throughout organizations, auto- or war-dialers (which dial a range of numbers and record those that answer with handshake tones) will locate access points from the inside—far easier than trying to break in from the outside. Once a LAN-connected PC is under a perpetrator's control, all network resources are at risk, including back office networks.

Password controls and protections have become somewhat of a joke to those within the corporate environment. User IDs and passwords scribbled on Post-it Notes and stuck on top of monitors or PCs offer no security. Even your cleaning crews know to look for them. Aside from not keeping login information secret, typical users aren't that good at creating passwords in the first place. Easily guessed passwords or those that readily give way to brute-force attacks only add to their vulnerability.

Let's examine the two types of hacking: technical intrusion and nontechnical intrusion.

Technical Intrusion

Technical intrusion is often perpetrated using highly polished game plans or methodologies that employ tricks easily learned in the hacker underground. These tricks elevate what were once the pranks and hijinks of late-night computer nerds to a big business in attacking computer sites.

Organized hackers typically follow a methodical approach when attacking a site:

1. Target acquisition
2. Network discovery

3. Scanning for vulnerabilities
4. Hacking the system to gain root or administrator privileges
5. Disabling auditing and removing traces of intrusion from log files
6. Stealing files, modifying data, and stealing source code or other valuable information
7. Installing back doors and Trojan horses that permit undetectable reentry
8. Returning at will to inflict more damage

Before hackers begin an attack, they may know nothing about your network. By the time they're finished, they often know more about your systems than your systems administrator knows!

During the initial phase of an attack, the hacker creates a list of networks, domain names, and IP (Internet Protocol) addresses that may include a particular targeted system. Using a variety of queries and searches readily available on the Internet, the hacker can, with time and patience, build a repository of information about a particular company's internal network topology. This likely would include information about system aliases, functions, internal addresses, and potential gateways and firewalls. The hacker can also trace the paths that IP packets follow as they traverse the network. Next, the hacker focuses on systems within the targeted address space that respond to the network. A number of different tools allow him to test for a server response or ping the network in order to determine which systems are active. Once he has targeted his system, the hacker scans the system's ports, either sequentially or randomly. By doing so, he can determine what services are running on the targeted system, possibly revealing vulnerable services, which he can then exploit.

Where does the hacker get his tools? The answer, paradoxically enough, is the Internet. It makes the tools readily available as freeware or as commercially available software that the hacker can download to his PC. For example, in order to scan ports, he can easily obtain scanners such as strobe, netcat, jakal, nmap, or Asmodeus (Windows NT). (A theme that's repeated throughout this book is that the open architecture of the Internet imposes few restrictions on the user community. It's simply too massive an undertaking to patrol the activities of each and every user. That means that vigilance and caution are imperatives when considering opening your internal network to the Internet.)

In a further attempt to learn as much as he can about the targeted system, the hacker taps into program banners and prompts created by remote access and convenience services to help identify platforms, system types, and other useful information. The remote access banners are most typically associated with FTP, Telnet, pop (post office protocol), HTTP, and mail; several of the convenience services are finger, rusers, and rwho, to help learn more about legitimate computer user accounts. Popular freeware tools are strobe, SATAN (Security Administrator Tool for Analyzing Networks), and netcat, which the hacker can use to assemble a target matrix. This matrix contains IP addresses, active ports, protocols, and useful banner information.

Finally, as the last step of the discovery phase, the hacker gleans as much information as possible about target systems—information generally not intended for public viewing. Using more freeware and commercially available tools, the hacker gathers usernames, names of system files, mount points, and as much other useful information as he possibly can. The idea here is to refine the number of possible entry points and develop a strategy for attacking target systems.

Another technique that hackers use to determine the vulnerability of systems is called dial-in penetration. In one scenario, the hacker determines the dial-in phone number ranges from external sources such as the Internet, the company receptionist, and even corporate publications such as a prospectus. In yet another scenario, the hacker obtains phone numbers or a list of known ranges by contacting a knowledgeable employee inside the company. With this information, he can use a tool such as ToneLoc to create a list of numbers to try and test access. He can compile information such as the dial-in number, type and name of system, IP address, and passwords. Any number of tools (e.g., PCAnywhere, ProComm Plus, ReachOut, Crosstalk) allow the hacker to penetrate the system. This threat of penetration is insidious because it avoids most of the measures taken to prevent unauthorized access from the outside. With auto-answer modems on desktop systems, a successful takeover of a trusted user PC on the local area network could prove disastrous.

At this point the hacker has identified system vulnerabilities based on his assessment of the hardware, operating systems, and application software. He is now ready to exploit systems using manual techniques or any number of commercially available tools (e.g., CyberCop Scanner). How the hacker proceeds from this point to exploit a targeted system (and cover his tracks!) is the subject of chapters to follow.

However, we should mention in advance some of the basic techniques that hackers use to gain access to confidential information. The least elegant technique is the brute-force attack on a system. In this case the hacker uses a tool such as LophtCrack to attack encrypted passwords. Other techniques include session hijacking, keystroke recording, spoofing e-mail and Web sites, and installing Spartan horses, Trojan horses, or back doors. It should be clear by now that the experienced hacker has at his disposal a number of different and popular tools generally available as freeware or shareware that he can use to scan, identify, and target systems. The nature of his attack depends upon the particular vulnerability of a given system and his objectives.

Nontechnical Intrusion

Nontechnical intrusion, or social engineering, hasn't garnered the kind of attention it deserves in the world of network security, perhaps because it is the more obvious but less glamorous of the ways a hacker can break into a network. The hacker in this case uses trickery, chicanery, smooth talking, and persuasion to beguile and deceive a trusting, gullible, or otherwise unsuspecting coworker.

A recent case involving the FBI, foreign espionage, and possible smuggling of U.S. nuclear research by a Taiwanese-born physicist dramatically highlights the seriousness of insider threats. Wen Ho Lee was relieved of his position in March 1999 from the Los Alamos National Laboratory when he was suspected of transferring data without authorization from a classified government computer system to his unclassified and accessible desktop system. Lee was indicted on fifty-nine counts of mishandling sensitive information. His possible actions alarmed government security analysts as a serious breach in security.

In some instances, hackers with malicious or criminal intent are hired by information brokers to infiltrate a corporation. They may pose as janitors, administrative help, even programming contractors who have equal access to the company's data as full-time employees but are not subjected to the same kind of background checks. As one technical security consultant put it, "The problem with contractors is that they're brought in and given employee-like access, but [they're] not subjected to the same background checks, nondisclosures, and policy directives that employees are." Once inside an organization, the hacker can download files, steal passwords, locate root directories, or put sniffer programs on the network, among other things. She can also pose as someone conducting a telephone survey about security and, if she finds the right person, can wear her prey down with a long train of tedious questions until she gets the information she is looking for.

Frequent targets of social engineers are help-desk staff and end-users. Both groups are usually eager to assist the caller by providing passwords, user IDs, and names and phone numbers of network system administrators. The truly inventive and creative hacker has been known to pose as a telephone company repairman who puts a sniffer on a wire while the office revels on a Friday afternoon.

Dumpster Diving and Other Methods

Hackers also target physical facilities as an easy way to gain access to a company's secrets. They sometimes enter doors that employees use for smoking breaks or finagle a security pass from an unsuspecting guard. (Remote facilities generally have less security than main offices and are easier prey for hackers.) Another phrase that has crept into hackerspeak is *dumpster diving,* which means exactly what it sounds like: rummaging through trash cans, recycling bins, or dumpsters for scraps of paper that might hold passwords, account numbers, or any clues to the company's network.

5

Peeking inside a Hacker's Toolbox

In Chapter 4, you learned about the two most common forms of attacks on computer resources—technical intrusions and social engineering (nontechnical intrusions). Chapter 5 builds upon the details of technical intrusions by looking inside the wide array of readily available tools and techniques to disrupt networks or steal information. Here you'll find examples of programs that help hackers during the stages of an attack, namely:

- Target acquisition
- Network discovery
- Scanning for vulnerabilities
- Hacking the system to gain root or administrator privileges
- Disabling auditing and removing traces of intrusion from log files
- Stealing files, modifying data, and stealing source code or other valuable information
- Installing back doors and Trojan horses that permit undetectable reentry
- Returning at will to inflict more damage

Recall that hackers often begin by knowing nothing about your network, but by the time they're finished, they often know more than your own personnel.

This chapter shows the simplicity of hacking with only a tiny representative fraction of the readily available (and mostly free) weapons that are used to attack computer systems, locate vulnerabilities, or demonstrate attack mechanisms. Here you'll see several classes of tools that are used in different phases of attack, including:

- Password cracking tools
- Web and session hijacking tools
- E-mail spoofing tools
- Keystroke recording tools
- Rogue and hostile active languages programs

An important concept to understand about hacker tools is that the primary danger lies in who's operating them. Just as a hammer in a carpenter's toolbox could be used both to create and destroy, hacker tools can be used by both security specialists looking to close down holes prior to releasing a system into the wild, and by ne'er-do-wells hell-bent on causing damage or disruption to Internet services. One prime example of this paradox is SATAN.

SATAN

The Security Administrator Tool for Analyzing Networks, or SATAN, is one of the many general purpose UNIX system administrator's tools that proves dangerous in the wrong hands. When the developers of SATAN were asked why they developed it, they said:

> Why did we create SATAN? Quite simply, we wanted to know more about network security, particularly with respect to large networks. There is an enormous amount of information out there, and it is definitely not clear by examining informa-tion and hosts by hand what the real overall se-curity picture is. SATAN was an attempt to break new ground, to promote understanding, and to have fun writing such a program. . . .

With SATAN, people can find the security weaknesses of any computer system, locally or remotely—even un-skilled hacking amateurs. SATAN is used primarily in the network discovery phase of an attack. It performs the work of port scanning, ping sweeping, TCP (Transmission Con-trol Protocol) scanning, UDP (User Datagram Protocol) scanning, and other security assessments. SATAN is now a bit dated and has been replaced with a new version, called SAINT. (As you know, a race is under way between those people developing new and improved hacking techniques and those trying to detect and close vulnerabilities before they're exploited.)

Modern intrusion detection systems (IDSs) look for patterns of known attack signatures, including those from SATAN, and act upon them accordingly. For example, depending on the severity of an attack (or risk from damage if the attack is successful), the IDS may prevent further communications from that IP (Internet Protocol) address (called shunning), or it may record the fact for later investigation, if deemed appropriate. Because SATAN has been out there awhile and was commonly used for scanning, security product manufacturers began to look for its signature on Internet-based traffic passing through their IDS and now alert the users of their products when the pattern is found.

Because IDSs appear from many different manufacturers, the identification systems used on newly found vulnerabilities are unique to a manufacturer or security advisory board. As you'll see in Chapter 7, a recent effort to standardize the nomenclature of security vulnerabilities and exposures—called the Common Vulnerabilities and Exposures (CVE)—is under way, led by the MITRE Corporation.

HACKING YOUR WAY THROUGH THE INTERNET

Before looking at some specific classes of hacking tools, it's important to realize that when hackers are left to their own devices, only a low-to-moderate level of expertise is needed to configure and use common hacking tools properly. And unfortunately, the hacking community is rather helpful in training and simplifying the lives of their own kind. Consider the *Hackers' Handbook* CD from Dark Bay, Ltd. According to its makers, the handbook, which costs only $9.95, contains "over 800 hacking tools developed and used by the world's top hackers to exploit all types of computer security! Including: password crackers, Trojan horse wrappers, UNIX and LINUX scripts, Win 95/98 remote hacking, nuking, ICQ hacks, Win NT administrator crackers, virus labs, and much more!" The opening screen of the *Hackers' Handbook* is shown in Figure 5-1.

The "Hack/Phreak Library" on the CD contains everything a novice or expert hacker could want, without wasting time and bandwidth to download them. The most frightening entry is the "Beginners Step by Step Security Guide," version 0.1.32, written by Overlord. It's available free online at *http://www.cyberarmy.com*. What's most troubling about this guide is that it's a Web-based system of forms that makes hacking easy. It walks you through a strategy for an attack, explains the technique and reasons why it works, then offers you a choice of learning more about it or exercising the information on remote targets

Figure 5-1. The opening screen of the *Hackers' Handbook*.

that you supply. Hacking is now as simple as point and click! What's worse is that kits like this one offer anyone a conveniently available, straightforward, and effective hacking methodology, with rapid results, and is pervasively distributed.

The focus of the beginner's guide is to help a user to gain root access on a remote system, effectively controlling the target and rendering the host network susceptible to a free-for-all attack. Remember, no previous experience at hacking is required to use the guide. Here's a high-level look at its contents:

- Introduction
- Anatomy of a hack
- "Don't get caught"
- Information gathering
- Dirt digging stage
- Case the joint
- The old bouncing mail trick
- Traceroute
- Whois
- Give 'em the finger
- The deadly port scan
- Telneting
- Running lame programs
- Hacking through the password
- Easy things first
- Using the login names
- Getting the password file
- Ancient Chinese FTP method
- The old style PHF technique
- Finger box hacking

Once you've made it to the end, the program concludes:

Congratulations: You have gained access.
    If you now have the login code and password, you may use the user's mail account, FTP

privileges (change their Web pages), and HTTP access. . . .

All this and more for only $9.95 (plus shipping).

For additional information about the specific types of attacks listed, read *Hacking Exposed* by Stuart McClure, Joel Scrambray (*InternetWeek* journalists), and George Kurtz (an instructor for Ernst & Young's Extreme Hacking class). The book is second to none for building an effective Internet security defense to known problems and vulnerabilities in virtually all popular operating systems, network operating systems, and application programs. For each attack method, the authors include a clever risk rating that averages an attack's popularity, simplicity, and impact on the target system. As a reference guide in a complete library on information security, *Hacking Exposed* is indispensable!

POPULAR HACKING TOOLS

Everyone loves the latest and greatest cool tools, and hackers are no exception. The following is a small representation of some popular hacking tools, categorized by the type of misdeed they're capable of performing. Programs discussed in this chapter are readily available for free downloading on the Internet. Their appearance here does not constitute an endorsement, and users assume any risks inherent with their downloading, installation, or use.

Password Crackers

A sizable class of modern programs exist only to crack passwords that are stored in encrypted forms and are thought to be secure. All that's needed is a copy of the UNIX/etc/passwd file or NT Server SAM file, a cracker program, and a dictionary file. During the network discovery or scanning phase of an attack, an intruder will likely try running the FTP (File Transfer Protocol) or TFTP (Trivial File Transfer Protocol) services to grab a copy of a password file from either a UNIX or NT host system. If she's successful, she's only one step away from logging into the system using the credentials from an authorized user.

On server- or host-based systems, the file containing the list of authorized users stores passwords using a technique called hashing, which transforms real passwords into a form that cannot be read directly. The password is passed through a one-day hashing algorithm that cannot be reversed. Think of a one-way hash in the same vein as a meat grinder. You can run meat through a grinder to make ground beef, but you can't turn the ground beef back into the original chunks of meat. When a user enters his password, the server runs the entry through the hashing algorithm (built into the operating system) and compares the entry to that stored in the password file.

Pattern matching—through a brute-force attack that tries all possible combinations—encrypts every entry in a dictionary or a number of dictionaries, then compares the results to the encrypted passwords that are stored. Successful matches are recorded for later abuses. Dozens of free programs exist in this category and are readily found throughout the Internet. LophtCrack, shown in Figure 5-2,

Figure 5-2. The LophtCrack NT password cracker.

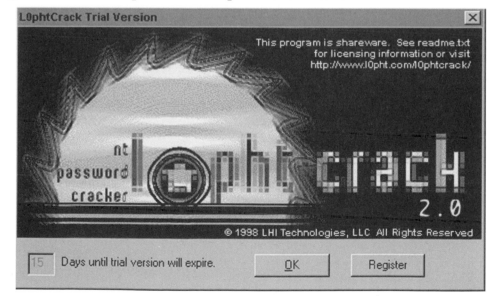

is but one example of programs in this class. LophtCrack converts LANMAN and NT password hashes into plaintext using a dictionary and a brute-force attack.

Another neat little tool is SnadBoy's Revelation program, which reveals hidden passwords that are stored in connection dialog boxes by users who check the "store my password in the password list" box. Figure 5-3 shows just how easy Revelation is to use. Worse still, the developers of Revelation believe that they've provided a valuable service to forgetful people!

Session Hijackers

Using packet-sniffing technology with useful interface, a "Man-in-the-Middle" attack makes it possible for an attacker's computer to receive data that's intended for an authorized user's computer. When it's in use, the program responds to the sender as though she's the authentic user. For example, an adversary could gain control of a Web server and send back faked Web pages to requesters. These Web pages might try to collect sensitive, private, or confidential information from the user or simply defame the company they're attacking. These methods of attack are useful for network discovery, hacking root, pilfering, or installing back doors.

Figure 5-3. The SnadBoy Revelation program.

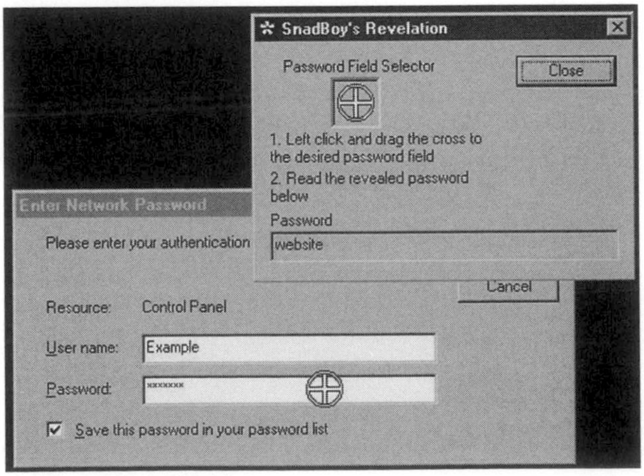

Still another type of a Man-in-the-Middle attack might occur on an intranet, where a Telnet session is taken over by an adversary using a sophisticated packet-sniffing application. Figure 5-4 shows an easy-to-use graphical interface to a tool that simplifies a session hijacking effort.

Spartan Horses

Everyone has heard of Trojan horse programs that offer for free some irresistible utility or service. It's only after a user downloads, installs, and runs the program that its true purpose is revealed. Often these Trojan horses damage the system (format disks, crash the operating system, alter the contents of the registry, etc.) or implant themselves into the system to wreak havoc later on (imbed a virus, collect keystrokes, transfer files to a remote computer, etc.).

There are also Spartan horse programs. One favorite Spartan horse causes the user to believe his system is disconnected from the network and requires a reconnection and reauthentication prior to proceeding with work. These

Figure 5-4. A Graphical User Interface screen for hijacking a Telnet session.

```
Connection Data: 10.0.0.1 [1027] <-> 10.0.0.3 [23]                    _ □ ×

File  Edit

lrwxrwxrwx  1 mcn        35 Sep 22 17:36 identify -> /home/candide/dmn/proje      LP: 10:26:14
cts/identify/                                                                        10/27/97
drwxrwsr-x  2 mcn       512 Apr 17  1997 lanl/
-rw-rw-rw-  1 mcn    209703 Sep 22 17:26 libpcap.tar.Z                          Status:
-rw-rw-r--  1 mcn     23552 Dec 12  1995 ms_statwork.fm                         Active
drwxrwsr-x  2 mcn       512 Dec 19  1995 newlic/
-rw-rw-r--  1 mcn     44032 Jun 16 13:44 product_rationale.fm                   Countermeasures
drwxrws---  6 mcn       512 Sep  2 19:54 projects/
-rw-rw-r--  1 mcn     36948 Sep 10 09:52 rawlog                                   Terminate
-rwxr-xr-x  2 mcn     49152 Oct 30  1996 rb*
-rwxr-xr-x  2 mcn     49152 Oct 30  1996 rz*                                      Take Over
-rw-rw-r--  1 mcn      4252 Jul  2  1996 standard.mcn
drwxrwsr-x  2 mcn       512 Dec  5  1995 stuff/                                 M-0           ▼
drwxrwsr-x  6 mcn      1536 Oct 26 00:46 trans/
drwxrwsr-x  6 mcn      1536 Jul 29 14:26 watcher/                                 Send (Client)
-rw-rw-rw-  1 mcn    962308 Aug 28 18:29 webpage.tar.gz
-r-xr-xr-x  1 mcn     57344 Oct 30  1996 xcomm*                                   Send (Server)
.candide.mcn,~ {4} > id
uid=100(mcn) gid=0(wheel) groups=0(wheel),10(staff),30(security),31(www),40(sour
ce),41(ppp),42(identify)
.candide.mcn,~ {5} > su
Password:
Sorry
.candide.mcn,~ {6} >
^M^J^M^J^M^Jls -l^M^Jid^M^Jsu^M^Jrootpw^M^J
```

attacks are launched using a number of different means. Legitimate Web pages may be hacked with a Spartan horse program that tells the user that their network connection has been severed and asks them to login again with their ID and password. This data is usually collected on a remote computer and recalled later for illegitimate uses. Vulnerable attack points for Spartan horses include Web-based guest books, message boards, Internet Relay Chat (IRC) clients, Usenet groups, FTP sites, and even e-mail. In fact, anywhere HTML (HyperText Markup Language) can be embedded is vulnerable to a Spartan horse attack.

Figure 5-5 shows an example of the message that users see when the Spartan horse activates. Figure 5-6 shows the new login dialog box that appears after users dismiss the error message. Only users who pay very close attention to the details and appearance of the dialog box may realize that something's amiss. Unfortunately, most users have grown so accustomed to seeing these dialog boxes that they offer up their authentication data freely and without suspicion.

Keystroke Recording Programs

Keystroke recording programs are another class of programs that are touted as being "helpful." Intended for parents who want an "automatic babysitter" while their children type at the keyboard, keystroke recording programs—like the one shown in Figure 5-7—can be particularly insidious. When such a program is implanted on a

Figure 5-5. An example of the error message that users see when a Spartan horse activates.

www.thetopoftheworld.com - [JavaScript Application]   ☒

⚠ Error 630: You have been disconnected from the computer you dialed. Please re-enter sign-on information to reconnect.

[OK]

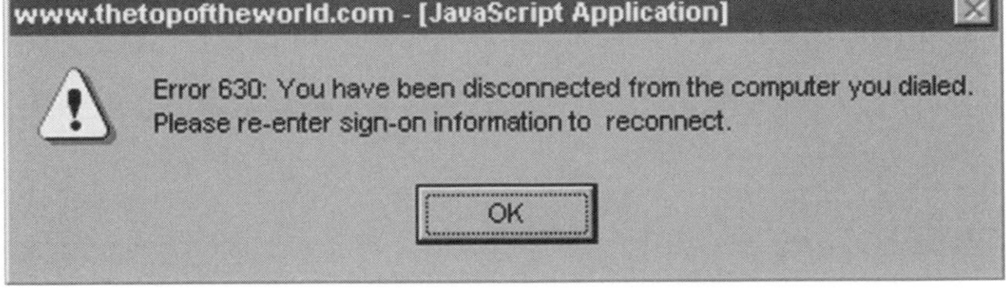

Figure 5-6. The Spartan horse login dialog box.

victim's computer system, IDs and passwords can be easily collected and sent to a remote computer for illegal purposes, thus saving the time to explore the network or crack password files. Grab the password as it's being typed, and you're in!

Skeleton-key is another good example of a program in this class that exploits PC-based networks. It loads itself at boot-up time and waits until it "sees" the word "LOGIN" or "login" typed. It then begins recording a 256-byte buffer of whatever the user types in following the word LOGIN or login. Once the buffer is full, it writes the data to a file for later retrieval.

Rogue and Hostile Active Languages Programs

Literally thousands of programs in this class are readily found with little effort around the Internet. Java, Java-Script, and ActiveX present a terrific set of opportunities for those who would harm us. For example, several incidents aimed at Hotmail.com used rogue JavaScript forms to col-

Figure 5-7. An example of a keystroke recording program control panel.

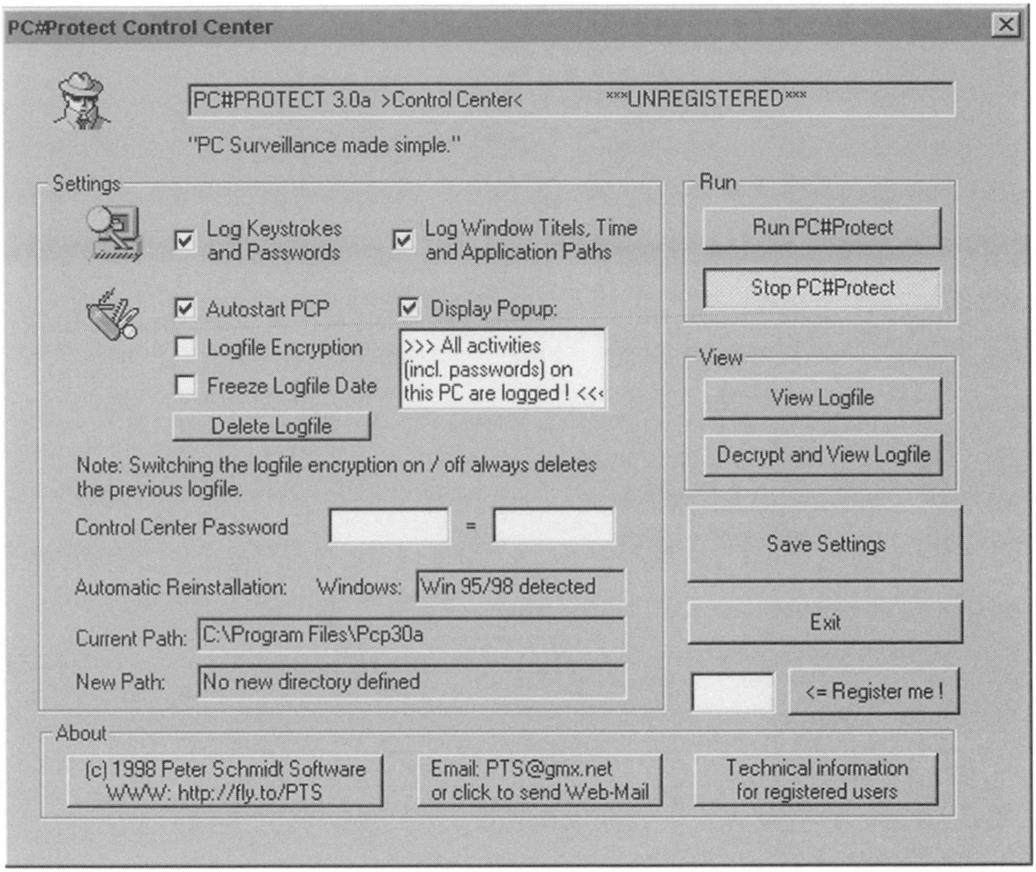

lect login IDs and passwords, then used the data to compromise the e-mail accounts of hundreds of users. In addition, hostile Java applets can gain control of a user's browser and prevent any further productive uses until the program is terminated and restarted—amounting to a denial of service attack while it's active.

Let's not forget Back Orifice, recently updated for the Windows 2000 operating system. With Back Orifice, a rogue remote user can take control over a target host system, after the simple act of convincing an unwary user to download a small piece of program code, called a Back Orifice client. Once installed, the program permits a remote user to take control of the system interface and have her way with the machine. Similar programs like PCAnywhere, Microsoft's remote system administrator manager, and others accomplish the same feats, but Back Orifice has gained notoriety because of its propensity for abuse.

E-Mail Spoofing

Want to send an impostor e-mail message to someone? It's simple: Just fill out a form like the one shown in Figure 5-8. Even without any tools, the act is still simple. The mail handling daemon, smtpd, was never built with the need for security or user authentication. Consequently, it gladly accepts whatever is typed in (providing syntax rules are followed), and then gladly delivers the e-mail. This is one of the reasons that e-mail spamming has become so common, widespread, and untraceable.

Other Handy Tools

So you think that your Excel spreadsheets are safe from prying eyes when you encrypt them prior to saving them? Guess again! Figure 5-9 shows just how unsafe those spreadsheets really are. All that's needed is the name of the file to decrypt and the name of the file in which to save the decrypted spreadsheet. Users would never even know that they've become a victim until it's too late because nothing is changed in the original file.

Although it's impossible and impractical to cover them all within the scope of this book, a variety of other threatening tools are also available for:

- Domain Name Service (DNS) poisoning and redirection
- Address Resolution Protocol (ARP) broadcast attacks for redirection purposes
- Exploiting weaknesses in Virtual Private Network (VPN) technologies like Point-to-Point Tunneling Protocol (PPTP)
- Building viruses or variants of other viruses

Figure 5-8. A Web form to send fake e-mail.

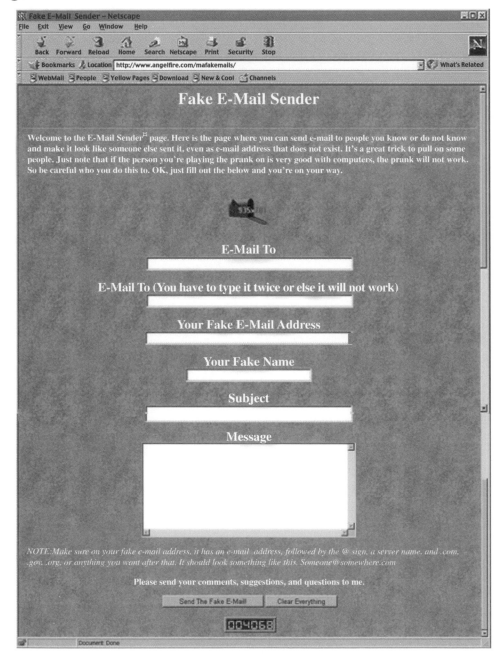

Figure 5-9. A program to decrypt Excel spreadsheets.

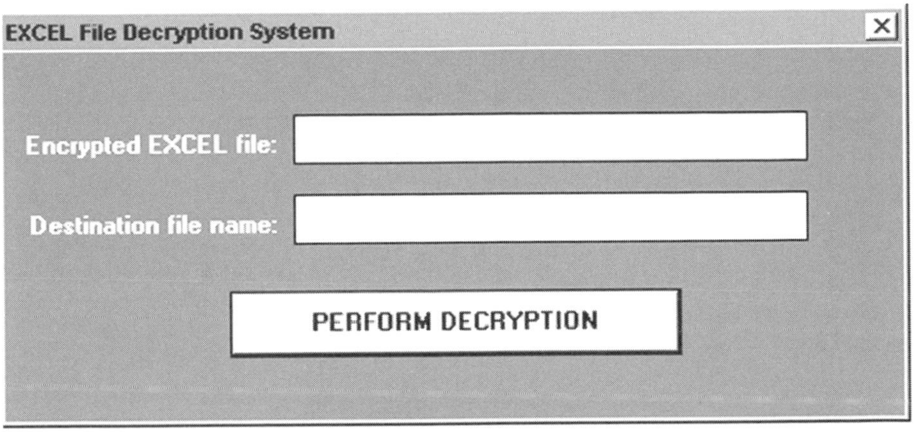

- Network packet sniffing
- War-dialing

TESTING YOUR HACKING IQ

Perhaps you're ready to test your hacking abilities. Try the irreverent "computer hacking test" below. The Hacker Test—Version 3.0 was conceived and written by Felix Lee, John Hayes, and Angela Thomas in 1989. Late that year, it was made into an interactive computer program by Rich "Crash" Lewis at Miami University in Oxford, Ohio. In 1992, the final version of the Hacker Test was released free to the world. It has since received rave reviews from the industry. You can find a copy of the complete test on the *Hackers' Handbook* CD. An image of the program's interface is shown in Figure 5-10.

Here's an excerpt of the more than 500 questions composing the Hacker Test:

> *0001 Have you ever used a computer?*
> **Have you ever used a computer:*
> *0002 . . . for more than 4 hours continuously?*
> *0003 . . . for more than 8 hours?*

Figure 5-10. The interface of the Hacker Test.

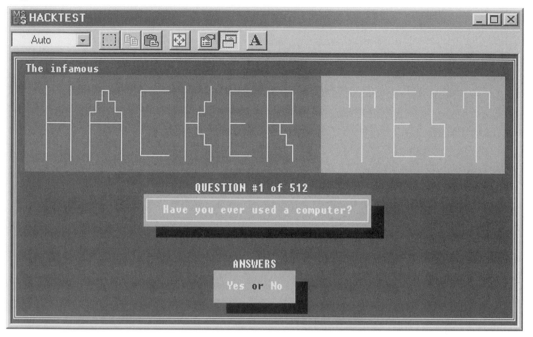

0004 . . . *for more than 16 hours?*

0005 . . . *for more than 32 hours?*

0006 *Have you ever patched paper tape?*

0007 *Have you ever missed a class while programming?*

* *While programming, have you ever:*

0008 . . . *Missed an examination?*

0009 . . . *Missed a wedding?*

0010 . . . *Missed your own wedding?*

0011 *Have you ever programmed while intoxicated?*

0012 . . . *Did it make sense the next day?*

0013 *Have you ever written a flight simulator?*

0014 *Have you ever voided the warranty on your equipment?*

0015 *Ever change the value of 4?*

Ever change the value of 4:

0016 . . . *Unintentionally?*

0017 . . . *In a language other than Fortran?*

0018 *Do you use DWIM to make life interesting?*

0019 Have you named a computer?

0020 Do you complain when a "feature" you use gets fixed?

0021 Do you eat slime-molds?

0022 Do you know how many days old you are?

0023 Have you ever wanted to download pizza?

0024 Have you ever invented a computer joke?

0025 . . . Did someone not 'get' it?

0026 Can you recite "Jabberwocky"?

0027 . . . Backwards?

0028 Have you seen "Donald Duck in Mathemagic Land"?

0029 Have you seen "Tron"?

0030 Have you seen "Wargames"?

0031 Do you know what ASCII stands for?

0032 . . . EBCDIC?

0033 Can you read and write ASCII in hex or octal?

0034 Do you know the names of all the ASCII control codes?

0035 Can you read and write EBCDIC in hex?

0036 Can you convert from EBCDIC to ASCII and vice versa?

0037 Do you know what characters are the same in both ASCII and EBCDIC?

0038 Do you know maxint on your system?

0039 Ever define your own numerical type to get better precision?

0040 Can you name powers of two up to 2**16 in arbitrary order?

*Can you name powers of two in arbitrary order:

0041 . . . up to 2**32?

0042 . . . up to 2**64?

0043 Can you read a punched card, looking at the holes?

0044 . . . feeling the holes?

0045 Have you ever patched binary code?

0046 . . . While the program was running?

0047 Have you ever used program overlays?

0048 Have you met any IBM vice president?

0049 Do you know Dennis, Bill, or Ken?

0050 Have you ever taken a picture of a CRT?

0051 Have you ever played a videotape on your CRT?

0052 Have you ever digitized a picture?

0053 Did you ever forget to mount a scratch monkey?

0054 Have you ever optimized an idle loop?

0055 Did you ever optimize a bubble sort?

0056 Does your terminal/computer talk to you?

0057 Have you ever talked into an acoustic modem?

0058 . . . Did it answer?

*Can you whistle:

0059 . . . 300 baud?

0060 . . . 1200 baud?

0061 Can you whistle a telephone number?

0062 Have you witnessed a disk crash?

0063 Have you made a disk drive "walk"?

0064 Can you build a puffer train?

0065 . . . Do you know what it is?

0066 Can you play music on your line printer?

0067 . . . Your disk drive?

0068 . . . Your tape drive?

0069 Do you have a Snoopy calendar?

0070 . . . Is it out-of-date?

*Do you have a line printer picture of:

0071 . . . Woody Allen?

0072 . . . the Mona Lisa?

0073 . . . the Enterprise?

0074 . . . Einstein?

0075 . . . Oliver?

0076 Have you ever made a line printer picture?

0077 Have you ever had your face on a line printer picture?

*Do you know what this stands for?

0078 . . . DASD

0079 . . . Emacs

0080 . . . ITS

0081 . . . RSTS/E

0082 . . . SNA

0083 . . . Spool

0084 . . . TCP/IP

*Have you ever used:

0085 . . . TPU?

0086 . . . TECO?

0087 . . . Emacs?

0088 . . . ed?

0089 . . . vi?

0090 . . . Xedit (in VM/CMS)?

0091 . . . SOS?

0092 . . . EDT?

0093 . . . Wordstar?

0094 Have you ever written a CLIST?

*Have you ever programmed in:

0095 . . . the X windowing system?

0096 . . . CICS?

0097 Have you ever received a fax or a photocopy of a floppy?

0098 Have you ever shown a novice the "any" key?

0099 . . . Was it the power switch?

*Have you ever attended:

0100 . . . Usenix?

0101 . . . DECUS?

0102 . . . SHARE?

0103 . . . SIGGRAPH?

0104 . . . NetCon?

0105 Have you ever participated in a standards group?

0106 Have you ever debugged machine code over the telephone?

0107 Have you ever seen voice mail?

0108 . . . Can you read it?

Use the following scoring grid to see how you've done. Count 1 for each item that you have done or each question that you can answer correctly.

SO WHAT CAN YOU DO TO SAVE YOURSELF?

Of course, there's no single answer to that question, any more than there is an effective single weapon against an arsenal of the adversary's weapons. Typical attacks are launched using a combination of techniques and tools, making them far more difficult to detect and respond.

If your score is between:	You are:
0x00 and 0x010	Computer Illiterate
0x011 and 0x040	a User
0x041 and 0x080	an Operator
0x081 and 0x0C0	a Nerd
0x0C1 and 0x100	a Hacker
0x101 and 0x180	a Guru
0x181 and 0x200	a Wizard

Note: If you don't understand the scoring, stop here.

What's important is that you're prepared to defend yourself in the event of an attack.

Beginning with Chapter 6, you'll start to uncover some of the programs, principles, and technologies behind warding off intruders from your network.

6

Instrumental Effects for Security Assurance

Now that you've seen some of the threats you're up against and you understand just how vulnerable Internet-attached networks are, your first instinct may be to start installing security technologies to help cut attackers off at their knees. But before you rush out to hire a security consultant or fall prey to the seduction of security products, it's imperative that you know how to shop for products intelligently.

How can you effectively compare security products (firewalls, intrusion detection systems, etc.) across product lines and among different suppliers when all you have to go on is advertising and hype? How can you know that a product actually lives up to your expectations and provides the levels of security that you require? Wouldn't it be great if the information technology (IT) industry and security professionals had a metric to use that truly helps consumers to compare apples to apples when selecting security products for general and e-commerce purposes?

Thanks to ongoing international efforts, that metric exists today and is shaping how you'll purchase security systems tomorrow. Before we uncover specific security products in upcoming chapters, let's look at how to compare like products. This will place you at a distinct advantage when you're ready to start finding solutions to your security concerns.

THE COMMON CRITERIA (CC) FOR INFORMATION TECHNOLOGY SECURITY EVALUATION

The Common Criteria (CC), commonly known as ISO 15408, combines the best features of three separate criteria: (1) from the United States, the Trusted Computer Security Evaluation Criteria (TCSEC, also known as the National Security Agency's Orange Book); (2) from Europe, the Information Technology Security Evaluation Criteria (ITSEC); and (3) from Canada, the Canadian Trusted Computer Product Evaluation Criteria (CTCPEC). These have been synergized into a new, single international standard.

Some of the countries and organizations involved in the development of the Common Criteria are:

- *Canada:* Communications Security Establishment *(www.cse-cst.gc.ca/cse/english/cc.html)*
- *France:* Service Central de la Securité des Systèmes d'Information
- *Germany:* Bundesamt fur Sicherheit in der Informationstechnik *(www.bsi.de)*
- *Netherlands:* Netherlands National Communications Security Agency
- *United Kingdom:* Communications–Electronics Security Group *(www.cesg.gov.uk/cchtml)*
- *United States:* National Institute of Standards and Technology (NIST—*csrc.nist.gov/cc*) and National Security Agency (NSA—*www.radium.ncsc.mil/tpep*)

The Common Criteria Version 1 was released for public comment in 1996. Version 2 embodies revisions after extensive reviews and trials and was submitted to the International Standards Organization (ISO) in 1998. CC Version 2 was approved as an ISO standard on June 8, 1999.

The CC provides a common language and structure to express IT security requirements and enables the creation of catalogs of standards, broken down into components and packages. Packages permit the expressing of requirements that meet an identifiable subset of security objectives. Packages are reusable and can be used to construct larger packages as well. Using the CC framework, users and developers of IT security products create what are called Protection Profiles (PPs) as an implementation-independent collection of objectives and requirements for any given category of products or systems that must meet similar needs (e.g., firewalls). Protection Profiles are needed to support the defining of functional standards and serve as an aid in specifying needs for procurement purposes.

While Protection Profiles serve as a generic description of product and environment requirements, Targets of Evaluation (TOEs) are the specific products or systems that fall into an evaluation against an existing PP. The sets of evidence about a TOE and the TOE itself form the inputs to a Security Target (ST) that's used by certified independent evaluators as the basis for evaluation.

Security requirements appear as two types: functional and assurance. *Functional requirements* describe what a product needs to do, and *assurance requirements* describe how well it meets functional requirements. Consumers need both of these pieces of data to effectively judge the merits of one product over another.

In defining security requirements for a trusted prouct or system, users and developers need to consider the threats to the environment. The CC provides a catalog of components (Part II of the CC) that developers of PPs use to form the requirements definition. Assurance requirements (defined in Part III of the CC) contain two classes from which evaluation assurance requirements may be selected, along with a class for assurance maintenance.

Organization of the Protection Profile

A Protection Profile is organized as follows:

1. *Introduction,* which provides descriptive information that's needed to identify, catalog, register, and cross-reference a PP. The overview provides a summary of the PP as a narrative.

2. *Target of Evaluation (TOE),* which describes the TOE to aid in understanding its security requirements and addresses the product type and the general features of the TOE, providing a context for the evaluation.

3. *Security Environment,* which consists of three subsections: Assumptions, Threats, and Organizational Security Policies. These subsections describe the security aspects of

the environment in which the TOE is to be used and the manner in which it is to be used. The Assumptions subsection describes the security aspects of the environment in which the TOE is to be used, including information about the intended usage, aspects about the intended applications, potential asset value, and possible limitations of use. The Threats subsection covers all the threats where specific protection within the TOE or its environment are needed. Only those threats that are relevant for secure TOE operation are included. The Organizational Security Policies subsection identifies and explains any security policies or rules that govern the TOE or its operating environment.

4. *Security Objectives*, which address all of the security environment aspects identified in earlier sections of the PP. These objectives define the intent of the TOE to counter identified threats and include the organizational security policies and assumptions.

5. *Security Requirements*, which consist of: Functional Requirements and Assurance Requirements. This section defines in detail the security requirements that must be satisfied by the TOE or its environment and describes what supporting evidence is needed to satisfy security objectives. Functional Requirements are selected from the CC functional components (Part II). Assurance requirements are stated as one of the Evaluation Assurance Levels (EALs) from the CC Part III assurance components.

6. *Rationale*, which presents the evidence used by a PP evaluation. This evidence supports the claims that the PP is a complete and cohesive set of requirements and that a compliant TOE provides an effective set of IT security countermeasures within the security environment.

Security Functional Requirements

The classes of security functional requirements (component catalog) found in Part II of the CC include:

- Audit
- Cryptographic support
- Communications

- User data protection
- Identification and authentication
- Security management
- Privacy
- Protection of the TOE security functions
- Resource utilization
- TOE access

Evaluation assurance classes found in Part III of the CC include the following:

- Configuration management helps ensure that the integrity of the TOE is preserved through required discipline and control in the processes of refinement and modification of the TOE and other related information. Configuration management prevents unauthorized modifications, additions, or deletions to the TOE and provides assurance that the TOE and documentation used for evaluation are the ones prepared for distribution.

- Delivery and operation classes define the requirements for the measures, procedures, and standards concerned with secure delivery, installation, and operational use of the TOE, assuring that the security protection offered by the TOE is not compromised during transfer, installation, start-up, and operation.

- Development classes define the requirements for the stepwise refinement of the TOE Security Functions (TSF) from the summary specification in the Security Target (ST) down to the actual implementation. Each of the resulting TSF representations provide information to help the evaluator determine whether the functional requirements of the TOE have been met.

- Guidance documents define the requirements for understandability, coverage, and completeness of the operational documentation provided by the developer. This documentation, which provides two categories of information—for users and for administrators—is an important factor in the secure operation of the TOE.

- Life Cycle Support defines the requirements for the adoption of a well-defined life-cycle model for all the steps of the TOE development, including flaw remediation procedures and policies, correct use of tools and techniques, and the security measures used to protect the development environment.

- Tests cover the testing requirements needed to demonstrate that the TSF satisfies the TOE security functional requirements. This class addresses coverage, depth of developer testing, and functional tests for independent lab testing.

- Vulnerability Assessment defines the requirements directed at identifying exploitable vulnerabilities. Specifically, it addresses those vulnerabilities introduced in the construction, operation, misuse, or incorrect configuration of the TOE.

- Protection Profile Evaluation has the goal of demonstrating that the PP is complete, consistent, and technically sound and that an evaluated PP is suitable as the basis for developing an ST.

- Security Target Evaluation has the goal of demonstrating that the ST is complete, consistent, and technically sound and is suitable as the basis for the corresponding TOE evaluation.

- Maintenance of Assurance provides the requirements intended for application after a TOE has been certified against the Common Criteria.

These requirements help to assure that the TOE will continue to meet its Security Target as changes are made to the TOE or its environment. Such changes include the discovery of new threats or vulnerabilities, changes in user requirements, and the correction of bugs found in the certified TOE.

Evaluation Assurance Levels

Evaluation Assurance Levels (EALs) define a scale for measuring the criteria for evaluating PPs and STs. EALs provide an increasing scale that balances the levels of assurance claimed with the cost and feasibility of acquiring such assurance. Table 6-1 indicates the CC EAL levels, compared to the criteria levels in the Orange Book (or TCSEC) and the ITSEC (discussed earlier in this chapter).

Evaluation Assurance Level 1

EAL1 applies where some confidence in correct operation is required, but the threats to security are not viewed as serious. It's of value where independent assurance is required to support the contention that due care has been exercised in protecting personal or similar types of information. It's intended that an EAL1 evaluation could be successfully conducted without assistance from the developer of the TOE, and for minimal outlays of investment. An evaluation at this level provides evidence that the TOE functions in a manner consistent with its documentation and that it provides useful protection against identified threats.

Table 6-1. **A comparison of the Common Criteria Evaluation Assurance Levels, Orange Book criteria levels, and ITSEC criteria levels.**

Common Criteria Evaluation Assurance Level	Orange Book Criteria Level	ITSEC Criteria Level
—	D: Minimal protection	E0
EAL1	—	—
EAL2	C1: Discretionary Security Protection	E1
EAL3	C2: Controlled Access Protection	E2
EAL4	B1: Labeled Security Protection	E3
EAL5	B2: Structured Protection	E4
EAL6	B3: Security Domains	E5
EAL7	A1: Verified Design	E6

Think of EAL1 as kicking the tires on a product you're considering for purchase.

Evaluation Assurance Level 2

EAL2 requires the cooperation of a developer in terms of the delivery of design information and test results, but it does not demand more effort on the part of the developer than is consistent with good commercial practice and should not require a substantially increased investment of cost or time. EAL2 is applicable where developers or users require a low to moderate level of independently assured security in the absence of ready availability of the complete development record. Such a situation may arise when securing legacy systems or where access to the developer may be limited.

Evaluation Assurance Level 3

EAL3 permits a conscientious developer to gain maximum assurance from positive security engineering at the design stage without substantial alteration to existing sound development practices. EAL3 applies in those circumstances where developers or users require a moderate level of independently assured security, and it requires a thorough investigation of the TOE and its development but without substantial reengineering.

Evaluation Assurance Level 4

EAL4 permits a developer to gain maximum assurance from positive security engineering based on good commercial development practices that, though rigorous, do not require substantial specialist knowledge, skills, or other resources. EAL4 is applicable in those circumstances where developers or users require a moderate to high level of independently assured security in conventional off-the-shelf TOEs and are prepared to incur additional security-specific engineering costs.

Evaluation Assurance Level 5

EAL5 permits a developer to gain maximum assurance from security engineering based upon rigorous commercial development practices supported by moderate application of specialist security engineering techniques. Such a TOE is likely to be designed and developed with the intent of achieving EAL5 assurance. EAL5 is applicable in those circumstances where developers or users require a high level of independently assured security in a planned development and require a rigorous development approach without incurring unreasonable costs for special security engineering techniques.

Evaluation Assurance Level 6

EAL6 permits developers to gain high assurance from application of security engineering techniques to a rigorous development environment in order to produce a premium TOE for protecting high-value assets against significant risks. EAL6 is applicable to the development of security TOEs for application in high-risk situations, where the value of the protected assets justifies additional costs.

Evaluation Assurance Level 7

EAL7 applies to development of security TOEs for application in extremely high-risk situations, where the value of such assets justifies the costs for higher assurance levels.

Once a Security Target is independently evaluated and is found to meet the desired assurance level, the CC provides for a certification process that's recognized across all CC-using countries. The implication is that products developed and tested abroad can compete on equal footing with similar products developed within the United States.

THE CONUNDRUM OF SECURITY TESTING

For the moment, consider the problem of security testing. When developing software, the goal is to write it to do something that provides a needed function. Testing then becomes a matter of determining if the product performs as it was intended by checking for what it does.

With security testing, the approach turns this model

on its head. At his April 1999 presentation on "Flaws in Cryptographic Systems" at Certicom, Bruce Schneier—a leading industry expert on security—points out some of the stickier issues related to security and testing. According to Schneier, security engineering is different from any other type of engineering because:

- Most products are useful for what they do, but security products are useful precisely because of what they do not allow to be done.
- Most engineering involves making things work, but security engineering involves figuring out how to make things *not* work, and then preventing those failures.
- Safety engineering involves making sure things do not fail in the presence of random faults, but security engineering involves making sure things do not fail in the presence of an intelligent and malicious adversary who forces faults at precisely the wrong time and in precisely the wrong way.

Schneier continues with the challenges that testers of security products face:

- Security is orthogonal to functionality.
- Just because a security product functions properly does not mean that it's secure.
- No amount of beta testing can ever uncover a security flaw.
- Experienced security testing is required to discover security flaws.

THE NATIONAL INFORMATION ASSURANCE PARTNERSHIP (NIAP)

Independent security testing is needed by everyone who wants to design, build, market, procure, or use products or systems that claim some level of security or trust. Testing adds value—but it's neither easy nor cheap to perform.

To help in addressing some of these issues and challenges, the National Information Assurance Partnership (NIAP) was formed to foster the availability of objective measures and testing methods for evaluating IT security products. NIAP also promotes the development of commercial testing labs to provide internationally recognized formal independent testing and validation services.

NIAP is a collaborative effort between the National Institute of Standards and Technology (NIST) and the U.S. National Security Agency (NSA), but its goals are designed to serve more than the U.S. government alone. Those goals include:

- Promoting the development and use of evaluated, security-enhanced IT products
- Furthering the growth and development of a common security testing industry
- Supporting a framework for international recognition and acceptance of standardized security evaluation methods
- Fostering research and development in security specifications, tests, tools, and metrics

NIAP's efforts have just begun, but as of early 2000, the following programs and activities are planned or already under way:

- Establishing a Common Criteria Evaluation and Validation Scheme (CCEVS) and lab accreditation programs for IT security
- Supporting the formal, international mutual recognition scheme rooted on Common Criteria–based tests and evaluation
- Maintaining lists of accredited labs, evaluation reports, and validated products
- Serving as a general center of expertise and resources for the security testing community
- Assisting organizations wishing to establish testing and validation programs for standards, products, or classes of products

- Developing tools for use by IT product developers and test labs
- Collaborating with industry or testing labs on research into advanced techniques of specification-based testing
- Developing Common Criteria Protection Profiles and associated test sets for selected classes of security products (e.g., firewalls, routers, DBMSs [Database Management Systems])
- Facilitating or sponsoring workshops and classes related to system and product testing and evaluations.
- Issuing Common Criteria certificates for IT products that successfully complete evaluation and verification

THE COMMON EVALUATION METHODOLOGY (CEM)

The Common Evaluation Methodology (CEM) Editorial Board, with members from all of the organizations that produced the Common Criteria (CC) for Information Technology Security Evaluation, is responsible for producing an agreed-upon methodology for conducting evaluations to apply the CC to security targets. The CEM is a companion document to the CC. It's focused on the actions that evaluators must take to determine that CC requirements for a TOE are present. CEM is a tool that's used by evaluation schemes to ensure consistent application of the requirements across multiple evaluations and multiple schemes. As such, it is an important component of the Mutual Recognition Arrangement (MRA) that enables any country to accept a certified evaluation from any other member country. So far, agreement has been reached for evaluation levels EAL1 to EAL4, which are deemed adequate for most commercial security products. The CEM Editorial Board is continuing the work on common evaluations for levels EAL5, EAL6, and EAL7.

The CEM Approach

Portions of the CEM are still in development and are out for review, and public comments are welcome. You can find a copy of it in its current state at the NIST Web site (*csrc.nist. gov/cc/cem*).

In its next release sometime in 2000, the CEM will contain three parts:

- Part I: *Introduction and General Model.* Describes agreed-upon principles of evaluation and introduces agreed-upon evaluation terminology dealing with the process of evaluation.
- Part II: *CC Evaluation Methodology,* based on CC Part III evaluator actions. Uses well-defined assertions to refine CC Part III evaluator actions and tangible evaluator activities to determine requirement compliance. In addition, it will offer guidance to further clarify the intent of evaluator actions. Part II provides for:
  - Methodology to evaluate PPs (Protection Profiles)
  - Methodology to evaluate STs (Security Targets)
  - Methodology to evaluate EAL1
  - Methodology to evaluate EAL2
  - Methodology to evaluate EAL3
  - Methodology to evaluate EAL4
  - Methodology to evaluate EAL5
  - Methodology to evaluate EAL6
  - Methodology to evaluate EAL7
  - Methodology to evaluate components not included in an EAL
- Part III: *Extensions to the Methodology.* These are needed to take full advantage of the evaluation results. It will include topics such as guidance on the composition and content of evaluation document deliverables.

NIAP ACTIVITIES

Classes

NIAP is currently offering three classes to the public at its Gaithersburg, Maryland, facility as an aid in promulgating the CC and the CEM.

- Class 1, on developing CC Protection Profiles, is offered as a four-day class to provide introductory information to IT product developers and consumers on the use and application of the CC. Students learn about naming conventions and concepts and work through a real-world example on developing a PP for a biometrics system.
- Class 2, on familiarization with the CC, is a one-day seminar that focuses on terminology and usage concepts of the CC.
- Class 3, on understanding the CEM, is a one-day class for IT product developers, consumers, and evaluators on the basic concepts of the CEM and its fit in the NIAP Common Criteria Evaluation and Validation Scheme. The Mutual Recognition Arrangement (MRA) is also discussed.

Other Activities

NIAP has contracted with Sparta Inc. (*cctoolbox.sparta. com*) for the development of the CCToolbox as an automated tool to apply the CC. It provides for:

- Top-down and bottom-up development of PPs and STs
- Online reference materials
- Mutual recognition support
- EAL selection, interviews, and dependency analysis support

Incremental releases of the CCToolbox will provide support for:

- Security environment interviews and a dictionary of threats, policies, and assumptions
- Security objective suggestions to address basic threats and policies
- Enhanced integration of the CC to support extensibility of CC requirements

- Suggested safeguards for common problems related to threats and assumptions

Approved Protection Profiles

Currently, approved Protection Profiles are available at NIAP's Web site *(niap.nist.gov)* for:

- Packet filter and application gateway firewalls
- Telecommunication switch protection
- National Aerospace Systems (NAS) Infrastructure Management System (NIMS)
- Commercial security profile template
- Profile to replicate Orange Book C2 and B1 requirements
- Role-based access control
- Relational databases

Other industry PPs are under development through NIAP's cooperation and guidance.

From all indications, the future of security product definition and testing is bright. With worldwide efforts to improve global IT product security, the major criticisms of e-commerce's ability to protect private and confidential information may well evaporate as these efforts succeed. With clear metrics in mind, you're ready to begin wading through the advertising and hype that promote security technologies, products, and services. In Chapter 7, we begin dissecting the landscape of security technologies to better help you plan your own defense strategies and know that they'll indeed protect you when you need them most.

7

Security Technologies

Corporate networks are built assuming certain levels of trust in how the information traversing them is accessed and used. When they're hooked into public networks, like the Internet, a safer and more intelligent route leads security administrators to trust no one on the outside.

Up to now, this book has focused on security principles, open holes in commonly used servers, popular tools and techniques for attacking computer installations, and security assurance activities needed for today's security software- and hardware-based systems. With these in mind, we can begin to examine the pieces of the security puzzle to see how best to fit them together for effective defenses and coverage. This chapter explores several types of approaches to security that are usually present wherever the Internet and corporate networks intersect. These include the uses of:

- Routers
- Firewalls
- Intrusion detection systems

Figure 7-1 illustrates the basic design for network security. As you can see, the infrastructure relies upon layers of devices that serve specific purposes and provide multiple barriers of security that protect, detect, and respond to network attacks, often in real time.

The following sections focus on each of the building blocks needed to complete the network security picture.

ROUTERS

A router is a network traffic managing device that sits between subnetworks and routes traffic intended for or ema-

Figure 7-1. The basic network security model.

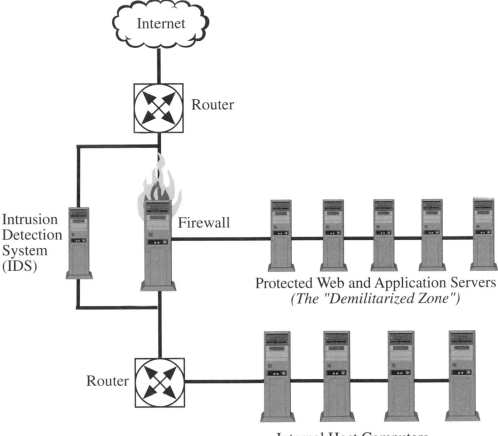

Protected Web and Application Servers
(The "Demilitarized Zone")

Internal Host Computers,
including Mainframe Access Servers

nating from the segments to which it's attached. Naturally, this makes routers sensible places to implement packet-filtering rules, based on the security policies that you've already developed for the routing of network traffic.

Packet Filtering

A packet filter is a simple and effective form of protection that matches all packets against a series of rules. If the packet matches a rule, then an action is performed (packet is accepted, rejected, logged, etc.).

Straight Packet Filtering

Straight Packet Filtering mechanisms allow communication originating from one side or the other. To enable two-way traffic, you must specify a rule for each direction. Packet-filtering firewalls identify and control traffic by examining the source, destination, port number, and protocol types (Uses Datagram Protocol, or UDP; Transmission Control Protocol, or TCP; etc.).

Stateful Inspection Packet Filtering

Stateful Inspection Packet Filtering is a more complex packet-filtering technology that filters traffic on more than just source, destination, port number, and protocol type. Stateful Inspection keeps track of the state of the current connection to help assure that only desired traffic passes through. This allows the creation of one-way rules (for example, inside and outside).

A packet-filtering router yields a permit or deny decision for each packet that it receives. The router examines each IP (Internet Protocol) datagram to determine whether it matches one of its packet-filtering rules. The filtering rules are based on packet header information that's made available to the IP forwarding process. This information consists of:

- IP source address
- IP destination address
- Encapsulated protocol (TCP; UDP; Internet Control Message Protocol, or ICMP; or Virtual Private Network, or VPN, IP Tunnel)
- TCP/UDP source port
- TCP/UDP destination port
- ICMP message type
- Incoming interface of the packet
- Outgoing interface of the packet

If a match is found and the rule permits the exchange, the packet is forwarded using the information in the network routing table. If a match is found and the rule denies the packet, the packet is discarded. If there are no matching rules, a user-configurable default parameter determines whether the packet is forwarded or discarded.

Service-Dependent Filtering

Packet-filtering rules establish when a router will permit or deny traffic based on a specific service, since most service listeners reside on well-known TCP/UDP port numbers. As you saw in Chapter 3, services listen for remote connections on particular ports. For example, a Telnet server listens for remote connections on TCP port 23, and an SMTP (Simple Mail Transfer Protocol) server listens for incoming connections on TCP port 25. To block all incoming Telnet connections, the router simply discards all packets that contain a TCP destination port value equal to 23. To restrict incoming Telnet connections to a limited number of internal hosts, the router must deny all packets that contain a TCP destination port value equal to 23 and that do not contain the destination IP address of one of the permitted hosts. Your policies spell out these rules.

One set of typical filtering rules may include:

- Permit incoming Telnet sessions only to a specific list of internal hosts.
- Permit incoming FTP (File Transfer Protocol) sessions only to specific internal hosts.
- Permit all outbound Telnet sessions.
- Permit all outbound FTP sessions.
- Deny all incoming traffic from specific external networks.

Service-Independent Filtering

Certain types of attacks are difficult to identify using basic packet header information because these attacks are service-independent. Routers may be configured to protect against these types of attacks, but they're more difficult to specify because filtering rules require additional information that's available only by carefully examining the routing table, inspecting for specific IP options, checking for a special fragment offset, etc. Some examples of these types of attacks include:

- *Source IP Address Spoofing Attacks.* For this type of attack, an intruder transmits packets from the outside that pretend to originate from an internal host. These packets falsely contain the source IP address of an inside system. The attacker hopes that the use of a spoofed source IP address will allow penetration of systems that employ simple source address security, where packets from specific trusted internal hosts are accepted and packets from other hosts are discarded. Source spoofing attacks can be defeated by discarding each packet with an inside source IP address if the packet arrives on one of the router's outside interfaces.

- *Source Routing Attacks.* In a source routing attack, the source station specifies the route that a packet should take as it crosses the Internet. This type of attack is designed to bypass security measures and cause the packet to follow an unexpected path to its destination. A source routing attack can be defeated by simply discarding all packets that contain the source route option.

- *Tiny Fragment Attacks.* For this type of attack, the intruder uses the IP fragmentation feature to create extremely small fragments and force the TCP header information into a separate packet fragment. Tiny fragment attacks are designed to circumvent user-defined filtering rules; the hacker hopes that a filtering router will examine only the first fragment and allow all other fragments to pass. A tiny fragment attack can be defeated by discarding all packets where the protocol type is TCP and the IP FragmentOffset is equal to 1.

Benefits of Packet-Filtering Routers

A number of Internet firewall systems are deployed using only a packet-filtering router. Other than the time spent planning the filters and configuring the router, there is little or no cost to implement packet filtering since the feature is included as part of standard router software releases.

Since Internet access is generally provided over a WAN (wide area network) interface, there is little impact on router performance if traffic loads are moderate and few filters are defined. Finally, another benefit is that packet-filtering routers are generally transparent to users and applications, eliminating the need for specialized user training or specific software on each connected host system.

Limitations of Packet-Filtering Routers

These routers also have drawbacks. Defining packet filters can be a complex task because network administrators need to have a detailed understanding of the various Internet services and packet header formats, as well as the specific values they expect to find in each field. If complex filtering requirements must be supported, the filtering rule set can become robust and complicated, increasing its difficulty to manage and comprehend. Finally, there are few testing facilities to verify the correctness of the filtering rules after they are configured on the router. This can potentially leave a site open to untested vulnerabilities.

Any packet that passes directly through a router could potentially be used to launch a data-driven attack. Data-driven attacks occur when seemingly harmless data are forwarded by the router to an internal host. The data may contain hidden instructions that cause the host to modify access control and security-related files, making it easier for the intruder to gain access to the system.

Generally, the packet throughput of a router decreases as the number of filters increases. Routers optimized to extract the destination IP address from each packet, make a relatively simple routing table lookup, and then forward the packet to the proper interface for transmission. If filtering is enabled, the router must not only make a forwarding decision for each packet but also apply all of the filter rules to each packet. This can consume CPU (Central Processing Unit) cycles and impact the performance of a system.

Another limitation is that IP packet filters may not be able to provide enough control over traffic. A packet-filtering router can permit or deny a particular service, but it is not capable of understanding the context/data of a particular service. For example, a network administrator may need to filter traffic at the application layer in order to limit access to a subset of the available FTP or Telnet commands, or to block the import of mail or newsgroups concerning specific topics. This type of control is best performed at a higher layer by application-level gateways that are often called firewalls.

FIREWALLS

A firewall insulates a private network from a public network using carefully established controls on the types of requests they'll route through to the private network for processing and fulfillment. For example, an HTTP (Hypter-Text Transfer Protocol) request for a public Web page will be honored, while an FTP request to a host behind the firewall may be dishonored. Firewalls typically run monitoring software to detect and thwart external attacks on the site. They are needed to protect internal corporate networks. Firewalls appear primarily in two flavors: application-level gateways and Bastion hosts.

Application-Level Gateways

An application-level gateway allows the network administrator to implement stricter security policies than packet-filtering routers can manage. Rather than relying on a generic packet-filtering tool to manage the flow of Internet services through the firewall, special-purpose code (a proxy service) is installed on the gateway for each desired application. If the network administrator does not install the proxy code for a particular application, the service is not supported and cannot be forwarded across the firewall. Also, the proxy code can be configured to support only those specific features of an application that the network administrator considers acceptable while denying all other features.

This enhanced security comes with increased costs in terms of:

- Purchasing the dedicated gateway hardware
- Configuring the proxy service applications
- Time, knowledge, and skills required to configure the gateway system
- Degradation in the level of service that may be provided to users as a result of the overhead of firewall operation
- Lack of transparency for remote users, resulting in a less user-friendly system

Note that users are permitted access to the proxy services, but they are never permitted to login to the application level gateway itself. If users are permitted to login to the firewall system, the security of the firewall is threatened, since an intruder could potentially perform some activity that compromises the effectiveness of the firewall. To that end, it's crucial that the firewall software you purchase is operated exclusively on a hardened server, with all unnecessary services eliminated from the host.

Bastion Hosts

Unlike packet-filtering routers, which allow the direct flow of packets between inside systems and outside systems, application-level gateways allow information to flow between systems but do not allow the direct exchange of packets. The primary risk of allowing packet exchange between inside systems and outside systems is that the host applications residing on the protected network's systems must be secured against any threat posed by the allowed services.

An application-level gateway is often referred to as a Bastion host because it is a designated system that is specifically armored and protected against attacks. The dual-homed (connected to two subnetworks) Bastion host firewall configuration is illustrated in Figure 7-2.

Several design features are used to provide security for a Bastion host. The Bastion host hardware platform operates a secure (hardened) version of its operating system. For example, if the Bastion host is a UNIX platform, it exe-

Figure 7-2. The dual-homed Bastion host firewall configuration.

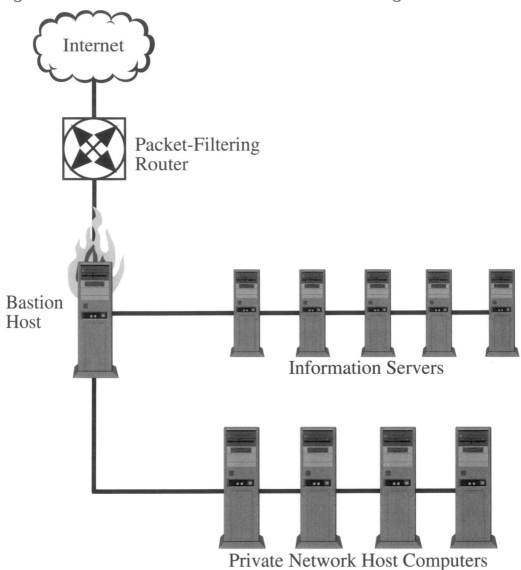

cutes a secure version of the UNIX operating system that is specifically designed to protect against operating system vulnerabilities and ensure firewall integrity. Often these operating systems comply with Orange Book B2 criteria.

Only the services that network administrators consider essential are installed on the Bastion host. The reasoning is that if a service is not installed, it can't be attacked. Generally, a limited set of proxy applications—such as Telnet, DNS (Domain Name Service), FTP, SMTP, and user authentication—are installed on a Bastion host. The Bastion host may be configured to require additional authentication before a user is allowed access to the proxy services. For example, the Bastion host is the ideal location for installing strong authentication using a onetime password technology, where a SmartCard or token generates a unique access code. In addition, each proxy service may require its own authentication before granting user access.

Each proxy is configured to support only a subset of the standard application's command set. If a standard command is not supported by the proxy application, it is simply not available to the authenticated user. Each proxy is configured to allow access only to specific host systems. This means that the limited command/feature set may be applied only to a subset of systems on the protected network. Each proxy maintains detailed audit information by logging all traffic, each connection, and the duration of each connection. Thus, audit logs are essential tools for discovering and terminating intruder attacks. Each proxy is a small and uncomplicated program specifically designed for network security.

Each proxy is independent of all other proxies on the Bastion host. If there is a problem with the operation of any proxy, or if a future vulnerability is discovered, it can be uninstalled without affecting the operation of the other proxy applications. Each proxy runs as a nonprivileged user in a private and secured directory on the Bastion host. If your users require support for new services, your network administrator can easily install the required proxies on the Bastion host. A proxy generally performs no disk access other than to read its initial configuration file. This makes it difficult for an intruder to install Trojan horse sniffers or other dangerous files on the Bastion host.

Using a Firewall for a Telnet Proxy

Figure 7-3 illustrates the operation of a Telnet proxy on a Bastion host. In this example, the outside client wants to Telnet to an inside server protected by an application-level gateway. The Telnet proxy never allows the remote user to login or have direct access to the internal server. The outside client Telnets to the Bastion host, which authenticates the user employing onetime password technology. After authentication, the outside client gains access to the user interface of the Telnet proxy. The Telnet proxy permits only a subset of the Telnet command set and determines which inside hosts are available for Telnet access. The outside user specifies the destination host, and the Telnet proxy makes its own connection to the inside server and forwards commands to the inside server on behalf of the outside client. The outside client believes that the Telnet proxy is the

Figure 7-3. The operation of a Telnet proxy on a Bastion host.

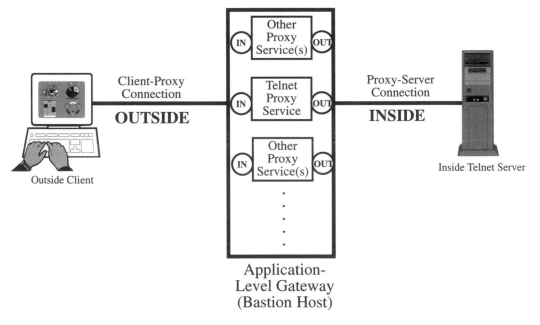

real inside server, while the inside server believes that the Telnet proxy is the outside client.

Figure 7-4 shows the output to the outside client's terminal screen as the connection to the inside server is established. Note that the client is not performing a logon to the Bastion host: The user is being authenticated by the Bastion host, and a challenge is issued before the user is permitted to communicate with the Telnet proxy. After passing the challenge, the proxy server limits the set of commands and destinations that are available to the outside client.

Authentication can be based on something the user knows (like a password), something the user physically possesses (like a SmartCard), or both. Since both techniques are subject to theft, using a combination of both methods increases the likelihood of correct user authentication. In the Telnet example, the proxy transmits a challenge, and the user—with the aid of a SmartCard—obtains

Figure 7-4. The output to the outside client's terminal screen as the Telnet connection to the inside server is established.

```
Outside-Client > telnet bastion_host
Username: John Smith
Challenge Number "237936"
Challenge Response: 723456
Trying 200.43.67.17 ...

HostOS UNIX (bastion_host)

bh-telnet-proxy> help
Valid commands are:

connect hostname
help/?
quit/ exit

bh-telnet-proxy> connect inside_server

HostOS UNIX (inside_server)

login: John Smith
Password: ######
Last login: Wednesday April 15 11:17:15
```

a response to the challenge. Typically, a user unlocks the SmartCard by entering her PIN (Personal Identification Number). The card, based on a shared "secret" encryption key and its own internal clock, then returns an encrypted value for the user to enter as a response to the challenge.

Benefits of Application-Level Gateways

There are many benefits to the deployment of application-level gateways. They give the network manager complete control over each service, since the proxy application limits the command set and determines which internal hosts may be accessed by the service. Also, the network manager has complete control over which services are permitted, since the absence of a proxy for a particular service means that the service is completely blocked.

Application-level gateways have the ability to support strong user authentication and provide detailed logging information. Finally, the filtering rules for an application-level gateway are much easier to configure and test than for a packet-filtering router.

Limitations of Application-Level Gateways

The greatest limitation of an application-level gateway is that it requires either that users modify their behavior, or that specialized software be installed on each system that access proxy services. For example, Telnet access via an application-level gateway requires two user steps to make the connection rather than a single step. However, specialized end-system software could make the application-level gateway transparent by allowing the user to specify the destination host rather than the application-level gateway in the Telnet command.

Examples of Firewall Implementation

The following are a few examples of common implementation using firewall technologies.

Packet-Filtering Router Firewalls

The most common Internet firewall system consists of nothing more than a packet-filtering router deployed between the private network and the Internet. This configuration is shown in Figure 7-5. The packet-filtering router performs the typical routing functions of forwarding traffic between networks as well as using packet-filtering rules to permit or deny traffic. Typically, the filter rules are defined so that hosts on the private network have direct access to the Internet, while hosts on the Internet have limited access to the systems on the private network. The external posture of this type of firewall system dictates that all traffic that is not specifically permitted be denied.

Although this firewall system has the benefit of being inexpensive and transparent to users, it possesses all the

Figure 7-5. A packet-filtering router firewall.

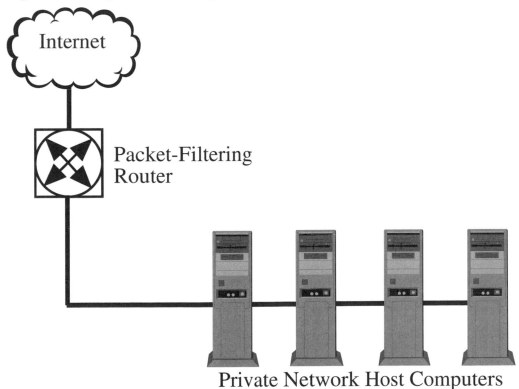

Internet

Packet-Filtering Router

Private Network Host Computers

limitations of a packet-filtering router, such as exposure to attacks from improperly configured filters and attacks that are tunneled over permitted services. Since the direct exchange of packets is permitted between outside systems and inside systems, the potential extent of an attack is determined by the total number of hosts and services to which the packet-filtering router permits traffic. This means that each host directly accessible from the Internet needs to support sophisticated user authentication and needs to be regularly examined by the network administrator for signs of an attack. Also, if the single packet-filtering router is penetrated, every system on the private network may be compromised.

Screened Host Firewalls

The second firewall example employs both a packet-filtering router and a Bastion host, as illustrated in Figure 7-6. This screened host firewall system provides higher levels of security than the previous example because it implements both network-layer security (packet filtering) and application-layer security (proxy services). Also, an intruder has to penetrate two separate systems before the security of the private network can be compromised.

For this firewall system, the Bastion host is configured on the private network with a packet-filtering router between the Internet and the Bastion host. The filtering rules on the exposed router are configured so that outside systems can access only the Bastion host; traffic addressed to all other internal systems is blocked. Since the inside hosts reside on the same network as the Bastion host, the security policy of the organization determines whether inside systems are permitted direct access to the Internet, or whether they are required to use the proxy services on the Bastion host. Inside users can be forced to use the proxy services by configuring the router's filter rules to accept only internal traffic originating from the Bastion host.

One of the benefits of this firewall system is that a public information server providing Web and FTP services can be placed on the segment shared by the packet-filtering

Figure 7-6. A screened host firewall system employing both a packet-filtering router and a Bastion host.

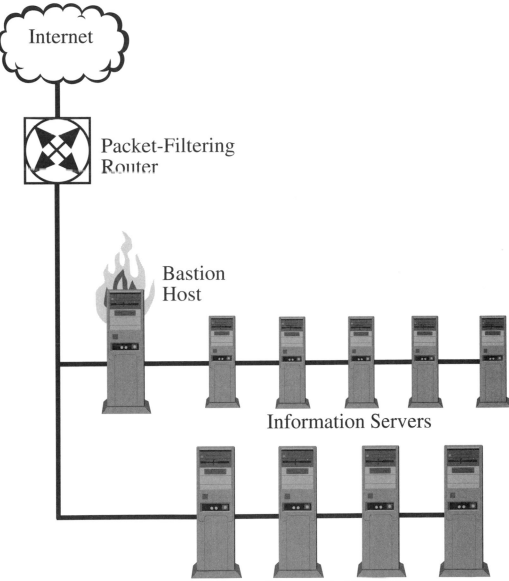

router and the Bastion host. If the strongest security is required, the Bastion host can run proxy services that require both internal and external users to access the Bastion host before communicating with the information server. If a lower level of security is adequate, the router may be configured to allow outside users direct access to the public information server.

An even more secure firewall system can be constructed using a dual-homed Bastion host system, like the one illustrated in Figure 7-2. A dual-homed Bastion host has two network interfaces, but the host's ability to forward traffic directly between the two interfaces bypassing the proxy services is disabled. The physical topology forces all traffic destined for the private network through the Bastion host and provides additional security if outside users are granted direct access to the information server.

Demilitarized Zone (DMZ), or Screened Subnet, Firewall

The final firewall example discussed here employs two packet-filtering routers and a Bastion host, as shown in Figure 7-7. This firewall system—sometimes called a screened subnet firewall—creates the most secure firewall system, since it supports both network- and application-layer security while defining a "demilitarized zone" (DMZ) network. The network administrator places the Bastion host, information servers, modem pools, and other public servers on the DMZ network. The DMZ network functions as a small, isolated network positioned between the Internet and the private network. Typically, the DMZ is configured so that systems on the Internet and systems on the private network can access only a limited number of systems on the DMZ network, but the direct transmission of traffic across the DMZ network is prohibited.

For incoming traffic, the outside router protects against the standard external attacks (source IP address spoofing, source routing attacks, etc.) and manages Internet access to the DMZ network. It permits external systems to access only the Bastion host (and possibly the information server). The inside router provides a second

Figure 7-7. A DMZ, or screened subnet, firewall system employing two packet-filtering routers and a Bastion host.

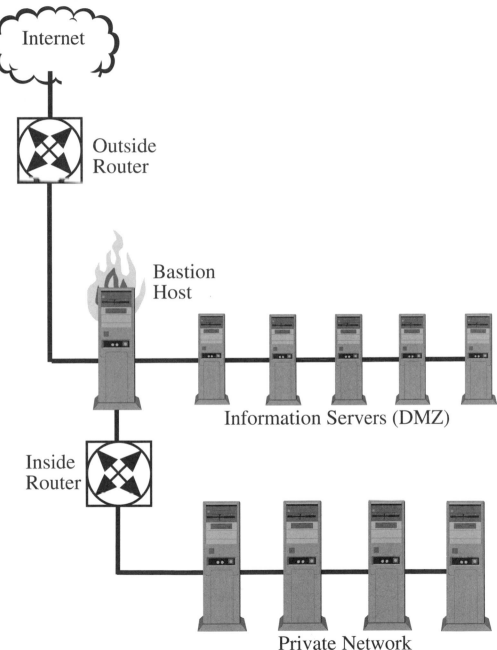

line of defense, managing DMZ access to the private network by accepting only traffic originating from the Bastion host.

For Internet-bound traffic, the inside router manages private network access to the DMZ network. It permits internal systems to access only the Bastion host (and possibly the information server). The filtering rules on the outside router require use of the proxy services by accepting only Internet-bound traffic on the Bastion host.

There are several key benefits to the deployment of a screened subnet firewall system:

- An intruder must crack three separate devices (without detection) to infiltrate the private network: the outside router, the Bastion host, and the inside router.

- Since the outside router advertises the DMZ network only to the Internet, systems on the Internet do not have routes to the protected private network. This allows the network manager to ensure that the private network is "invisible" and that only selected systems on the DMZ are known to the Internet via routing table and DNS information exchanges.

- Since the inside router advertises the DMZ network only to the private network, systems on the private network do not have direct routes to the Internet. This guarantees that inside users must access the Internet via the proxy services residing on the Bastion host. Packet-filtering routers direct traffic to specific systems on the DMZ network, eliminating the need for the Bastion host to be dual-homed. The inside router supports greater packet throughput than a dual-homed Bastion host when it functions as the final firewall system between the private network and the Internet. Since the DMZ network is a different network than the private network, a Network Address Translator (NAT) can be installed on the Bastion host to eliminate the need to renumber or resubnet the private network.

The Choice Is Yours

There is no single answer nor any one correct design and deployment of an Internet firewall. Your decision on how to build your firewall architecture is influenced by many different factors related to your corporate security policies, staff's technical background, costs, and the perceived threats of an attack. Since the benefits of connecting to the Internet are certain to exceed the related costs of implementation and maintenance, network managers should be encouraged knowing that networks—with the proper precautions—can be as safe as you need.

But wait. By adding one more element to your building blocks for secure networks—intrusion detection systems—you can keep an eye out for problems before they get out of hand. Intrusion detection systems work in conjunction with routers and firewalls by monitoring and standing as a sentry on guard to protect your networks against attacks.

INTRUSION DETECTION SYSTEMS (IDSs)

An intrusion detection system (IDS) attempts to detect an intruder breaking into your system or a legitimate user misusing system resources. The IDS operates constantly on your system, working in the background, and notifies you only when it detects something it considers suspicious or illegal.

There are two major classifications of potential intruders:

1. Outside intruders
2. Inside intruders

IDSs are needed to detect both types of intrusions—break-in attempts from the outside, and knowledgeable insider attacks. Effective intruder detection systems find both.

As this book has preached all along, security policies define what's permitted and what's denied on your computer systems. The two basic philosophies behind all policies are:

1. Prohibit everything that is not expressly permitted.
2. Permit everything that is not expressly denied.

Generally, people more concerned about security exercise the first option. Policies are put in place that describe exactly what operations are allowed on a system. Any operation that is not detailed in the policy is considered banned on the system. Other people, who operate their systems under the spirit of cooperative computing, are likely to adopt the second philosophy. Unfortunately, this philosophy does not work well in today's hostile computing environments.

What Kind of Intrusions?

Before discussing the detection of intrusions, it's important to understand what's meant by an intrusion. Intrusions are defined relative to your security policy. Unless you've already decided what is and is not allowed on your system, it's pointless to try and catch intrusions.

An intrusion is defined as any set of actions that attempt to compromise the integrity, confidentiality, or availability of a resource. Intrusions can be categorized into two main classes:

1. *Misuse intrusions* are well-defined attacks on known weak points within a system. They can be detected by watching for certain actions being performed on certain objects.
2. *Anomalous intrusions* are based on observations of deviations from normal system usage patterns. They are detected by building up a profile of the system under concern and detecting significant deviations from this profile.

Because misuse intrusions follow well-defined patterns, they can be detected by doing pattern matching on audit-trail information. Anomalous intrusions are detected by observing significant deviations from normal behavior. An anomaly may be a symptom of a possible intrusion. Given a set of metrics that can define normal system usage, security violations may be detectable from abnormal patterns of system usage. Anomaly detection is also performed using other mechanisms, such as neural networks, machine learning classification techniques, and even trying to mimic biological immune systems.

Anomalous intrusions are harder to detect than misuse intrusions. There are no fixed patterns that can be monitored for, and so a more fuzzy approach is needed. Ideally, a system that combined humanlike pattern-matching capabilities with the vigilance of a computer program could eliminate most problems. Many intrusion detection systems base their operations on analysis of operating system audit-trail data. These data form a footprint of system usage over time. Audit trails are convenient sources of data and are readily available on most systems. Using audit-trail observations, the IDS can compute metrics about a computer network's overall state and decide whether an intrusion is occurring.

Characteristics of Good Intrusion Detection Systems

An intrusion detection system should address the following issues, regardless of what mechanisms you use:

- It must run continuously without human supervision. It should be reliable enough to allow it to run in the background of the system being observed.
- It must be fault-tolerant to survive a system crash without requiring the rebuilding of the IDS's knowledge base each time the system is restarted.
- Similarly, it must resist subversion. The system should monitor itself to assure that it has not been subverted.
- It must impose minimal overhead on the attached network.
- It must observe deviations from normal behavior.
- It must be easily tailored to the network in question. Every system has different usage patterns, and the defense mechanisms should adapt easily to these patterns.
- It must cope with changing system behavior over time as new applications are being added. The sys-

tem profile will change over time, and the IDS must be able to adapt.
- It must be difficult to fool.

Perhaps you're wondering what types of errors may occur with IDSs. IDS processing errors can be categorized as false positives, false negatives, or subversion errors.

- A *false positive* occurs when the system classifies an action as anomalous (a possible intrusion) when it is a legitimate action. False positive errors will lead users of the intrusion detection system to ignore its output, because it will classify legitimate actions as intrusions. The occurrences of this type of error should be minimized (it may not be possible to completely eliminate them) so as to provide useful information to the operators. If too many false positives are generated, the operators will come to ignore the output of the system over time, which may lead to an actual intrusion being detected but ignored by the users.

- A *false negative* occurs when an actual intrusive action has occurred, but the system allows it to pass as non-intrusive behavior. The action proceeds even though it is an intrusion. False negative errors are more serious than false positive errors because they give a misleading sense of security. By allowing all actions to proceed, a suspicious action will not be brought to the attention of the operator. The intrusion detection system is now a liability because the security of the system is less than it was before the intrusion detector was installed.

- A *subversion error* occurs when an intruder modifies the operation of the intrusion detector to force false negatives to occur. Subversion errors are more complex and tie in with false negative errors. An intruder could use knowledge about the internals of an intrusion detection system to alter its operation, possibly allowing anomalous behavior to proceed. The intruder could then violate the system's operational security constraints. This may be discovered by a human operator examining the logs from the intrusion detector, but it would appear that the intrusion detection system still seems to be working correctly.

Another form of subversion error is fooling the system over time. As the detection system is observing behavior on the system over time, it may be possible to carry out operations, each of which, when taken individually, pose no threat, but taken as an aggregate form a threat to system integrity. How would this happen? As mentioned previously, the detection system is continuously updating its notion of normal system usage. As time goes by, a change in system usage patterns is expected, and the detection system must cope with this. But if an intruder could perform actions over time that were just slightly outside normal system usage, then it is possible that the actions could be accepted as legitimate whereas they really form part of an intrusion attempt. The detection system would have come to accept each of the individual actions as slightly suspicious, but not a threat to the system. What it would not realize is that the combination of these actions forms a serious threat to the system.

BUILDING CONFIDENCE WITH A LAYERED APPROACH TO SECURITY

With packet-filtering routers, firewalls, proxies (i.e., proxy senses), and intrusion detection systems in place, you can rest better at night knowing that you're protected from both internal and external threats, while still keeping the channels of communication open for customers and employees on the outside. The hardware- and software-based security systems described throughout this chapter are manufactured by dozens of suppliers around the world, including Cisco, 3Com, AXCENT, and Intel.

The attack characteristics that these systems require to determine if attacks are occurring have been collected and analyzed through a variety of advisory boards, incident response centers, and product manufacturers. Because of the lack of a single authority on computer security threats and countermeasures, a number of differing naming conventions are commonly being used today.

As collections of attack characteristics grow, it becomes exceedingly difficult for all manufacturers of security products to scan for all known vulnerabilities, regardless of their source of discovery. Furthermore, the marketplace for security products has become confusing for consumers by overcomplicating information to help identify which tool scans for which vulnerabilities, and if these vulnerabilities are identified consistently across different product lines of similar equipment and software. To help eliminate some of these problems, an effort begun in 1999, called the Common Vulnerabilities and Exposures (CVE), is beginning to lead the way to naming and identification consistency. With CVE, both consumers and providers of security products alike stand to benefit through a unified approach to computer security problem enumeration.

CVE: A COMMON FRAMEWORK FOR COMPUTER SECURITY THREATS

CVE is the result of ten months' worth of collaborative efforts by the MITRE Corporation and CVE participants. The board consists of over fifteen security-related organizations that include tool vendors, academic institutions, government, and security experts. MITRE maintains the CVE List and serves as the coordinator of the editorial board, providing neutral guidance throughout the CVE development and maintenance process. CVE underwent a validation period at the same time the validation process was formalized. CVE Version 1 was released to the general public by MITRE at the end of September 1999.

CVE cleans up the messy world of known computer exploits by uniquely identifying them using an industry-wide naming scheme. This scheme cross-references the naming conventions adopted by security tool manufacturers, security advisory groups, discussion groups, and hacker underground sites. These new vulnerability identities serve as primary keys for relational database systems that contain known exploits. Using these as search criteria, users of the software are referred to the actual databases that contain the details about the vulnerability (symptoms, remediation steps, etc.).

CVE is vital in helping consumers of security tools and systems to compare products effectively using an apples-to-apples approach. You no longer need to concern yourself about which tool tests for which vulnerability. If a tool is CVE-compliant, you can immediately decide if a tool tests for the specific vulnerabilities that concern you without poring through the product's documentation.

CVE defines vulnerabilities and exposures as follows:

- *Vulnerabilities* are problems that are universally thought of as "weaknesses" in any security policy, software flaws that could directly allow serious damage, and specific known vulnerabilities in operating systems, utility, and network programs.

- *Exposures* are problems that provide stepping stones to successful hacker attacks. Examples include the running of services such as finger, poor logging practices, or misconfiguration problems.

CVE Goals and Benefits

The goals of the CVE initiative include:

- Enumerating all publicly known problems
- Assigning a standard, unique name to each problem
- Operating the list independent of product vendors, advisories, newsgroups, etc.
- Enabling open and shareable information without any distribution restrictions

CVE helps in providing a common language for security professionals when referring to problems. It facilitates the sharing of data among intrusion detection systems, assessment tools, vulnerability databases, academic research, and incident response teams. CVE helps to improve communication across the computer security community and helps to improve the mix of security tools in the marketplace by fostering interoperability among multiple vendor products.

Although many people may criticize CVE as being an aid to hackers, its benefits outweigh the possible risks in the following ways:

- CVE is restricted to publicly known problems.
- The sharing of information among security professionals is far more difficult than the sharing of information within the hacker community.
- CVE represents a shift in community opinion trends toward open sharing, rather than the former "cloak and dagger" operations of yesteryear.

CVE Acceptance Phases

According to CVE documentation, security information goes through the following phases as it's being considered for acceptance into CVE:

- *Discovery.* A potential vulnerability or exposure is discovered.

- *Public Announcement.* A public announcement is made about the potential vulnerability/exposure through postings to Bugtraq, newsgroups, security advisories, etc.

- *Assignment.* A Candidate Numbering Authority (CNA) obtains a candidate number for the potential vulnerability/exposure from the chair.

- *Proposal.* A board member (possibly not the original CNA) proposes the potential vulnerability/exposure to the editorial board, using the candidate number obtained during the assignment phase. The vulnerability/exposure then becomes a candidate for CVE acceptance. Members discuss the candidate and vote on it. They may *accept, reject, recast,* have *no opinion,* or say that they are actively *reviewing* the candidate.

- *Modification.* The candidate is discussed by the editorial board in light of CVE content decisions. In some cases, the candidate may need to be significantly altered in order to be accepted. The chair decides on what alterations need to be made, then resubmits the altered candidate to the board for additional voting. Some candidates may skip this phase if they do not need to be modified in any significant way.

- *Interim Decision.* The chair decides when it is appropriate to determine whether debate about the candidate is complete or has come to a standstill. The chair assigns a single *accept, reject,* or *recast* vote. The chair then gives the board a short amount of time to post any final comments or objections.

- *Final Decision.* If the chair decides that there are not sufficient grounds for changing the vote made in the interim decision phase, the decision becomes final. If the candidate is *accepted* or *recast*, the chair guarantees to all board members that the candidate shall be placed into CVE and identifies the CVE name(s) that will be produced.

- *Publication.* If the candidate is *accepted* or *recast*, a CVE name or names is or are assigned, and the candidate is added to CVE. It then becomes a CVE entry and is published via the CVE Web site. If the candidate is *rejected*, the chair notes the reason for rejection.

- *Deprecation.* In some rare cases, the editorial board may decide that a CVE entry should no longer remain active in the CVE. For example, the board may decide to modify the level of abstraction by splitting the entry into lower-level entries or merging it with others. In such cases, the vulnerability is annotated with a status of "deprecated." However, it is not deleted from CVE.

The CVE Web Site

On the CVE Web site (*http://www.cve.mitre.org*), you can find the following detailed information:

- Introduction to CVE
- CVE Terminology: vulnerabilities and exposures
- Using CVE
- Frequently asked questions

- CVE-compatible tools and databases
- CVE-related documents
- Editorial board
- Editorial board archives

You can also search, view, and download copies of CVE to import into your own database systems. If you're interested in the rationales behind the various content decisions for CVE, you can read the editorial board archives, where you'll find public record of the mailing list used to discuss CVE content issues.

Table 7-1. Supporters of CVE.

Product Name	Type of System	Manufacturer	URL
CERIAS Vulnerability Database	vulnerability database	CERIAS/Purdue University	www.cerias.purdue.edu
Centrax 2.3	Intrusion detection system and assessment tool	CyberSafe	www.cybersafe.com
CERT Advisories	archives	CERT Coordination Center	www.cert.org
Cisco Secure Intrusion Detection System (formerly NetRanger)	intrusion detection system	Cisco Systems	www.cisco.com
Cisco Secure Scanner (formerly NetSonar)	assessment tool	Cisco Systems	www.cisco.com
DOVES	vulnerability database	Computer Security Laboratory, Department of Computer Science, University of California—Davis	seclab.cs.ucdavis.edu
Expert	network risk analysis tool	L-3 Network Security, LLC	www.l3security.com
HackerShield	assessment tool	BindView Development	www.bindview.com
ISS Internet Scanner 6.0.1	assessment tool	Internet Security Systems, Inc. (ISS)	www.iss.net
NTBugtraq	vulnerability database	NTBugtraq	www.ntbugtraq.com
Retriever	network security management tool	L-3 Network Security, LLC	www.l3security.com
SANS SNAP Vulnerability Assessment Training	education material	SANS	www.sans.org
Security Focus Vulnerability Database	vulnerability database	Security Focus, Inc.	SecurityFocus.com
X-Force Alert	advisory archive	Internet Security	www.iss.net
X-Force Database	database	Internet Security Systems, Inc. (ISS)	www.iss.net

Support for CVE

Since CVE's release, many companies and organizations have pledged their support for it. Table 7-1 lists the product names, types of systems, manufacturers, and URLs supporting CVE.

8

Physical Security Control

So far, you have learned the importance of building a strong security foundation and have seen some of the threats you're certain to face with an Internet-attached network. You also began to understand the major issues related to security technologies and how they're used within a layered approach to integrate security into your overall computer operations. Now you will gain an understanding of the layering of security, helping you to construct a veritable fortress to protect your information-based assets.

Chapters 8 and 9 discuss the dual aspects of security—physical systems and logical systems—a distinction that isn't always as neat and tidy as one might like. In general, physical security deals with who has literal physical access to buildings, computer rooms, and the devices within them. Controlling physical security involves developing and implementing plans that secure devices from unauthorized physical contact. Logical security deals with the software and data in your systems and how it is accessed.

Security experts traditionally focus more on the problems related to logical security because of the likelihood that remotely located computer hackers will analyze, dissect, or break into computer networks without leaving their offices or homes. A hacker's physical proximity to a network has less to do with its vulnerability than do poorly written CGI (Common Gateway Interface) scripts or operating systems with more holes in them than Swiss cheese. Concerns over remote users breaking into networks are reflected in a July 1999 *InformationWeek* survey of 2,700 security professionals, shown in Figure 8-1. In 1998, some 17 percent of respondents cited computer hackers and terrorists as suspected sources of breaches or espionage—a

Figure 8-1. Results of an *InformationWeek* survey on suspected sources of security breaches.

	1998	*1999*
Computer hackers and terrorists	17%	48%
Authorized users/employees	58%	41%
Contracted service providers	10%	31%
Foreign governments	3%	25%
Unauthorized users/employees	24%	23%
Former employees	8%	5%
Suppliers	4%	5%
Customers	12%	15%
Competitors	3%	3%
Public interest groups	4%	6%
Information brokers	1%	1%
Others	3%	4%

figure that jumped to almost 50 percent in 1999. Meanwhile, employees or other authorized users as suspects fell from almost 60 percent in 1998 to a little more than 40 percent in 1999.

Do these numbers reflect reality? It's difficult to say without an increased awareness of security risks, more rigorous network monitoring, and more sophisticated network intrusion detection tools. Still, as we have stressed, a complete security plan cannot afford to overlook any aspect of network security—and that means both physical and logical security.

ASPECTS OF PHYSICAL SECURITY

Chapter 8 covers the following aspects of physical security:

- Physical accessibility
- Hardware solutions

- Securing personnel
- Biometrics techology (especially in conjunction with SmartCard technology)

Physical Accessibility

While it's intuitive to some corporations, others fail to see the need to restrict physical access to facilities and equipment. For example, you may read a story in your local paper about a company whose computer equipment was stolen or usurped. Why is it that some companies take the possibility of these kinds of thefts so lightly?

One reason may be that many shops do not even realize that equipment has been stolen. These shops may order replacement memory and processors under parts for equipment maintenance or repairs. Instead, they should tightly control parts replacement by auditing individual line items in a purchase order to verify the parts that are being ordered. The individual who is ordering replacements for bad parts should be required to turn the bad parts in. For example, an employee asking to replace memory does so most likely because memory has been stolen, not because it has gone bad. A company with such a problem should also compare its new hardware purchases with maintenance expenses. If they are roughly equal, the company has a problem.

Other companies simply point to their insurance companies as their protection against theft. However, with claims for high-value components on a dramatic rise, insurance companies are looking more closely at companies submitting claims repeatedly for stolen parts. In 1993, the Chubb Insurance Group paid out less than $3 million in claims because of stolen computer property. That figure jumped to $15 million a year later, a trend that has continued ever since. Companies that substitute an insurance claim for secure physical access will at the least see their premiums rise and will be required to secure their physical site. At the worst, they will lose their insurance coverage.

As a general rule, a company should give limited access to critical server areas. Areas within a facility should be categorized based on level of access: open, controlled, limited, or highly restricted or excluded access. Physical access to the following areas should be restricted:

- Computer server rooms
- Wiring closets
- Computer hub rooms
- Buildings and rooms containing production systems
- Cabinets, desk drawers, tape libraries, media archives, etc.

Companies should clearly define physical security policies and educate their employees on the importance of their buy-in to those policies. They should, for example, be required to sign in all visitors, to lock their PCs when stepping away (even if only for a moment to refill their coffee cups), and to be wary of the social engineering tactics used by many hackers (discussed in Chapter 4). After all, securing the physical site means protecting people in addition to equipment, materials, and documents.

Hardware Solutions

Many organizations are seeing an increase in the theft of computer components from within the organization as well as from without. Thieves can easily slip some parts into their pockets or carry them out in purses or briefcases. Bolder individuals walk innocently past security guards with an armload of equipment. Theft of equipment becomes even more problematic with an increasingly mobile workforce that carries a computer notebook in lieu of being stationed at a desktop workstation. Any sensitive data stored locally on an employee's hard drive can fall into the wrong hands if the laptop is left unattended at the airport or in the back seat of a car.

This latter point—the risk of losing what's on the computer—could cost a company far more than the cost of the equipment. Employees may be carrying sensitive corporate data, customer account numbers, strategic plans, or even data critical to the security of a country.

The case of Wen Ho Lee (previously discussed in Chapter 4), a scientist at the Los Alamos National Laboratory, is a dramatic example of lax security and improper investigations. Lee was accused of espionage for China at the nuclear weapons laboratory when it was learned that he had downloaded highly secret information about the U.S. nuclear program. Lee allegedly transferred government secrets from a classified network to his unclassified desktop computer from 1983 to 1995. When you consider the fact that nearly 8,000 researchers work at the Los Alamos campus, and that nearly every one has a computer—many more than one wired into sensitive laboratory networks—you may begin to wonder if such a thing doesn't happen more often. Perhaps it does.

Los Alamos officials, like those at other facilities performing classified work, thought they had addressed this problem by assigning scientists two computers: a black computer for their classified and secret material, and a white computer for communicating with the outside world. In practice, however, scientists found themselves downloading classified information to their white computers, thus coining the phrase "gray computers." They did so because the white computers were usually better and faster machines and the ones used for communication with other scientists. In other words, a well-intentioned attempt to secure the use of classified data by assigning separate physical devices to the Los Alamos researchers didn't work.

Military installations attempt to secure their networks and contain classified information by air gapping their networks. This involves fencing off their network from the outside world and cutting off any connection between the outside world and their data. The National Security Agency air gaps its computers by controlling physical devices such as modems, floppy disks, optical disks, Zip drives, Ethernet cards, and CD-ROMs by installing blocker boxes—devices that prevent data from leaking through power cables.

Perhaps the example of Wen Ho Lee will move companies to review their policies and procedures surrounding the use of computer equipment. At the least, they need to maintain accurate and current inventories of their PC equipment, components, and peripherals as well as how that equipment is used. Hardware solutions should include the use of locks on all computer equipment, desk mounts, disk locks, and secure enclosures. Can unauthorized personnel remove casing on the equipment? Are laptops and notebooks secured to desktops by using docking stations? Is peripheral equipment such as CD-ROM drives, speakers, and tape backup units also secured to the desktop? The general rule should be that every piece of equipment is accounted for and secure and can be accessed only by authorized personnel. Frequent reviews of hardware usage policies should be mandatory, and inventories should always be up to-date

Securing Personnel

The best weapon a company can have is an educated staff made aware of the potential for theft and misuse of facilities and equipment. Employees should be reminded periodically of the importance of helping to secure their surroundings, including:

- Being mindful of physical and environmental considerations required to protect the computer systems
- Adhering to emergency and disaster plans
- Monitoring the unauthorized use of equipment and services and reporting suspicious or unusual activity to security personnel
- Recognizing the security objectives of the organization
- Accepting individual responsibilities associated with their own security and that of their coworkers as well as the equipment they use and how they use it

A corporation can educate its staff on the importance of their physical security though the use of self-paced or formal instruction; through security education bulletins, posters, training films, and tapes; or through awareness days that drive home the importance of constant vigilance.

Biometrics Technology and SmartCards

One of the most critical steps a company can take toward securing its network and data is controlling who has access to it. This involves verifying the identity of users and authenticating them (known as I&A). The most obvious and prevalent form of I&A is the use of passwords, but passwords are proving increasingly ineffective. How often do users write their passwords down on a Post-it note stuck on a monitor? How often does someone send e-mail with IDs and passwords to a colleague, asking her to check his e-mail while he is on vacation? With each of these egregious security faux pas, an experienced cracker can easily steal an ID and password to pose as the authorized user.

I&A techniques typically include (1) something a user knows, such as a password or PIN (personal identification number); (2) something he possesses, such as a hard token or SmartCard; and (3) something he is, an identifying characteristic such as a fingerprint or voiceprint. This is referred to as multifactor authentication, with the idea that the more factors present, the more secure the system.

Many people are familiar with general recommendations about the use of passwords: how users should choose one that combines characters and numbers, how users should change them frequently, and how users should not give them out to coworkers or write them down and leave them on their desks. (See the accompanying "What Makes for a Good Password?") You may also be familiar with hard tokens. Token use is on the increase with the expanding population of mobile users who access their company's network remotely. Hardware-based or software-based tokens work by generating a onetime dynamic password that the user must enter in addition to her fixed ID to access the network. They operate by encrypting a time-stamp using a secret key that's embedded in the token. When presented to the authentication server within a fixed, short period of time after generation (e.g., ten to twenty seconds), the value is checked. Only after a successful decryption step occurs can access be granted. If a problem is encountered or a time-out period has elapsed, the entire process must begin anew.

What Makes for a Good Password?

Users typically choose poor passwords when they're left to their own devices. So what makes a good password? Passwords that aren't likely to fall victim to dictionary attacks use combinations of letters and numbers, are six or more characters in length, and are never based on personal information about the user (children's names, pets' names, hobbies, etc.). Furthermore, users should be forced to make regular password changes (every thirty to sixty days), and previously used passwords should never be reused. Any system-assigned passwords should require changing the first time they're used, and any password changes should require knowledge of the old password before any change requests are honored.

With adequate up-front planning, along with investments in technology, you should be able to reduce many of the vulnerabilities associated with password management.

Biometrics

The use of *biometrics* (Greek for "life measurements"), in conjunction with more standard forms of authentication such as fixed passwords and PINs, is beginning to attract attention as the cost of the technology decreases and its sophistication increases. In fact, the traditional scheme of password-based computer security could lose stature as the use of SmartCard-based cryptographic credentials and biometrics authentication become commercially viable. Once the domain of TV spy shows and science fiction pulp stories, the use of human characteristics to allow access to secure systems is quickly becoming a reality.

Any security system, especially biometrics systems, must balance convenience with security. A system that is too intrusive or cumbersome discourages if not prevents an authorized user from accessing a system. A security system should also be scalable. In other words, not all systems and users need the same level of security, and security procedures and techniques should reflect this. Still, any computer system requires a minimal level of security, and that is where authenticating the user at system log-on becomes an issue. SmartCards, biometrics, and other forms of logical access controls using cryptographic devices are discussed at length in Chapter 15.

A user's first access to a PC is during system logon; thus, much attention focuses on the use of passwords, PINs, and more recently biometrics. In Windows 95/98, no formal system log-on is required, and even if a user is not authenticated, the operating system is still available and ready for exploitation by rogue network connections or back office operations. Windows NT, however, offers a network-level logon that can be secured by authenticating a user's credentials on an authentication server.

How Can Authentication Best Be Achieved?

Some companies, such as the American Biometrics Co. (ABC), claim that using an individual's unique physical characteristics along with other I&A techniques can almost unequivocally authenticate a user. Biometrics authentication uses characteristics of the human face, eyes, voice, fingerprints, hands, signature, and even body temperature. Each has its own strengths and weaknesses. Today, the use of fingerprints appears to be the cheapest and most reliable form of biometrics authentication.

The tip of the finger has characteristics called friction ridges, minutia points, and valleys that uniquely identify it from the print of any other individual. Since a fingerprint can vary in appearance throughout the day because of changes in temperature, skin moisture, oiliness, cuts, and abrasions, any direct comparison of digital images of the fingerprint cannot guarantee true authentication. Doing so would also require storing a complete image of the fingerprint in a database, something that attracts the attention of civil liberties groups and government agencies.

Instead, another technique compares fingerprints based on their minutiae and are thus characterized. How does this process work? Here are steps involved in authenticating an individual using his fingerprint:

- Multiple images of the individual's fingerprint are taken, using the core of the image as the reference point for the orientation and placement of other features.

- The minutiae features of importance surrounding the core become vectors and are cataloged in a database. The minutia features are typically termination, intersecting, and splitting of lines.

- Each sample is scored based on the number and quality of vectors. The image with the highest score becomes the template for the individual. This template is stored in a database and becomes the user's enrollment template. Because it contains only a subset of the fingerprint detail, the template cannot be used to reconstruct the fingerprint.

- When a user wants to authenticate himself, an algorithm against the template stored in the database uses the minutiae of his fingerprint. The level of security determines the number of minutiae that must match.

This process of matching a user's finger image to a specific image is called one-to-one matching, a form of identification but not authentication.

In the case of physical access control, the goal may be to relieve the user of the burden of identifying himself before authentication begins. These techniques include requiring the user to enter his user ID and inserting his SmartCard into the card reader. The use of SmartCards, in fact, would be mandatory for a small percentage of the population whose fingerprints are not of sufficient quality to allow authentication of the individual. The American Biometrics Co. estimates, based on its studies of thousands of office workers, that approximately 2.5 percent of employees fall into this category. See *www.abio.com.*

SmartCards

A SmartCard looks like a regular payment or credit card with the major difference that it carries a semiconductor chip with logic and nonvolatile memory (see Figure 8-2). The card can have many purposes, including storing value

Figure 8-2. A SmartCard.

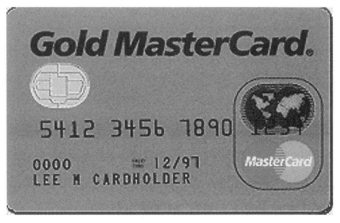

for consumer purchases, providing medical identification, travel ticketing, and building access control cards. The card may also store software that detects unauthorized tampering and intrusions. SmartCards—used much more extensively in Asia and Europe than in the United States—can also store banks of passwords. A user, for example, can store her desktop and Windows or Novell network passwords on her SmartCard. When integrated with a biometrics login, the user's fingerprint can replace the entering of her PIN.

SmartCards can also facilitate file encryption by storing the user's private key for use with a Public Key Infrastructure, or PKI (see Chapter 13). They work well for mobile users, who are inclined to carry their SmartCards with them as they would one of their credit cards. This means that the user's encryption keys are not stored on her workstation, thus providing a more secure environment than when the cryptographic functions are performed on the workstation itself, which are subject to Trojan horse attacks.

Still, SmartCards alone are not completely secure. If an attacker stole a user's PIN or password, he could gain complete access to the network by stealing the card. However, using a fingerprint along with the card to authenticate the user (three-factor authentication) would greatly reduce the chance for intrusion. Thus, a company that has already committed to using SmartCards for many of its applications could benefit from adding an additional level of security using a biometrics logon.

The use of SmartCards in conjunction with biometrics authentication techniques can be extremely effective, especially in situations where controlling physical access is of the utmost importance. This kind of three-factor–level security goes beyond the use of passwords alone or passwords and SmartCards together.

So why aren't these techniques more widely used? Several factors—namely cost, reliability, and practicality—have hampered the deployment of SmartCards and biometrics. However, as more companies build SmartCard readers into their workstations, and as the use of biometrics increases in manageability and flexibility and decreases in price, their use will become increasingly important and prevalent.

We've stressed the importance of controlling physical access to equipment and services in this chapter, along with promising technologies that help with authentication and identification. Chapter 9 discusses the more pernicious and widespread security issues: controlling what a legitimate user does once she logically accesses your systems.

9

Logical Access Control

Chapter 8 discussed policies on controlling the access to physical devices and how data is stored on those devices. This chapter focuses on the software and data that can be accessed from the lowest granular level (the user level), through user groups as they're defined by the systems administrator. However, the distinction between the domains of physical and logical access control are not always readily apparent.

Think of a computer as an automobile. In order to drive the car legitimately, you must have permission. You must either be the owner or have permission of the owner to drive it. Once you have this permission, you must also have the keys for the ignition and a valid driver's license (which is another kind of permission, this time from a recognized authority—the state that issued it). These are aspects of physical control.

Extending this analogy, logical control includes the rights and restrictions you have as a driver. If you are just learning to drive and have a learner's permit, you must have a licensed driver in the car with you at all times. If you wear glasses, you must wear them in the car at all times. Perhaps you are allowed to drive only during the day because you have poor night vision. Also, your basic driver's license does not give you the right to operate specialized vehicles such as limousines or big rigs. In those cases, you must belong to a different class of drivers. These are forms of logical control. You're at the wheel, but what exactly are you allowed to do?

As corporate networks continue to expand and grow well beyond their traditional boundaries—the extent of which most systems administrators would not have imagined a few years ago—the need to control internal access to the network increases as well. Some experts believe that more than 50 percent of network attacks occur from within—attacks that are becoming increasingly difficult to detect as the edge of the network perimeter grows fuzzier. As the number of telecommuters, consultants, clients, and supply-chain vendors connecting to the network by dial-up lines increases, a reliance on firewalls alone is insufficient.

DIMENSIONS OF LOGICAL ACCESS CONTROL

This chapter explores several of the logical controls network administrators should consider implementing to make an Internet-connected network more secure. You may be an authorized user of the system, with a valid user ID and password, but what exactly are you allowed to do on the system?

Logical access control includes these topics:

- File access permissions
- Execution privileges
- Automatic Directory Listing
- Access Control Lists (ACLs)
- Host name and IP address restrictions
- User and password authentication
- CGI scripts and Active Server Pages (ASPs)
- Software vulnerabilities

These controls comprise aspects of *server-side security.*

If you fail to properly secure your Web servers (or mail servers, remote login servers, etc.), seasoned hackers are more likely to ignore strong encryption that protects data while it transports the data when they're given any opportunity to exploit improperly misconfigured Web servers. As Anup K. Ghosh aptly points out in his primer *E-Commerce Security,* secure data transmission protocols or payment systems are frequently included as part of a commercial/ off-the-shelf (COTS) or ERP (enterprise resource planning) system, but the security of the hosting server must be actively configured, maintained, and reevaluated by knowledgeable IS (Information Systems) staff as business needs change. At a high level, an ERP system integrates all information flowing through a company.

The task of implementing server-side logical controls requires the active participation of the system administrator, business partners, and other key figures involved with controlling access to critical corporate and customer data. These individuals must understand where and how their servers are vulnerable, institute the appropriate policies to address the problems, and enforce them rigorously.

WEB SERVER SECURITY

The Web server or HTTP (hypertext transfer protocol) network daemon is an essential component of an electronic commerce infrastructure—one of the many network servers that you'll need (e.g., mail, remote login, FTP servers). Security and business specialists should review all the network services that they offer and decide which are truly necessary to their company's business and mission. Do you really need to provide network services on all available ports? Chances are, close scrutiny of these services will reveal that many of these services are unnecessary and only expose the company to excessive risks. The more doors and windows a house has, the more opportunity robbers are given to break in and steal.

However, a house without doors and windows is a bunker, a gloomy and uninviting fortress whose only purpose is security. Security is not an end-all-and-be-all but one of several aspects of the larger e-commerce model. This model must offer a rich set of services to its users and customers while at the same time preventing hostile attacks and intrusions by hackers. A sound security strategy must discourage intruders while reassuring customers.

How is this feat accomplished? As Ghosh points out, *defense in depth* is the best approach to securing a Web complex. The primary job of the system administrator is to understand and control access to the network and its resources through sound security policies, and to help guarantee that the network servers are not the weak links in the overall security chain. To do so, he must properly harden the complex.

On a UNIX system, administrators have *root* access and privileges. On the server, the system administrator is known as the *super user*—a role that enables him to grant access permission to files. He essentially owns the files and directories on the system and controls access privileges to individuals and user groups. A sound security policy requires close examination of file access by the system administrator and a determination of what access levels are required by users and departments within the company, as well as external users, in order to do business effectively and efficiently.

LOGICAL ACCESS CONTROL METHODS

Let's look at some specific methods of logical access control.

File Access Permissions

Two classes of files on Web servers—the *server root* and *document root* files—contain critical data whose access should be controlled by file permissions. The server root directory should contain those files that are included and needed as part of the Web server installation and other critical system files: configuration, administration, log, CGI (Common Gateway Interface) program source, and executable files. These files should be visible and accessible only to the system administrator and to no one else, internal and external users alike.

The second class of critical server files, the document root, contains the Web pages that are displayed to users as the Web daemon (httpd) patrols the network ports (usually port 80 and 443 for Secure Sockets Layer or https traffic). Usually written in the HyperText Markup Language (HTML), these sensitive documents are the most visible aspect of a company's e-commerce site. If a hacker gains access to the HTML files, she can easily modify them and embarrass—or even worse—expose a company to extreme losses.

In particular, log files on the server should be as secure as they can be to accurately keep track of who accesses the site, the number of requests made, and the source IP (Internet Protocol) address of the user, and they may be useful to calculate usage or other financial transaction costs. Hackers often cover their footprints before leaving a site by modifying or erasing any trace of their activity in the log files—yet another reason to secure them.

Execution Privileges

Execution privileges define what rights authorized users have to access, modify, create, or delete files on the server. If server processes are given the same access rights as the super user (root), an authorized user can wreck havoc on system files through privilege escalation. By exploiting holes in the network or application software, a hacker can gain access under the user ID that's running the vulnerable service. If the service is started using the root ID, an exploit may lead a hacker to a shell (terminal) session as root. In the security world, we call this situation "game over."

How can this happen? When the system administrator installs the Web server, she does so with super user authority in order to configure the network and listener ports. Network daemons can and do invoke subordinate processes, called child processes. These child processes often do everything from serving up Web pages to satisfying requests through invoking CGI scripts or API (application program interface) calls. If the system administrator is not careful, she can inadvertently grant authority to these lower-level processes as the daemon that invokes them.

You don't need to strain your imagination too hard to see the potential dangers here. A hacker would have little trouble exploiting a child process or a poorly written CGI script to gain super user access and control the system files. Once the door is open to the intruder, he can do everything—from stealing passwords to creating new accounts, pilfering sensitive corporate and customer information, or simply rendering the server useless.

The solution? System administrators should configure all servers to assure that subordinate processes execute as nonprivileged user—that is, *nobody*. This reduces the risk of exploitation by keeping security access at the correct levels—and nothing more!

Automatic Directory Listing

A danger lies in the absence (on some Web server software) of an index file (index.html). If the Automatic Directory Listing option is turned on when the server boots up, and an unwanted user browses the directory, he will automatically obtain a listing of the files in the directory. If this directory happens to contain or point to interface files such as CGI scripts, he could copy source code, examine its contents, find holes if they exist, and return to exploit them.

The safeguard here is to turn off Automatic Directory Listing when the server is installed and booted. Note that this option is turned *on* as the default on most configurations and must be actively reconfigured to *off*.

Access Control Lists (ACLs)

With the proliferation of intranets and extranets comes an increasing concern about company documents and files. Employees can now access human resources policies and guidelines, corporate strategies, white papers, organizational structures, and much internal and highly sensitive information on the company intranet. They can make travel arrangements, file travel and other expense reports, change their contributions to company 401(k) plans, and perform other financial transactions. Meanwhile, customer access is restricted to specific files and directories on the Web server: Customers can obtain only those privileges needed to transact their business. The system administrator's challenge is to grant privileges specific to both the employee and customer while preventing both from accessing files and documents that they shouldn't see. Access control mechanisms allow the system administrator to perform this task.

One of the most common techniques for controlling user access on the server is the Access Control List (ACL). ACLs contain names (IDs), passwords, and the types of operations that users are allowed to perform on each resource that's protected. ACLs can also define the hosts (IP addresses) that are permitted to access particular Web pages based on their host names or IP address; conversely, they can prohibit those same hosts from accessing a specific Web page. Some experts recommend that it is generally a good idea first to deny access to everyone and then to allow specific ones in. This can avoid some the problems of incorrectly identifying a valid host name during translation on the DNS (Domain Name Service) server. The ACL can work well if properly configured, although this is often a laborious task.

New products, such as Solsoft's Net Partitioner, a network security policy manager, appeared on the market that allow companies to apply security access stategically, across physical topologies if necessary, rather than at the application or network device level. Solsoft's makers advocate using ACLs to partition the network into *secure zones*. Without an internal compartmentalization of resources and clearly defined access rules, a disgruntled insider or hostile outsider can read and possibly modify or delete privileged files.

Once these secure zones have been determined, authorized IP flows are established. Solsoft's makers believe, as do other experts, that "all that is not expressly allowed is denied." Such network partitioning can protect it from internal attacks and unauthorized accesses by limiting access to its resources, and it can offer more granular protection than is offered by firewalls. Since the latter can protect only a single access point, the use of ACLs helps shore up defenses and prevent back-door intrusions to the system, and can complement the use of internal and external firewalls, routers, and intrusion detection systems.

Host Name and IP Address Restrictions

One of the techniques often used by hackers to break into networks is to mimic the IP addresses of trusted machines and exploit the system, particularly on systems that use packet-filtering routers. In this case, the firewall makes its decision based solely on the IP address in the IP header of the current packet. A basic access control mechanism is to restrict access to services based on the requester's IP address or host name. The server uses this information along with the Domain Name Service (DNS) to determine what access the requester is allowed to services, files, and documents.

DNS, a naming service provided to hosts on the Internet, connects IP addresses with machine names to determine the host's availability. If a machine name and IP address do not agree with what is in the DNS table, the system administrator is wise to block access as part of her security policy for host names and IP addresses.

User and Password Authentication

In its most rudimentary implementation, a user/password scheme associates a user with a transformed (hashed) password stored on a file on the server. The UNIX file system uses the /etc/passwd file for storing such data. This file is used to grant specific access rights to individual users or groups of users, depending upon the sophistication of the password database and system. The problem here lies in poorly chosen passwords by users that are easily guessed by an experienced hacker who has gained control of the password file. If the password file then is not properly protected using a *shadow password* file, the hacker's job of brute-forcing the password file is trivial.

Also, the system administrator must decide whether to store the ACLs centrally or distribute them across the resources they're designed to protect. In the first case, all files and directories that need access control are defined in a single file that is referenced anytime a request is made for one of the listed resources. Centralizing this control has the advantage of one-stop shopping (as with Single-Sign-On). The system administrator need only go to one location to make updates to the Access Control List.

The option is to distribute access control by placing the ACLs in the directory of each resource that requires security. The advantage here is that local users can control access at a privilege level they require while still being unable to access system files such as the configuration file. Also, as directories are moved to different file partitions, the system administrator does not need to update a central configuration file since access control moves with the directory. Best of all, distributed access control permits dynamic evaluation of resource requests. Every time a user requests a file, the ACL is checked to see if access is permitted, unlike the steady state of the centralized configuration file, which requires a reinitialization of the server whenever it is changed.

The downside of distributed access control, however, is the overhead involved with maintaining multiple files. Changes are not centralized, and the risk of losing or deleting control files is greater. The system administrator must evaluate his situation, consider the complexity of distributed file access control versus centralized control, and implement the security policy that best fits staffing and organizational needs.

CGI Scripts

The Web browsers of today are, in a sense, a higher touch-and-feel version of the old mainframe terminal sessions using an older conversation manager such as IBM's CICS. What has helped take the Web from the monotony of display-only pages to truly interactive sessions is the Common Gateway Interface (CGI) and application program interfaces (APIs) built into modern Web server software (NSAPI for Netscape Enterprise Servers and ISAPI for Microsoft's Internet Information Server, or IIS). These interfaces are protocols that act upon requests from a client to a server and are commonly associated with three-tier or n-tier client-server architecture.

When a user completes a form on a Web page and clicks on the *submit* button, the browser gathers the information on the form, inserts it in an HTTP message, and *posts* the appropriate HTTP command on the server, depending upon the nature of the transaction. The server, unfamiliar with the form, invokes the program or resource named in the URL (Uniform Resource Locator) and passes the request to the application server running CGI and other protocols. These requests typically ask to perform some actions on a database (update or retrieve information based on parameters supplied by the user).

CGI and active programming or scripting languages have helped make the Internet a robust e-commerce marketplace. But they have also left holes in the network that seasoned hackers try to exploit. Hackers can manipulate files to their hearts' content, send files to themselves, execute programs they have downloaded on the server, and even launch denial of service attacks that overwhelm the server's CPU (Central Processing Unit) with more instructions than it can feasibly process. Often, when you hear about malicious defacement of Web pages, chances are a hacker has found a vulnerability in the CGI processor. Unfortunately, this problem has been around for years. Abusing CGI scripts is a popular pastime of hackers, partly because faulty CGI implementations are so widespread. Some of the older CGI scripts, for example, can execute any command remotely under the ID of the user logged-in executing the HTTP daemon process.

Some of the steps you can take to help secure your systems against rogue uses of the programming and scripting features of Web servers include the following:

- Avoid running the HTTP daemon (httpd) as a privileged user. Never begin the service while logged-in as *root*, for example, on a UNIX-based host. Rather, create and use an innocuous ID—such as *nobody*—with severely restricted privileges on the server when starting the httpd service.
- Delete the sample CGI scripts supplied during software installation from the cgi-bin directory. Many of

the older scripts, such as phf.cgi, are easy targets for hackers.

- Store all your CGI scripts in a central directory (called something other than cgi-bin), and restrict the write and delete access to this directory only to system administrators.
- Convert your CGI scripts (often written in the Perl language) to compiled versions in languages such as C or C++, to prevent hackers from obtaining your program source code. Alternatively, you could use the APIs supplied with the major Web server software (Netscape and Microsoft) to take advantage of improvements in technology since the Web's infancy.
- Review your shell scripts used in the development of CGI scripts within your software QA (Quality Assurance) process, looking for file access errors and set user ID (SUID) usage.

Software Vulnerabilities

At this point we've looked at directory structures, Access Control Lists, passwords, file permissions, and holes in CGI scripts. Still, with the exception of Java applets that are intended to run in what is called the security *sandbox* to contain the damage they may cause, developers often write programs that put a server at risk.

Anup Ghosh recommends two commonsense policies to address the problem of software vulnerabilities. First, review server-side programs to assure design principles that reduce the possibility of security breaches. Second, analyze programs carefully as part of a QA process to ferret out design flaws or behaviors that could again result in security problems.

One design flaw that garners much attention in software security circles is the *buffer overflow* problem. Generally speaking, a buffer overflow exploit takes advantage of programs that improperly parse data and inadvertently attempt to store too much data in too small a storage (memory) area, thus causing an overflow. One result of the overflow allows a subversive programmer to execute whatever commands she desires. Buffer overflows can also force a system to abort because it is trying to perform illegal instructions. UNIX platforms are often the victim of programs that do not perform what is known as proper *bounds checking.* The most effective way to address buffer overflows is to ensure that all code performs rigorous bounds checking (values are within the normal ranges, data strings are of normal length, etc.).

Unfortunately, security is rarely a consideration when designing new software. One of the chief goals of this book is to change that paradigm. Security has been traditionally considered project overhead—an afterthought or "nice to have" if time and budget permit. As project lifecycles shorten in the age of Rapid Application Development (RAD) methodologies, developers have even less time to consider the implications of security in the software they build. Developers are simply more focused on what their code *should* be doing than on what it *should not* be doing.

The same applies to testing methodologies. The software community all too often tests expected conditions, not unexpected conditions. They attempt to validate that software functions perform as anticipated, while hackers perform their own kind of tests to show that the unanticipated is also possible. There is no replacement for a sound software development and testing methodology that makes security a fixture of the project planning landscape.

LOGICAL ACCESS CONTROL THROUGH NETWORK DESIGN

It's possible to further improve e-commerce network security through more than configuration work and sound program development work alone. Here's one fundamental concept that pervades all *secure* Internet-accessible installations: the three-tier or n-tier client-server architecture. A three-tier system is one implementation of the logical partitioning of an application across clients and servers. The three-tier model divides the processing load among the clients running the GUI (Graphical User Interface), the application server executing the business software, and the database or legacy system. Three-tier systems benefit everyone in the organization, especially people in IT (information technology) departments. The three-tier model is appealing for enterprisewide distributed transaction-processing applications in that it offers these advantages:

- *Centralization* permits IT to control and secure programs and servers using an already accepted, mainframe-like environment that's scalable, predictable, and easily monitored.

- *Reliability* is enhanced since equipment resides in a controlled environment that can be easily replicated or moved onto fault-tolerant systems.

- *Scalability* is easier since servers or processors can be added to achieve acceptable levels of performance. Centralized database services tend to be more optimal since constant monitoring leads to prevention and quick detection of server or network problems.

- *Flexible,* well-defined software layers permit the highest degrees of IT responsiveness to changing business needs. With lightweight and inexpensive client desktop requirements, wholesale changes to desktop systems can be made at any time without any effect on the program layer or the database layer, allowing companies to adopt improvements in technology quickly. In addition, non-PC clients (e.g., Point of Sale devices, voice-response units, handheld devices) can be used at any time since the interfaces to the application are based on open industry standards and are well-defined to the developer.

- A flexible *data layer* means that existing mainframe services can be reused. Mainframe services can be made to look just like any other data service layer, thus preserving the transaction-processing capabilities of the mainframe. This is significant since mainframes tend to be optimal environments for high-volume transaction processing.

- Systems based on *open industry standards* allow companies to rapidly incorporate new technologies into the operation without concern of interoperability problems that exist in products based on proprietary approaches.

Security people especially embrace three-tier systems for Internet, intranet, and extranet applications. When they're present, these three tiers—Web server(s), application server(s), and database server(s)—greatly reduce many of the threats to production back office systems and networks and empower you to perform an excellent job of "order protection." These concepts arise from industry best practices and recommendations from security experts around the world. Since by definition your e-commerce site must be security conscious, you're advised to utilize these principles as much as possible in your own designs. Figure 9-1 illustrates one example of a three-tier network architecture that's not only robust and flexible but highly secure too. The figure shows how it's possible to add security as traffic moves beyond the Web servers into deeper tiers. As you move through the inner firewalls, you can turn off pro-

Figure 9-1. An example of a security-conscious three-tier network architecture.

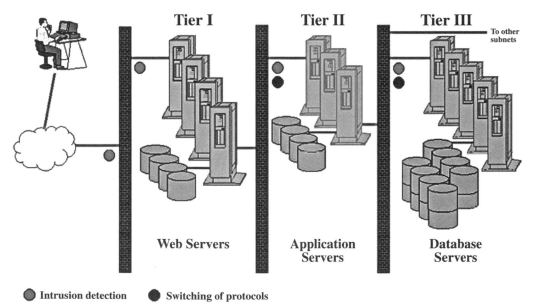

tocols that don't belong there. You can also force the uses of *trusted hosts* to help prevent unwanted requests from processing. You'll see how that's done shortly.

In Chapter 2, we discussed classifying data according to the level of protection it requires. This classification model should help you to decide instinctively where to properly place your data within the network. For performance reasons and the lack of any need for specific protection, you might opt to keep your materials "intended for the public" directly within the file systems of the Web servers themselves. Normally, this would include only information that people could otherwise locate via your other advertising channels (catalogs, images, marketing brochures, etc.). Any dynamically generated data (stored billing and shipping information, etc.) should be kept as far out of reach from the Internet as possible. Furthermore, any data that your customers supply via Web-based forms should immediately be removed from the Web server through as many firewalls as needed to safely secure it. It's this data that thieves want, so you must be extra careful with its handling. Your customers deserve no less! This is the *most* fundamental security precaution that you can take. Never store anything on the Web server itself because you can *never* really be sure the server will remain constantly in your control. Should a Man-in-the-Middle attack occur, perhaps a few Web pages will be spoofed, but your important assets will remain secure.

Another sound measure you can take is to switch the protocols your network supports as you move backward. Because of inherent HTTP vulnerabilities, you don't want it running past the outer firewall. Permitting HTTP routing into the back office places you at risk of hackers tunneling through HTTP to try and take over another server. Cut them off at the knees! Consider using protocols like CORBA/IIOP (Common Object Request Broker Architecture/Internet Inter-ORB Protocol) socket connections via TCP (transmission control protocol), or DCOM on Microsoft NT to gain access to services residing on the application tier. From the application tier to the database tier, switch the protocols on the firewalls again, allowing only Open

Database Connectivity (OBDC) for SQL Server, native database clients (e.g., Sybase's OpenClient), and message queuing protocols, like Microsoft's MSMQ and IBM's MQ-Series.

With the three-tier approach, you can begin to see how to add still more layers of security both between and within each tier. Before the outer firewall, consider using intrusion detection systems to scan for known attack signatures and to automatically alert those in charge of the network—in real time. The uses of cryptography for security both at the transport layer and the application layer are also possible without rewriting programs. In Chapters 10 and 12, you'll see how to use Secure Electronic Transaction (SET) for credit card information, Secure Sockets Layer (SSL) for encrypted communications of information, and Open Buying on the Internet (OBI) to help identify and authenticate people and their rights to access data. These and other protocols—running atop the architect described—can help turn your e-commerce site into a genuine citadel.

Trusted hosts (remote machines designated as secure in a configuration file) are another security measure that you may elect to use. Using ACLs on your application servers helps to thwart attempts at running or installing programs without the authority to do so. If your application software can somehow be identified as legitimate and trusted, you add still another layer of protection to your resources. Yet another approach might use server-to-server authentication with digital certificates (see Chapter 13) to provide two-way assurances that application requests and responses are legitimate.

Access control information (login IDs and passwords) that are stored on your servers should be kept in the most obscure forms possible. Never leave this type of information *in the clear* anywhere on the file systems. Move them to registries on the operating system in encrypted forms, or encrypt the configuration files themselves. Even if the server is hijacked, the attacker will still have a hard time accessing other systems or doing anything destructive.

On the database tier, consider encrypting the contents—at the field level, the row level, the table level, or the entire database level. Different data classifications call for different situations, so analyze your needs carefully. Where audit trails of activity are crucial, turn on database auditing to help in monitoring activity or for prosecution purposes.

MORE SETTINGS AT THE SERVER

We've covered switching protocols and closing ports on firewalls, but there's still more to do at the server level:

• Make certain that your e-commerce servers and any payment system processors are running on separate layers that are insulated both from the Internet and from other domains within your organization. Remove all unnecessary server software that's not specifically for operational purposes. This may include language compilers, Perl libraries, administrative utilities, and factory-supplied logins and passwords.

• Firewalls should disallow FTP (File Transfer Protocol), Telnet, or requests on any open ports.

• Don't operate software such as FTP, Telnet, or e-mail systems on any e-commerce server or Web server hardware.

• Whenever remote operations (Telnet, xterm, etc.) are needed, make sure the Secured Socket Handler (SSH) and Secure Copy (SCP) are used.

• Make sure httpd and merchant server software (catalog and shopping cart software) are protected against hostile browsers.

As much as possible, set up your servers to provide unique functions and capitalize on the distributed nature of the network.

PROTECT YOURSELF FROM YOURSELF

We've taken care of keeping intruders out from the Internet, but now what can we do to protect production systems from internal users attempting access using unauthorized means? More firewalls and intrusion detection systems (IDSs), of course! Add as many internal firewalls with ACLs and IDS sensors to prevent such attacks from your intranet.

You should now be able to see how many of the threats covered earlier are eliminated, or at least severely reduced, using the approaches above. Is the design practical? Sure! Is the implementation expensive? You bet! A bigger question, though, is whether you can afford to neglect it. You may have only one opportunity to get it right.

System administrators have a daunting task on their hands. Not only do they have responsibilities to carefully evaluate security needs, properly configure servers, and institute corporatewide policies. They also must constantly reevaluate and revisit all systems that are already built and operating. Fortunately, new tools, applications, and protocols are arriving on the scene almost daily to help sites to secure their operations more effectively.

In Chapter 10, we examine the highest layers of security—the application layer—where it's possible to implement robust or special-purpose systems that build upon the security features present at the physical and logical layers.

10

Application Layer Security

Application layer security primarily addresses access controls—those aspects of data security not specifically covered at the network or server levels. In some instances, an application may duplicate some security measures that are also performed at the network by other services, such as Remote Access Servers (RAS) or Remote Authentication Dial-In User Service (Radius), operating on your network's perimeter. Think of application layer security as the final door in a series of multiple locked doors that you must pass through to reach the programs and systems you need.

Often, these application layer controls rely upon industry standards for data content, context, and security. The next chapters of this book will acquaint you with the finer points of digital cryptography, but it's useful here to look at some protocols that manage business-specific processes securely.

Electronic purchasing requires additional safeguards for data as sensitive communications move through multiple networks of unknown reliability and security. Web servers are also playing an increasing role in application-level security through dynamically created Web pages that are based on user-specific requirements. This relates to the differences between user identification (authentication) and user authorization. Once a user has been authenticated, he will be provided only those choices that apply to his domain of use. These forms of access control increasingly rest upon the applications themselves. The network simply cannot handle all the specifics of security control at the application level.

INTRANETS AND EXTRANETS

Just as intranets and extranets have different purposes and characteristics, they also have different security requirements. Since these terms have entered the Internet vernacular, they often appear with conflicting or vague definitions. Thus, we will define them in the context of the following discussion.

Intranets

In his book *Building the Corporate Intranet* (New York: Wiley Computer Publishing, 1997), Steve Guengerich writes: "An intranet is a corporate network and the business applications that run on it that shares the 'DNA' of Internet computing technologies (e.g., Internet Protocol, browsers, Web oorvers) and exists behind the corporate security 'firewall.' "

Intranets enable a company to publish business information easily in forms that make the most sense for the type of information. They frequently house sensitive corporate information that's not intended to be viewed by anyone outside the company.

In a typical intranet, a local area network (LAN) is built with an application-proxy firewall (see Chapter 7) to offer employees outgoing access to the Internet. These proxy servers require those on the *trusted* side to login with proof of their authorization to use it. It's possible, however, to open the access to those on the Internet side with adequate security controls to assure its safe use. Through Access Control Lists (ACLs) on the server and router configuration settings, you can limit those who enter through the Internet to tightly controlled resources that you define as narrowly or as broadly as you desire.

IDs and passwords can be assigned in whatever ways work best for you. Many organizations ask someone wishing access to their site to complete a profile that gathers any information the organization would like to have about them. Once the person requesting access completes the profile and submits it, the organization reviews it to decide if it is acceptable and returns the ID and password back to the requester via e-mail.

If you gather this type of information, you can use it to your advantage. Building profiles of your visitors helps you to focus your advertising costs and the products that you offer in ways no mass-marketing approaches can begin to match. Customer profiles help you to build demographics on your clients, help you to understand how your click-through advertising is working, and might serve as the foundation for data-warehousing applications or customer information systems.

Even though it uses Internet and Web technologies, an intranet does not necessarily need to be connected to the Internet. This does not mean, however, that security is any less of a concern. Intranets still require strict internal security policies and procedures to control the access to sensitive corporate data from within. Who sets up each department's intranet? Who decides upon the content? Who maintains and controls access to each department's intranet? Intranets clearly illustrate how challenges to security are not so much technical as they are procedural.

Extranets

An extranet, according to Julie Bort and Bradley Felix in their book *Building an Extranet* (New York: Wiley Computer Publishing, 1997), is: "A bridge between a company and its most important business contacts, its partners." In this case, a company builds an extranet to share information with whom it deems its most strategic business partners, whether they be other companies working on a joint business project, an outsourcing firm, or a supplier of goods or services. The difference between an extranet and an intranet is one of audience. Where the intranet addresses the needs of the company as related to its employees, the extranet looks outward to its key business partners, establishing vital links in what might be a supply chain.

HOW MUCH E-COMMERCE SECURITY IS ENOUGH?

The OURS (Open User Recommended Solutions) Task Force (discussed in Chapter 4) states that Internet usage falls into one of three categories, as described by Vance

McCarthy in his article "Web Security: How Much Is Enough?" These are:

1. Advertising (brochureware)
2. Secure Internet/intranet
3. Electronic commerce

Since some Internet users are more "at risk" than others (e.g., a company's e-commerce site is arguably more than its online advertising), conscientious corporate users are encouraged to evaluate their data, determine how much that data is worth to them, and implement the appropriate levels of security for each type of data. For example, a company that has put its catalog of parts on the Internet where customers can order them online should understand what online payment protocols are all about and how to implement them. Another company that simply advertises its presence on the Internet for the purpose of entertaining its audience cares little about who enters its site. In the latter case, illegitimate users don't really exist.

Sound security strategies are based not on what the market has to offer in the way of security software packages but on what a company has to secure and from whom they need to protect it. To this end, the OURS guidelines identify six best weapons against security threats. They are:

1. *User ID/authentication,* anything from the use of simple passwords and callback systems to onetime passwords and challenge/response tokens, something that should be found in all but the most open Web sites.
2. *Authorization,* the concept of identifying the user to be who she says she is, through the use of privilege tables, authorization (digital) certificates, and directory services. OURS considers authorization to be a second-level protection against unauthorized access to a company's intranet or modification of Web content.
3. *Integrity control,* which focuses on the integrity of the data rather than the user. Integrity control is

extremely important to the kind of security features needed for e-commerce. Here, messages are verified and receivers can be assured that the data has not been altered in transit.

4. *Accountability,* the use of audits and Web server logs to enforce security policies. While these technologies by themselves do little to protect a Web site from threats, they can aid in the research of security violations.

5. *Confidentiality,* from forms of cryptography to the use of Virtual Private Networks (VPNs), which provide end-to-end encrypted links that can shield a site from the public Internet. Key escrow also falls into the category of confidentiality.

6. *Availability controls,* which involve how quickly a Web site can be restored in the event of catastrophic failure such as hardware failure. Solutions here include fault tolerance, backup/recovery plans, and capacity management systems.

This chapter focuses on concepts and industry standards and techniques to secure information and messages at the application level. With an understanding of these ideas, you'll begin to see how process and security protocols are mixed and matched to produce useful work.

SECURE ELECTRONIC TRANSACTION (SET)

Secure Electronic Transaction (SET) addresses most of the consumer demands for privacy when using a credit card to shop online. SET's uses are specific to the payment acceptance phases of what's called the *shopping experience*. It covers the steps from the point a particular payment card is selected for use through the point the merchant completes the transaction and requests actual payment (charge capture) from its acquirer bank and charge processor.

The Roots of SET

Back in the early 1990s, when the Web was first thought of as the marketer's Holy Grail, banks refused to accept or process charges originating on it and required merchants to use existing infrastructures for charge authorizations, point-of-sale phoned-in requests, and batch-processed requests. These banks, led by pressures on two sides (merchants and consumers), began to demand that the Visa and MasterCard associations develop a secure standard for using credit cards over any insecure channel, such as the Internet.

Visa and Microsoft responded with a standard they released in September 1995. The Secure Transaction Technology (STT) specification was posted to the Visa Web site for download by interested parties. At the same time, Microsoft announced that it would develop STT implementation tools for Windows 95 and Windows NT that could be licensed by developers. Tools for other desktop platforms would be developed by Spyglass Technology.

Meanwhile, MasterCard and its allies—Netscape Communications Corp., IBM, CyberCash, and GTE—had developed the Secure Electronic Payment Protocol (SEPP) as a proposed specification and posted it to the MasterCard Web site for a public comment period. MasterCard had hoped that SEPP could be in use for Internet transactions as early as April 1996.

STT and SEPP generated such heated debates and finger-pointing between the two opposing factions that the entire industry was at odds as to which way to turn. Both sides claimed their standard was defined with "openness in mind" and was designed in cooperation with the Internet standards–setting bodies—the W3 Consortium, the Internet Engineering Task Force (IETF), CommerceNet, and the Financial Services Technology Consortium. Industry and financial services observers at the time believed that STT and SEPP were similar, yet different enough to render them incompatible. This meant that separate implementation efforts were required, and all parties desiring to support Visa and MasterCard products needed two separate processing facilities.

Both STT and SEPP attempted to achieve the same objectives, but they did so from different directions. Those objectives included:

• Changing Internet-based credit card transactions from the risky card-not-present scenario (such as Mail Order/Telephone Order transactions) to the less risky card-present situation (such as retail shopping and eateries) to reduce the chances of fraud and increase the potential to lower the fees that merchants must pay for maintaining merchant accounts.

• Requiring all parties in a transaction (customer, merchant, credit card processor or bank) to possess digital certificates that establish their identities and their authority to conduct transactions.

• Requiring that public key certification agencies (Certificate Authorities) manage the certificate distribution processes on behalf of the card association or member banks.

• Using industry-standard public key cryptography techniques, as developed by Ron Rivest, Adi Shamir, and Leonard Adelman of RSA Data Security.

• Encrypting only credit card numbers and transactional data rather than encrypting the entire browser and shopping session.

• Concealing credit card data from all merchants to prevent merchant-initiated fraud.

• Enabling use of any type of credit card product, regardless of issuer. The card associations, however, reserved the right to specify that only their protocol be permitted for transactions with their cards.

By the latter part of 1995, banks that issued both Visa and MasterCard were up in arms with the attempt to force two separate standards that accomplish the same task. The banks persisted and finally forced Visa and MasterCard to work together on a single standard, since supporting two separate ones appeared ridiculous.

In February 1996, the announcement rocked the Internet community: "*Visa & MasterCard Combine Secure Specifications for Card Transactions on the Internet into One Standard.*" According to Edmund Jenser, president of CEO of Visa International:

> This is the first step in making cyberspace a profitable venture for banks and merchants. A single standard limits unnecessary costs and builds the business case for doing business on the Internet. Further, our work with MasterCard demonstrates our unwavering commitment to address the needs of our member financial institutions and their merchants and cardholders.

The SET Consortium and Its Work

Upon the agreement, Visa and MasterCard—along with GTE, IBM, Microsoft, Netscape, SAIC, Terisa Systems, VeriSign, and RSA Data Security—formed the SET Consortium. Their goal was to resolve the differences and conflicts between STT and SEPP and develop a new unified standard.

The development of SET—a relatively quick response to an explosive growth of Internet development (although some consider it an eternity in Web-years)—arose not so much from the spirit of mutual cooperation as from the intervention of major banks when the industry giants, Visa and MasterCard, were heading in separate development directions. Obviously, for any pragmatic solution to the problems of electronic commerce, a single, standard approach, both flexible and platform-independent, was absolutely essential.

The SET Consortium's work, the Secure Electronic Transaction (SET), was released to developers in draft form on June 24, 1996. The draft release (Version 0.0), embodied in three separate books, was intended to be used for testing and to elicit comments from outside experts. These books contained sufficient preliminary specifications that developers could use to build components that would "bolt on" to existing cardholder browsers, merchant commerce servers, and financial institution credit authorization systems. This is how SET Version 0.0 appeared:

- *Book 1:* The business description, containing background information and processing flows. It was intended as a primer on software that interfaces with payment systems and employs public key cryptography.
- *Book 2:* The programmer's guide, containing the technical specifications for the protocol. It was intended for use by software developers who wish to build cardholder and merchant software components.
- *Book 3:* The formal protocol definition. It was intended for use by cryptographers analyzing SET's security aspects, writers producing programming guides for toolkits or components, and system programmers developing cryptographic and messaging primitives.

Upon its initial release, SET Version 0.0 was placed under change control with a January 1997 deadline for enhancement requests to Version 1.0, and a March 1997 deadline for proposed corrections to the testing version. On April 21, 1997, SET Version 0.2 was released to the public containing those requests for enhancements that satisfied the additional needs of non-Visa/MasterCard issuers, such as American Express, Japan Commerce Bank (JCB), and Novus/Discover. On May 31, 1997, SET Version 1.0 was released to the public.

SET's Objectives

Like its predecessors, STT and SEPP, SET addresses seven major business requirements:

1. Provide confidentiality of payment information, and enable confidentiality of order information that is transmitted along with the payment information.
2. Ensure the integrity of all transmitted data.

3. Provide authentication that a cardholder is a legitimate user of a branded payment card account.

4. Provide authentication that a merchant can accept payment card transactions through its relationship with an acquiring financial institution.

5. Ensure the use of the best security practices and system design techniques to protect all legitimate parties in an electronic commerce transaction.

6. Create a protocol that neither depends on transport security mechanisms nor prevents their use.

7. Facilitate and encourage interoperability among software and network providers.

Since payment cards and their systems have been around since the 1950s, banks and issuers have had plenty of time deciding how to secure their processing. These vast private networks, using leased lines and dial-up connections, helped in assuring their safety and security, building merchant and consumer confidence. SET does the same using insecure public communications channels, such as the Internet. To better understand how SET achieves this privacy and security, think of its operation using the following context: Take a secret, write it on a piece of paper, seal the paper in an envelope, place the envelope in a safe, place the safe in a vault, and ship the vault to your recipient using a common carrier. While it's possible that your secret could be discovered en route, what are the chances that this will happen? SET secures information so thoroughly that the costs to discover it far outweigh the benefits of knowing it.

With SET's official release as a standard, work toward its implementation continues across the globe with pilot testing between and among dozens of software developers, hardware developers, financial services companies, and a handful of pioneering merchants. As Robert Marczak, president of Marczak Business Services in Sharon Springs, New York, says, "Once secure transactions become more prominent, the Web will be for people of this century what the Sears Roebuck catalog was for consumers in the last century."

Participants of SET

SET defines transactions as activities between three parties: cardholders, merchants, and acquirer payment gateways.

Cardholders

Users of credit- and charge-card accounts need digital certificates to transact in the online world of SET, in the same way they need a plastic representation in the offline world. Cardholders interact with two other parties in the SET umbrella: (1) Certificate Authorities (discussed below), to obtain new certificates and renew existing ones, and (2) merchants, where they intend to shop and buy.

To use a Web browser to visit and shop, a component called an Electronic Wallet (E-wallet), which understands how to carry out the salient SET messages, is a fundamental requirement. These wallets embody the SET protocol and provide a means to store and manage the certificates to digitally sign messages, along with the security aspects consumers demand to keep private data private. How an E-wallet interfaces with a Web browser is not specified within the SET standard and is left to the discretion of E-wallet developers.

Cardholders visit a Web site that has SET E-wallets available for download and "grab" a copy of an E-wallet. After installation, the E-wallet is configured for the specific Web browser(s) the cardholder wishes to use for shopping. Once the E-wallet is properly working, it's time to obtain a digital certificate for each charge card or credit card the cardholder wants to use in the online world. To do this, cardholders visit a Certificate Authority (CA) to request a SET digital certificate. Once they're at the brand CA site, they present certain information presumably only they possess to prove their identity and their right to obtain a certificate. This authentication information is not defined under the SET standard. It is left up to the card issuers to decide how to authenticate. Some card companies insist on strong authentication to verify proof of identity up-front, while others rely on weak authentication, relying on back-end system processing during a transaction to catch questionable uses of their cards.

Cardholders must ensure that their PC-resident E-wallet is protected at least as well as their real wallet is protected in the offline world. This means keeping their private key component private (through password protection) and using a browser that supports Secure Sockets Layer (SSL) encryption when sending any personal information across the Internet (see Chapter 12).

Merchants

Merchants, like cardholders, communicate with a CA to obtain their requisite merchant SET certificates. Merchants require two certificates for every brand of payment card they accept: (1) a key-exchange certificate and (2) a signature certificate. Together, these two certificates serve as an electronic equivalent to the brand decal that's displayed in a merchant's establishment.

Merchant server Point of Sale (POS) software performs the tasks of cryptographic processing, message preparation, and merchant certificate management. Merchant servers communicate with both the cardholder's Web browser/E-wallet and the acquirer payment gateways that serve the bank(s) and payment card companies.

When a cardholder initiates a purchase request to a merchant server, the merchant server POS component determines the brand selected and forwards a copy of the appropriate brand payment gateway certificate (which it stores) and the merchant certificate back to the cardholder's E-wallet. The E-wallet uses these certificates to encrypt payment instructions and order information back to the merchant server.

With the delivery of goods or completion of services, the merchant can request the completion of the sale by using the Capture Request and Response message pair. A charge can be captured only once the goods have shipped, and only if a previously approved authorization response code is contained in the Capture Request. The Capture Response contains all the data the merchant needs to settle the transaction with its acquiring bank.

Acquirer Payment Gateways

Payment gateways serve as the interface between an acquiring bank and the banking network that supports card issuer authorization and settlement systems. Payment gateways are typically operated on the behalf of many financial institutions. Some gateways are operated directly by the banks or card companies, while others are outsourced to third parties, such as First Data Merchant Services (a subsidiary of First Data Corporation in Omaha, Nebraska). The primary purposes of the payment gateway include checking the currency and legitimacy of all certificates presented and maintaining an appropriate interface to traditional banking systems that permit the Internet to behave as though it's a private leased-line connection into the banking networks. The interfaces between payment gateways and acquirer back office systems are not defined by SET and are left to the financial institutions for implementation details.

Specific Uses of SET

Although its adoption is not quite what the industry expected (or hoped for!) thus far, what's integral to the success of SET is its full acceptance in the marketplace as an open standard for conducting electronic commerce on the Internet. SET's uses are specific in the course of a shopping and buying transaction. Its processing is identified to support only certain phases in the e-shopping model:

- *Phase 1.* Cardholder browses for items via the Web, through a CD-ROM–based catalog, or through a mail-order paper-based catalog.
- *Phase 2.* Cardholder selects items for purchase.
- *Phase 3.* Cardholder completes an order form, including total costs, shipping, handling, and taxes (if any). This form may be presented electronically via the Web, or it may be created offline on the cardholder's PC.
- *Phase 4.* Cardholder selects the form of payment

card to use for the order. SET is initiated at this point.

- *Phase 5.* Cardholder sends completed order form and payment instructions to the merchant. SET is used to digitally sign these order forms and payment instructions using the cardholder's digital certificate to prove they came from the cardholder and no one else.
- *Phase 6.* Merchant requests payment authorization from the issuer of the payment card using its merchant account through its acquirer's payment system. SET wraps these messages in cryptography to assure their privacy and confidentiality.
- *Phase 7.* Merchant ships goods or performs requested services based on the order.
- *Phase 8.* Merchant requests to capture the payment that was previously approved for processing in Phase 6. SET wraps these messages in cryptography to assure their privacy and confidentiality.

Those phases not included under SET are considered out-of-band (or out of scope) activities, which are left up to the specific parties on deciding their implementation. In addition, those interfaces to systems required for using SET are also out-of-band to the specification. SET provides open and robust data structures and corresponding security to handle virtually any type of order processing. It establishes an infrastructure for participants to plug into, using software they customize to meet infrastructure requirements. How that software is developed and any affected systems remain outside SET's definition.

SET is designed for use with 1,024 bit cipher keys, making it one of the strongest encryption applications around. The time it would take to break the encryption described here, especially with all the various layers of encryption that occur, is upward of 2.8 trillion years using one hundred computers each able to process 10 million instructions per second. Even then, only a single message could be broken, and with the next message, the entire process would need to start over. While it may seem like overkill, the protocol is rather attractive to those wanting to conduct widespread business over the Internet, especially card issuers (banks, etc.) who have the most to lose from credit card fraud.

SET has been approved for export from the United States provided that it's used only in financial transactions and not as a mechanism to pass secret or sensitive information to those outside the United States. Giants in the industry offer software that meets the needs of each of SET's constituents. Suites of SET-compliant software are available from IBM, GlobeSet, VeriFone, CyberCash, and others. For more detailed information about SET and its implementation, read *Building SET Applications for Secure Transactions* by Mark S. Merkow, James Breithaupt, and Ken Wheeler (Wiley Computer Publishing, 1998).

SET is poised to end problems associated with consumer purchasing, but its scope is narrowly defined to best serve retail operators. With corporate purchasing expected to dominate the volume of sales conducted via the Internet, other equally important protocols are needed to satisfy corporate needs.

THE CORPORATE PURCHASING LANDSCAPE

A recent Gartner Group study shows that Boeing 747 airline customers can lose up to $40,000 per minute while their planes wait on the ground for spare parts. Typical American businesses expend 80 percent of their purchasing efforts on 20 percent of their total purchasing dollars on Maintenance, Repair, and Operations (MRO) items that don't directly contribute to company profits. Modern purchasing systems have become nightmare operations with the complexities of business reengineering and supply-chain management. A general lack of technology to support these efforts contributes to the agony.

To simplify matters, many large purchasing departments have reduced their base of suppliers with the goals of achieving a tighter integration of the supply chain, establishing sets of *preferred suppliers*. As a select group, these goods-providers are expected to be highly responsive to customer demand or face losing their "preferred status." Examples of the types of demands being placed on selling organizations include:

- Custom catalogs
- Custom products
- Custom pricing
- Value-added services

In response to these demands, supply companies have developed a slew of highly customized, *one-off* electronic catalogs and purchasing systems, creating other technology maintenance nightmares such as software compatibility problems. New products and services, like corporate purchasing cards, can help in achieving MRO cost and quality goals, but alone they can't go far enough. Many of the services that use these products are based on proprietary systems and mechanisms that lack standardized processing and systems support. Interoperability among these systems is rare, thus leading buying and selling organizations to seek easy-to-use, open, standards-based solutions to common business problems.

OPEN BUYING ON THE INTERNET

In 1998, the Internet Purchasing Roundtable—a group of *Fortune* 500 companies and their leading suppliers— heeded the call to help and announced the Open Buying on the Internet (OBI) standard to eliminate some problems with today's systems and processes. According to Thayer Stewart, vice president of marketing for American Express Corporate Services, "The OBI standard should break through the gridlock that has prevented corporations and suppliers from transacting business over the Internet. Having a common standard will facilitate Internet commerce and should deliver significant savings for users."

The Internet Purchasing Roundtable created OBI as a freely available set of specifications for software developers.

Copies of OBI Version 2.0 are currently available. Within the constructs of OBI are:

- An architectural approach for e-commerce systems
- Detailed technical specifications and guidelines for development
- Record layout formats
- File formats
- Communications structures and protocols
- Compliance testing guidelines
- Implementation assistance

The ongoing maintenance of OBI is carried out by the nonprofit OBI Consortium, whose membership is open to any buying and selling organizations, technology companies, financial institutions, or other interested parties.

The OBI Framework

OBI's underlying design relies on the notion that buying organizations are responsible for the profiles of those who request goods and services, accounting procedures, tax status information, and internal approval processes. Selling organizations are responsible for electronic catalogs, pricing, order entry and fulfillment systems, and inventory systems. Rather than require the selling organization to maintain profile data on potentially thousands of different buyers, OBI requires the use of authentication digital certificates that store those unique user profiles. These digital certificates, based on the X.509 Version 3 standard for digital certificates (see Chapter 13), are used to authenticate buyers, describe their roles and permissions within the buying organization, and offer selling organizations the highest level of assurance that they're dealing with whom they think they're dealing. These certificates also benefit sellers by helping them test the integrity of purchase order information through its signing by the digital certificate's cryptography.

Where the Secure Electronic Transaction (SET) standard governs the security of credit-card presentation and authorization usage over the Internet, it does not govern any of the processing or customization of the user's "shopping experience," which OBI does. OBI's intent is not to standardize the payment methods in use, but it does support the use of SET for actual payment (using SET digital certificates), as well as any other means as specified by the "payment authority" established by the OBI standard within each buying organization.

The Trading Web

OBI's ultimate goal is the establishment of a common ground for what the ODI Consortium refers to as the "Trading Web," where OBI standard adopters establish trading relationships with other OBI standard adopters through secured access to extranet facilities connected via the Internet. These companies, in turn, establish new relationships with others, and the Trading Web expands, forming dynamic sets of interoperable systems.

Software support for OBI from various e-commerce solution providers is currently available. For example, Open Market's Transact system offers OBI-compliant order management, online customer service, security services, authentication services, flexible payment processing, and secure transaction processing. Transact is intended to aid in the movement of online product catalogs to complete end-to-end Internet commerce systems that form the core of the Trading Web.

In August 1997, the Motorola Space and Systems Technology Group in Tempe, Arizona, ran the first pilot test of OBI using the Intelipro System. Employees at Motorola accessed Office Depot's online catalog in the first business-to-business electronic commerce pilot compliant with the OBI standard. Intelipro was developed by Intelisys Electronic Commerce, LLC, a joint venture between Chase Manhattan Bank and software developers BVR, LLC. In late August 1999, OBI Version 2.0 was released, intended to move OBI from pilot testing to full-bore production. In addition, there was an announcement of the OBI Interoperability Showcase, in time for CommerceNet 99. The OBI

Compliance Program was featured there to help vendors demonstrate their products' compliance to the standard.

What do companies think of OBI? Here's what Brian Buckley, director of business solutions for barnesandnoble.com, has to say:

> For companies like barnesandnoble.com, whose business is Web-based, adding OBI functionality to procurement solutions will increase the productivity of our operations. The new solution will also allow us to better serve our corporate customers by integrating with the initiatives they have under way to reduce the "soft costs" associated with purchasing. For a category like books that is high-volume and low dollars per transaction, OBI is an excellent solution.

David Liggett, chair of the OBI Standards Track, and vice president of Epic Systems Inc., explains:

> OBI lowers overall acquisition costs, decreases time to implementation, and increases user productivity. In Version 2.0, OBI now supports multivendor requirements, customer-specific catalogs, and secure processing on the Web. Purchase orders fed directly into the customer's local procurement or finance systems are returned to the seller via the Internet, eliminating the need for duplicate data entry by either the customer or the seller.

Future planned enhancements for OBI include adding further XML support (see below), international support, and expansion of the compliance testing and certification programs.

OBI-based extranets wring out costs in the supply chain. These same extranets can help companies to finally realize the benefits of Just-in-Time (JIT) inventory systems, a goal that Electronic Data Interchange (EDI) failed to achieve. Once willing companies begin to participate in the types of information sharing that OBI encourages, collaborative environments are bound to prosper and flourish.

While industry efforts like SET and OBI continue maturing, extranets continue finding their way into all walks of life, from automobile manufacturing to X-ray devices. Where technology we now consider obsolete often inhibited innovative business practices, extranets are enabling new practices, the likes of which have never been seen before in information systems. Further contributing to intranet and extranet evolution is the eXtensible Markup Language (XML), which is at the forefront of new development efforts.

XML

As businesses move to customer self-servicing, partnering with external companies, and adopting three-tier Web-based client-server systems (see Chapter 9), the complexities of processing increase by orders of magnitude. Managing and using business data is a precarious task since data is found under multiple formats:

- Corporate documents
- Messages from customers or external partners
- Interfaces to transaction-based systems
- Databases (all varieties)
- Web pages

Because of the lack of a universal and secure interchange format, companies are often prevented from taking advantage of automation that adds seamlessness between internal applications and external partner applications. As a result, IT departments spend upward of 40 percent of their time in extracting, redefining, and updating data to serve specific needs, according to an industry survey from Forrester Research.

Serving up XML

The next horizon for XML (a "meta-markup" language that defines a standard set of rules for describing data, not just how it appears) appears in solutions using middle-tier specialized application servers. A slew of new XML servers are available, bringing with them the promises of simplified integration, improved data management, and enhanced operating efficiencies. As XML further matures and finds its way into today's Web-based applications to address interoperability and security problems, it's becoming critical to architect XML into computer operations using intelligent designs and specialized processing. The new breed of XML data servers are designed specifically to meet these needs.

What Do XML Servers Do?

As a middle-tier device, XML servers provide:

- Storage and manipulation of native XML data
- High-performance querying capability on large sets of XML-based components
- Integration of disparate data sources into unified XML databases that permit querying and updating using well-defined standards
- Execution of Document Object Model (DOM)–compliant applications using XML data types
- Standard interfaces to Web development languages, including JScript, VBScript, and Java
- Single points of administration
- Scalable data distribution functions

Depicted graphically, XML middle-tier servers are typically implemented as shown in Figure 10-1. The XML server is in tier II.

XML-based services will likely supplant many of those systems we call traditional e-commerce today. The World Wide Web Consortium (W3C), Internet Engineering Task Force, and software developers worldwide are embracing XML, not only as a solution to the universal data exchange quandary but for security concerns as well. XML is finding its way into a host of industry-specific data standardization formats. Document Type Definitions (DTDs) in various stages of development have been defined for:

Figure 10-1. An XML middle-tier server.

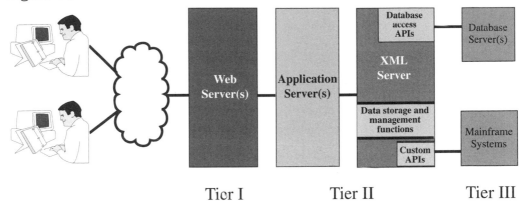

Tier I   Tier II   Tier III

- Ad Markup, defined by the NAA Classified Advertising Standards Task Force for the exchange of classified ads for media-independent formats.

- AECMA Specification 1000D, defined by the European Association of Aerospace Industries, to establish a standard for documentation of civil and military air vehicles and equipment.

- BizTalk, defined (as led by Microsoft) as a content framework to support the Microsoft Network (MSN) to bring businesses and consumers together.

- Microsoft's Channel Definition Format (CDF), to enable Web publishers to "push" collections or channels of information from any Web server to any Web client.

- Commerce XML (cXML), for product, catalog, and transaction data related to maintenance, repair, and operations (MRO) goods and services.

- Information and Content Exchange (ICE), for a common format for sharing and managing information assets between affiliates in syndicated publication networks, Web superstores, and online resellers.

- MathML, to describe mathematical notations, along with a taxonomy to describe structures and contents. MathML is intended for software developers writing media-independent rendering and editing software for math equations.

- News Industry Text Format (NITF), to enable the markup and transfer of electronically published news and content.

- OAGIS (Open Applications Group Integration Specification), developed by the Open Applications Group (OAG), to provide XML application program interfaces for financial, human resources, manufacturing, logistics, and supply chain applications to promote interoperability at the business process level among various ERP systems.

- Open Financial Exchange (OFX) (developed in 1997 by CheckFree, Intuit, and Microsoft), to support electronic exchange of financial data among financial institutions, businesses, and consumers via the Web. OFX is being used today for consumer and small business banking, bill payment, bill aggregation and presentment, and stocks, bonds, and mutual funds investments. Financial planning and insurance will be added to OFX in the future.

- Open Trading Protocol (OTP), defined as a software interoperability specification for electronic purchasing data that's independent of specific payment mechanisms, thus simplifying large corporate electronic purchasing systems.

- Platform for Privacy Preferences (P3P), to enable users to tailor their Web browsers to their sensitivity on private and confidential information collection practices and content. Once preferences are established, the Web browser alerts or automatically filters out content and practices that do not meet preferred selections.

- Real Estate Listing Markup Language (RELML), defined by OpenMLS and 4th World Telecom, to provide standardized format for media-independent real estate listings.

- RosettaNet, to define IT industry product and catalog data for recurring or large-volume purchasing of computer-related parts and equipment.

- Synchronized Multimedia Integration Language (SMIL), to enable the integration of individual multimedia objects into a synchronized multimedia presentation. SMIL enhances the compatibility of existing authorware programs by providing a consistent definition of multimedia objects and user interactions with them.

- vCard, to define a standardized format for electronic business cards.

- XML/EDI, to define durable and unambiguous business transaction data for commercial electronic interchange without the high costs and barriers in using traditional EDI systems.

- XwingML, from Bluestone Software Inc., for Java's Swing/JFC GUI (Graphical User Interface) components that enable developers to define menus, frames, and dialog boxes using XML. It dynamically creates Java GUI presentation layer program code.

XML as a Security Tool

Nearly everyone is turning to XML to solve even the stickiest of Internet communications problems. Significant security-related work comes from IBM with its XML Security Suite.

At the heart of the suite you'll find DOMHASH as a reference implementation for computing digital signatures on XML documents. IBM is offering the XML Security Suite as the basis for the digital signature discussions occurring at both the Internet Engineering Task Force (IETF) and the World Wide Web Consortium (W3C). IBM provides support for element-wise encryption on XML data, digital signatures on entire XML documents, and access control features that aren't possible under SSL (Secure Sockets Layer) transport layer security.

DOMHASH is intended as a canonicalizer (i.e., it reduces to canonical terms) for XML digital signatures. The sample implementation provided with the security suite is based on a draft submitted to the IETF by Richard Brown of GlobeSet. You can find the draft at *draft-brown-XML-dsig-XX.txt* on the IETF Drafts Site (www.IETF.org). You can also download the XML Security Suite from IBM's alphaWorks site in its Resources:Tools section.

Digital Signatures

For business-to-business e-commerce to supplant traditional, costly, and time-consuming exchanges with low-cost and readily available Internet technology, the security of business documents must be ramped up considerably and comprehensively. With digitally signed documents, both senders and receivers are assured that messages originated at their advertised source and that no tampering of message contents occurred en route.

Although you'll find additional details about PPK (Public-Private Key) cryptography later (see Chapter 13), it's useful to take a brief look now at the digital signing process to better understand the initiatives described here. Fundamental to the uses of digital signatures are pairs of public and private cryptographic keys that people possess in lieu of credentials in the offline world. Typically, private keys remain private under exclusive control of the keyholder, while the public key is shared when the keyholder wishes to conduct secure communications. Public keys are wrapped up in the form of a digital certificate that binds the key-pair to an individual after she's presented proper credentials to prove her right for such attestation. A Certificate Authority (a trusted party that operates on behalf of a corporation or entity) creates a digital certificate for the requester under what's called a Public Key Infrastructure (PKI). Once these key-pairs are in the hands of all those participating in a transaction, digital signatures on messages passed among the parties protect the contents and also provide sender authentication and message integrity checks.

Using a standard message digest creation algorithm (MD5, SHA-1, etc.), a sender creates a unique "fingerprint" of a message and then encrypts the result using the *sender's private key*. Message digest computations provide a 160-bit (20-byte) value that's guaranteed to be unique for a given message. If even a single bit is changed within the message, roughly half the bits in the digest also change, preventing someone from believing that the message arrived unaltered.

When you attach the encrypted message digest (digital signature) to the original message and further encrypt it using the *receiver's public key* (from his digital certificate), you create what's called a digital envelope, adding the three elements—sender authentication, message integrity, and confidentiality (privacy)—to complete the security picture that's required for effective electronic commerce. As you begin to appreciate the value of enabling this degree of security on Internet communications, you can also begin to appreciate their value, especially where e-commerce is concerned.

SDML

XML as a potential security solution doesn't stop with IBM's XML Security Suite. The Signed Document Markup Language (SDML) is also working its way through the IETF process. Its intent is fourfold:

1. Tag individual text items within a document.
2. Group the text items into document parts that can have business meaning and can be signed individually or together.
3. Allow document parts to be added and deleted without invalidating previous signatures.
4. Allow signing, cosigning, endorsing, coendorsing, and witnessing operations on documents and document parts.

SDML is a part of the Electronic Check Project from the Financial Services Technology Consortium (FSTC). Another initiative from FSTC is called the Bank Internet Payment System, or BIPS. It includes a protocol for sending payment instructions to banks via the Internet, along with a payment server architecture for processing those payment instructions. An appendix of the specification includes the XML structures and DTDs for BIPS.

In addition, the FSTC is promoting a standard series of message formats that describe the contents and behavior of an electronic payment transaction. Known as the Network Payment Protocol (NPP), some of the characteristics are:

- All messages are in XML.
- All messages begin with a BIPS XML header.

- All fields are self-identifying.
- All messages are signed.
- All messages include the originator's certificate.
- All request messages include a user-supplied transaction number.
- All message responses include the signature of the user on the original request.
- All response messages include a bank-supplied transaction number and the user-supplied transaction number.

As industry leaders respond to the demands of corporate suppliers and financial services institutions, a synergy forms, enabling far more than either could possibly achieve alone. Once the security requirements are met with industrial-strength solutions that are reliable, predictable, and impervious to attacks, the dreams of global electronic commerce come that much closer to bearing irresistible fruits.

Beginning with Chapter 11, we'll drill deeper into how digital cryptography protects Internet communications. It's time to pull out the old cloak and dagger!

11

An Introduction to Cryptography

In the offline world, it's easy to ask someone for an ID to prove she is who she claims to be. As a society, we've grown generally to trust photo IDs and written signatures as proof of someone's claim that she has rights—to use a credit card, to drive a car, etc.

In the online world, checking the same claims to rights can be performed only through technology, primarily cryptography. From the broadest overview, this is accomplishing by binding a person to a pair of cryptographic keys, using tightly controlled and secure conditions. Once a trusted key issuance process is complete, these keys are used to keep messages private, to authenticate the sender, and to test the integrity of messages. Since most Internet-related application-level security relies on cryptography, it's essential to lay a foundation for its understanding.

Applied cryptography—*the science of secret writing*—enables the storage of information in forms that reveal it only to those permitted and hide it from everyone else. In the 20th century, international governments began to adopt the use of cryptography for protecting their private and sensitive information and for communications purposes. Up until the last twenty years or so, governments and military organizations were the exclusive users of cryptography to secure private data and to try and crack everyone else's. The U.S. National Security Agency (NSA) is an example of the lengths the government goes to in developing and protecting robust cryptography. Today, cryptography is considered a munition and, as such, its uses and export are tightly controlled by various U.S. government agencies, including the NSA. The U.S. government continues its struggle to approve forms of strong cryptography for domestic and export purposes.

Since the 1970s, academic interest in cryptography grew at tremendous rates, and with the research, private citizens gained access to various cryptography techniques, permitting personal information protection and enabling the conduct of secure electronic transactions.

Advancements in the field continue. With the aid of supercomputers (massively parallel processors), communities of hackers working together to try and crack the strongest cryptosystems, and the increasing sophistication of modern computer technology, cryptography stands to become more tried and true, evolving into highly reliable and well-established practices.

BASIC TERMS AND CONCEPTS

Here are some of the basic terms and concepts involved in cryptography.

- *Cryptography* is the science (or art) of designing, building, and using cryptosystems.
- A *cryptosystem* disguises messages such that only selected people can see through the disguise.
- *Cryptanalysis* is the science (or art) of breaking a cryptosystem.
- *Cryptology* is the umbrella study of cryptography and cryptanalysis.
- *Cryptographers* rely on two basic methods of disguising messages: (1) *transposition*, where letters are rearranged into a different order, and (2) *substitution*, where letters are replaced by other letters.
- *Plaintext* is the message that is passed through an encryption algorithm, or *cipher*, at which point it becomes *ciphertext*. When ciphertext is passed through a decryption algorithm, it becomes plaintext again.

A strong cryptosystem is considered strong only until it's been cracked. While that may sound like common sense, you can never *prove* that a cryptosystem is strong. All you can do is assure that certain properties are present within it. Each defeat of an attempt to crack a cryptosystem serves to strengthen the belief in its ability to secure. Similar to currency, a cryptosystem has value because its users believe in its worth. Once that worth is proved to be unfounded, the cryptosystem collapses, and no one relies upon it anymore.

All strong cryptosystems have similar characteristics. Their algorithms are made well-known to the public (through published standards and public posting), and the strength of the algorithm rests in the keys used to encrypt and decrypt (the longer the key, the better) The basic idea is to keep the keys a secret rather than keep the algorithm a secret.

Strong cryptosystems produce ciphertext that always appears random to standard statistical tests. They also resist all known attacks on cryptosystems and have been brutally tested to ensure their integrity. Cryptosystems that have not been subjected to brutal testing are considered suspect.

Random Number Requirements

Perfectly random numbers, while thought to exist in nature, are impossible to achieve using deterministic devices, like computers. The best a computer can do is generate *pseudorandom* numbers. Cryptography demands far more from pseudorandomness than most other applications (for example, computer games). For a string of bits to be considered cryptographically random, it must be computationally infeasible to predict what the nth random bit will be, given full knowledge of the algorithm and the values of the bits already generated. Since computers are deterministic, at some point a random number generator becomes periodic— i.e., it begins to repeat. The challenge, then, is to build random number generators that won't repeat sequences of bits predictably often. Some of the pseudorandom number generators available today show randomness through 2 raised to the 256th power (a very large number), making them more suitable for use in cryptography than the kinds of random number generators built in to programming languages, like the rnd( ) functions in C or C++.

When the same key is used both to encrypt and decrypt messages, it's called *symmetric key* cryptography. When different keys are used, it's called *asymmetric key* cryptography. The Data Encryption Standard (DES) uses the former technique, while RSA (named after its inventors—Ron Rivest, Adi Shamir, and Leonard Adelman) uses the latter technique. Pretty Good Privacy (PGP), a public-domain cryptosystem invented by Phil Zimmerman, also uses asymmetric key cryptography.

A Simple Example

Although knowing the actual mechanics of cryptosystems is not directly required to understand how cryptography is used in security products, a grasp of the complexities involved helps one to appreciate what's going on within the software. Using the transposition technique with a symmetric key (shared secret), let's take a look at how encryption and decryption might operate manually.

Assume the plaintext message we want to encrypt is:
ATTACK AT SUNSET

We'll use the word "CAUTION" as our key and send the keyword to our intended recipient, using a secure channel that assures he has it when the ciphertext arrives.

Encrypt the message through the following steps:
1. Write the key horizontally as the heading for columns.

C   A   U   T   I   O   N

2. Assign numerical values to each letter based on the letter's appearance in the alphabet. (The first letter in the key that appears in the alphabet is 1, the second letter in the key that appears in the alphabet is 2, and so on.)

C   A   U   T   I   O   N
2   1   7   6   3   5   4

3. Align the plaintext message across each key/value column heading, skipping to the next line when the last column of the matrix is reached.

C	A	U	T	I	O	N
2	1	7	6	3	5	4
A	T	T	A	C	K	A
T	S	U	N	S	E	T

4. Read down along each column in the ordinal value of the column to produce the ciphertext (A-1 is the first column, C-2 the second, and so forth).

TS   AT   CS   AT   KE   AN   TU

5. Send the ciphertext to the recipient using any channel desired. Since he already possesses the shared secret, we don't need to worry about getting it in his hands again.

Upon receipt of the ciphertext, the recipient decrypts it through the following steps:

1. Write the key horizontally as the heading for columns.

C	A	U	T	I	O	N

2. Assign numerical values to each letter based on the letter's appearance in the alphabet.

C	A	U	T	I	O	N
2	1	7	6	3	5	4

3. Transpose the ciphertext, two letters at a time, using the ordinal value of each column to determine its placement. Since A is Column Value 1, the first group of letters, TS, is written vertically under A-1. The second group of letters belongs under C-2, and so forth.

C	A	U	T	I	O	N
2	1	7	6	3	5	4
A	T	T	A	C	K	A
T	S	U	N	S	E	T

4. Read the message horizontally to reveal the plaintext message.
ATTACK AT SUNSET

Had the message been longer, for example, ATTACK AT SUNSET TUESDAY, the ciphertext groups would have consisted of three letters instead of two, and would have grown with the length of the message. If the message had included the use of numbers or special characters, we'd have to treat them separately and agree on their positional values in the alphabet we're using; otherwise, our algorithm goes out the window.

Even with a simple example like this, you can begin to see the protocol developed to make it work. Steps must be performed in order, cannot be skipped, and cannot be altered in any way. Computer-based cryptography, while far more robust than anything that could be accomplished by hand, uses the same approaches, if not the same algorithms themselves.

Cryptography itself becomes *extremely* complicated extremely *quickly,* but it need not be totally intimidating to the casual observer. Those with a keener interest in the application of strong cryptography should read *Applied Cryptography* by Bruce Schneier, considered by many as the bible of modern cryptographers and cryptanalysts.

CRYPTOSYSTEMS AS THE ANSWER TO THE NEEDS OF TODAY'S E-COMMERCE

Before we discuss specific implementations of data encryption and secure electronic transmissions in upcoming chapters, it's important to understand that different situations call for different levels of security. A college student sending an e-mail home to his parents asking for money is mainly concerned that the note reaches its intended destination and that no one tampers with its contents. An internal corporate memo to all employees, on the other hand, might contain sensitive information that should not go beyond the company's intranet. The CEO assumes that when he sends the note, only the intended audience will read it. Likewise, the employees assume that the note did indeed come from the CEO and no one else. No real authentication is performed because the company's e-mail system relies on the notion of *trust*. Each employee must have an ID and password to access the e-mail system, but beyond that any guarantees of authenticity require implicit trust in the users of the system.

Ensuring that electronic commerce is secure, however, requires an implicit *distrust* in users of the Internet. Most users are law-abiding citizens who use the network for legitimate purchases. They are who they say they are, and they enjoy the convenience that Internet shopping affords. Unfortunately, given the decentralized design of the Internet and the potential for the unscrupulous few to wreak havoc for everyone, electronic commerce can never be made too secure.

In summary, cryptography is needed by Internet-based applications to implement the privacy and security that most users demand. In the next few chapters, you'll see specific uses of cryptosystems that are built using the principles discussed here.

12

Transport Layer Cryptography

With a basic understanding of how cryptography is used to protect private conversations and data, you're ready to begin seeing how it's used on the Internet.

You will recall that the OSI (Open Systems Interconnection) communication stack is a layering of network protocols. Communication software vendors use these layers to break down the complexity of protocols. Each layer builds on the communication services provided by the layers beneath it. The fourth layer of the communication stack is the OSI transport layer. It is responsible for the transport of network packets. Services provided by the transport layer are transparent to the user and include:

- Multiplexing
- Data flow control
- Virtual circuit management
- Error checking
- Error recovery

These services help to:

- Manage the rate of data transmission between devices
- Enable data from multiple applications to share the same physical link
- Detect transmission errors
- Recover data when errors occur

A number of transport-layer protocols perform these functions within the TCP/IP (Transmission Control Protocol/Internet Protocol) stack, as discussed in Chapter 3. These protocols include Transmission Control Protocol

(TCP), Name Binding Protocol (NBP), and others. As you also saw in Chapter 3, the Internet Protocol (IP) by itself is insecure and cannot prevent a hacker from launching an attack. Known as a connectionless service, its job is to route messages to the specified destination without requiring a setup process, but it does not guarantee the delivery of the message or the correct ordering of message packets, and it certainly does not guarantee the integrity of the data within the message. It was designed to interconnect as many sites on the network as possible without taxing the hardware or software at any destination or anywhere along the way to a destination.

Because TCP/IP was developed with reliability—not security—in mind, new security services or layers must be added to offer varying degrees of security on packets as they traverse the network.

THE SSL PROTOCOL

Sitting on top of a reliable transport protocol such as TCP, the SSL Record Protocol is used to encapsulate other higher-level protocols prior to transmitting them via the network. SSL (Secure Sockets Layer) is a secured socket connection between a Web server and Web client that uses Public-Private Key (PPK) cryptography. It has become the standard security mechanism for authentication and encryption between Web browsers and servers and is supported by all of today's commercial Web browsers. One such protocol, the SSL Handshake Protocol, authenticates the server to a software-based client (such as a Web browser) and enables it to decide upon an encryption algorithm and cryptographic keys before a higher-level protocol sends or receives data.

SSL addresses many of the security concerns in sharing private or confidential information via the Internet. Its goals are to ensure the privacy of the connection, to authenticate a peer's identity, and to establish a reliable transport mechanism for the message using integrity checks and hashing functions. However, it does not go far enough in the eyes of most security analysts.

The SSL protocol was designed for client/server applications, preventing the unwanted tampering of data transmission through eavesdropping, data alteration, or message forgery. Its goal is to ensure the privacy and reliability of communication between two applications. To do this, SSL consists of two layers. It relies on a six-step handshaking approach between parties that is described as follows:

- *Step 1.* The client browser initiates an SSL session to an SSL-enabled Web server using an https:// request containing what encryption algorithms the browser supports, a cryptographic challenge, and a session ID if a previous session is continuing.
- *Step 2.* The server responds with the encryption algorithms it supports, the session ID, and the server's SSL digital certificate.
- *Step 3.* The client browser generates a key for the algorithm it selects to use, signs it using the server's public key, and returns it.
- *Step 4.* The client browser sends a notice to the server that it's ready to proceed using the encrypted session ID identifier.
- *Step 5.* The server sends a verify message including the challenge from Step 1, encrypted using the client-supplied key.
- *Step 6.* The server sends a finish message indicating a new session ID, placing the session in a state where higher-level communications will be securely encrypted as long as the session is maintained.

Your browser lets you know when your session is ready for secure communication by displaying a closed padlock, typically in the lower left-hand corner of the browser window.

It is worth noting that, unlike TCP/IP, SSL must be selectively used by the Web client and server in order to invoke the protocol. The user can designate an SSL Web page by either typing the appropriate URL (Uniform Resource

Locator) prefixed with https:// or by linking to a site that specifies an SSL-enabled Web page.

A benefit of SSL is that it allows higher-level protocols to sit on top of it and communicates with them without dictating a specific application protocol. For an illustration of the "handshake" between the various layers of protocol in SSL, see Figure 12-1.

One problem with SSL resides in the concept of "hierarchies of trust" involving the use of digital certificates. In a nutshell, a digital certificate is a stream of data, possibly several thousands bytes long, that encodes the user's public key and an endorsement by a Certificate Authority (CA). Digital certificates move the burden of verification off the user's shoulders and puts it squarely on that of the CA,

Figure 12-1. The SSL "handshake" between various layers of the protocol.

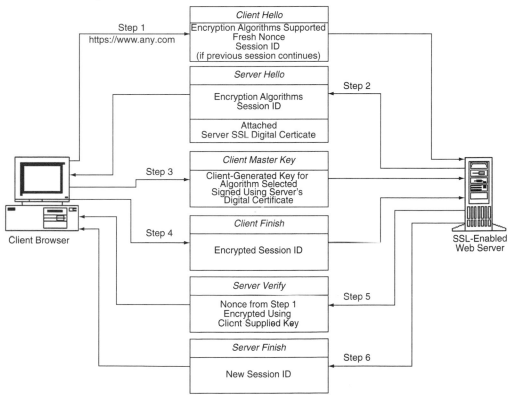

promoting the level of trust up to a higher rung on the security ladder (hierarchy).

As Peter Wayner pointed out in an article in *Byte* magazine, most users' computers that are SSL-enabled stop at this first level in the certificate hierarchy. If a user's Web browser, for example, connects to a server that uses SSL, the server establishes its identity by sending a copy of its public key wrapped in a certificate. The browser then sanctions the certificate by checking the signature. Unfortunately, the browser has no real way of knowing if the signature is valid. No further verification is performed up the hierarchy because most certificates used by SSL are known as "root" certificates.

An article entitled "Encryption Goes Mainstream" in *Computerworld Emmerce Webzine* (February 2, 1998; www.computerworld,com/home/Emmerce.nsf) cited the "Top 10" problems of SSL, according to Cryptography Research, Inc.:

1. SSL does not work well with proxies and filters.
2. SSL adds computational overhead, both at the client and the server.
3. SSL adds extra network round-trips to implement its handshake.
4. Migrating from non–Public Key Infrastructures requires significant efforts.
5. SSL does not work well with existing cryptography tokens.
6. SSL key management tends to be expensive.
7. SSL requires a Certificate Authority with appropriate policies for its use.
8. Encrypted SSL communications do not compress, slowing their transmission through devices such as modems.
9. International export restrictions complicate everything about SSL.
10. Few companies possess the expertise required to build, maintain, and operate secure systems.

Until it's matured and these problems are worked out—or worse, when SSL itself becomes unreliable from cryptanalysis—it can't provide the level of security that's needed to withstand the close scrutiny of the security community. By itself, SSL is inexpensive and well understood, so many companies will continue to rely on it (mainly with retail e-commerce systems) for a long time to come. But for those companies needing to ratchet up security features, especially where mission-critical application processing is performed, as with most extranets, VPN technology may be a better choice.

VIRTUAL PRIVATE NETWORKS

Virtual Private Networks (VPNs) are taking the industry by storm, helping to drive out proprietary networks and drive down the costs of doing business, especially where extranets are found. To answer some of the enhanced security requirements that are mandatory as Internet demand increases, certain vendors of networking systems are responding with both proprietary and nonproprietary (standardized) solutions that *tunnel* private traffic over public networks, like the Internet.

VPN Protocols

Common protocols found in today's VPN products include:

- Point-to-Point Tunneling Protocol (PPTP), from Microsoft
- Layer 2 Forwarding (L2F), from Cisco Systems
- Layer 2 Tunneling Protocol (L2TP), which combines PPTP and L2F
- SOCKS protocol, from NEC

PPTP

PPTP is a tunneling protocol that supports multiple other protocols by encrypting their traffic prior to submitting them to the Internet for transport. LAN (local area network) protocols, such as Novell's IPX and Microsoft's NetBEUI, are encapsulated (wrapped up) using PPTP and unwrapped on the receiving end before being routed to their destination. PPTP is built into Microsoft Windows NT 4.0, and client software for PPTP is available as a free add-on for Windows 95 users. PPTP lacks scalability and was found to contain several problems in its implementation, making it vulnerable to attacks. PPTP is intended for use over dial-up connections to the Internet.

L2F

In 1996, Layer 2 Forwarding (L2F) began competing with PPTP. L2F's essential technical difference is its ability to use protocols at Layer 2 of the TCP/IP protocol stack, including ATM (Asynchronous Transfer Mode) and Frame Relay for tunneling purposes. PPTP operates at Layer 3 of TCP/IP by wrapping IP packets themselves under PPTP protocol rules.

L2TP

Combining the best features of PPTP and L2F, Layer 2 Tunneling Protocol (L2TP) merges the two as a successor protocol that is supported and commonly used by today's network routing devices.

SOCKS

NEC has been advancing the uses of the SOCKS protocol as another alternative to PPTP, L2F, and L2TP. SOCKS is an authenticated firewall traversal protocol that was designed to permit traffic to pass through only after the user who sent it has been authenticated to the system, rather than relying upon any specific characteristics of an IP packet to decide if access is permitted or not. Some of the greatest advantages of SOCKS are its support for both UNIX and NT systems and its ability to establish application-specific tunnels for programs that are tied to specific TCP/IP server ports. SOCKS is an Internet Engineering Task Force (IETF) standard described in RFC 1928, RFC 1929, and RFC 1961. SOCKS Version 5 includes support for negotiating encryption uses between communicating parties.

IPSec

The current version of IP addressing, and the one in widest use today, is IP Version 4, or IPv4. The next generation of IP—called IP Version 6, or IPv6—mandates the use of a new set of security features that are optionally available for IPv4. These features, called IP Security, or IPSec, operate at both the network layer and session layers of the TCP/IP protocol stack.

Today's VPN solutions increasingly rely on IPSec. While other VPN protocols will remain commercially available for some time to come, the majority of VPN solution providers have incorporated IPSec into their products.

IPSec was developed by the IETF as RFC 1825-9, based on the work conducted in the Automotive Network eXchange (ANX) project from the Big 3 automakers. IPSec performs both encryption and authentication to address the inherent lack of security on IP-based networks. Its design supports all of the security goals: sender authentication, message integrity, and data confidentiality. IPSec operates by encapsulating an IP packet with another packet that surrounds it, and then encrypts the result. See Figure 12-2 for a view of repackaging IP packets for secure transfer. IPSec provides security without requiring organizations to modify their user applications. Figure 12-3 shows the relationship of some transport layer protocols to the TCP/IP protocol stack. For example, the lowest layer of the protocol stack, the physical layer, contains the communication software that belongs to device drivers. These drivers interface with several types of communication hardware adapters. Moving up the stack, the layers move from the physical model of wiring and hardware adapters to the higher layers that deal with the application "look and feel" and session behavior—that aspect of the computer with which the user is intimately familiar.

IETF RFCs Governing IPSec

The IPSec standard is defined in the Internet Engineering Task Force Request for Comments (RFCs) 1825 through 1829. Figure 12-4 illustrates the hierarchy of these RFCs,

Figure 12-2. Repackaging IP packets for secure transport using IPSec.

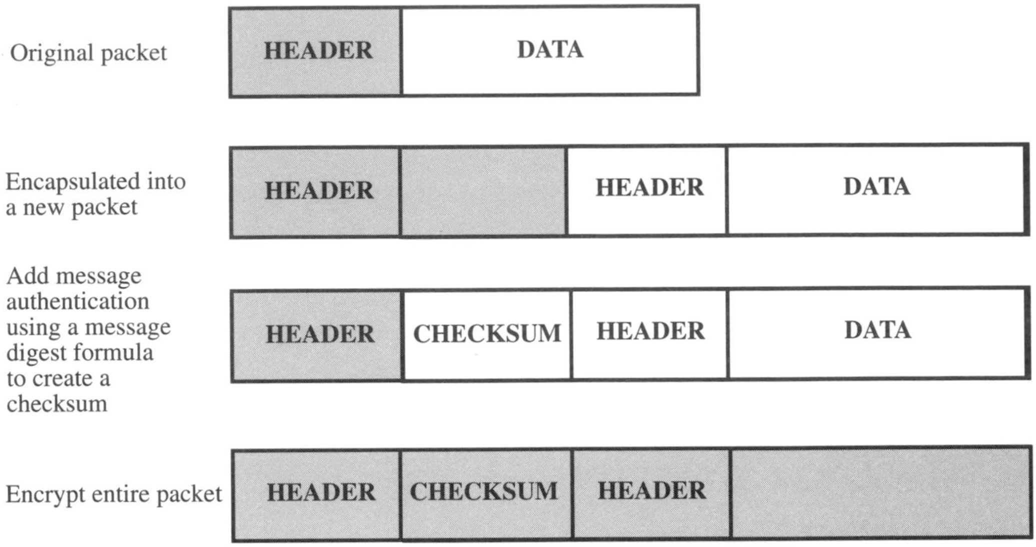

Original packet

HEADER	DATA

Encapsulated into a new packet

HEADER		HEADER	DATA

Add message authentication using a message digest formula to create a checksum

HEADER	CHECKSUM	HEADER	DATA

Encrypt entire packet

HEADER	CHECKSUM	HEADER	

grouped by the security services that IPSec offers. In general, Figure 12-4 shows the components of the IP Security Architecture. The IP Application header, for example, provides integrity and authentication without confidentiality. The Encapsulating Security Protocol (ESP) provides integrity, authentication, *and* confidentiality. Those who are interested in the other components of the IP Security Architecture in greater detail should go to the IETF Web site (*www.IETF.org*).

The IPSec Working Group of the IETF published the first proposed mechanisms for IPSec in 1995. Key management for IPSec was later added to the proposal in 1998. Today there are dozens of proposed enhancements to IPSec in the form of Internet Drafts.

How IPSec Ensures Security

Just as TCP/IP networks operate using a series of layers, security processing can also occur at one or more layers of the protocol stack. IPSec is designed to operate at the network layer of TCP/IP, enabling those applications operating at higher layers (e.g., public key cryptography) to enhance

Figure 12-3. The relationship between some transport layer protocols to the TCP/IP protocol stack.

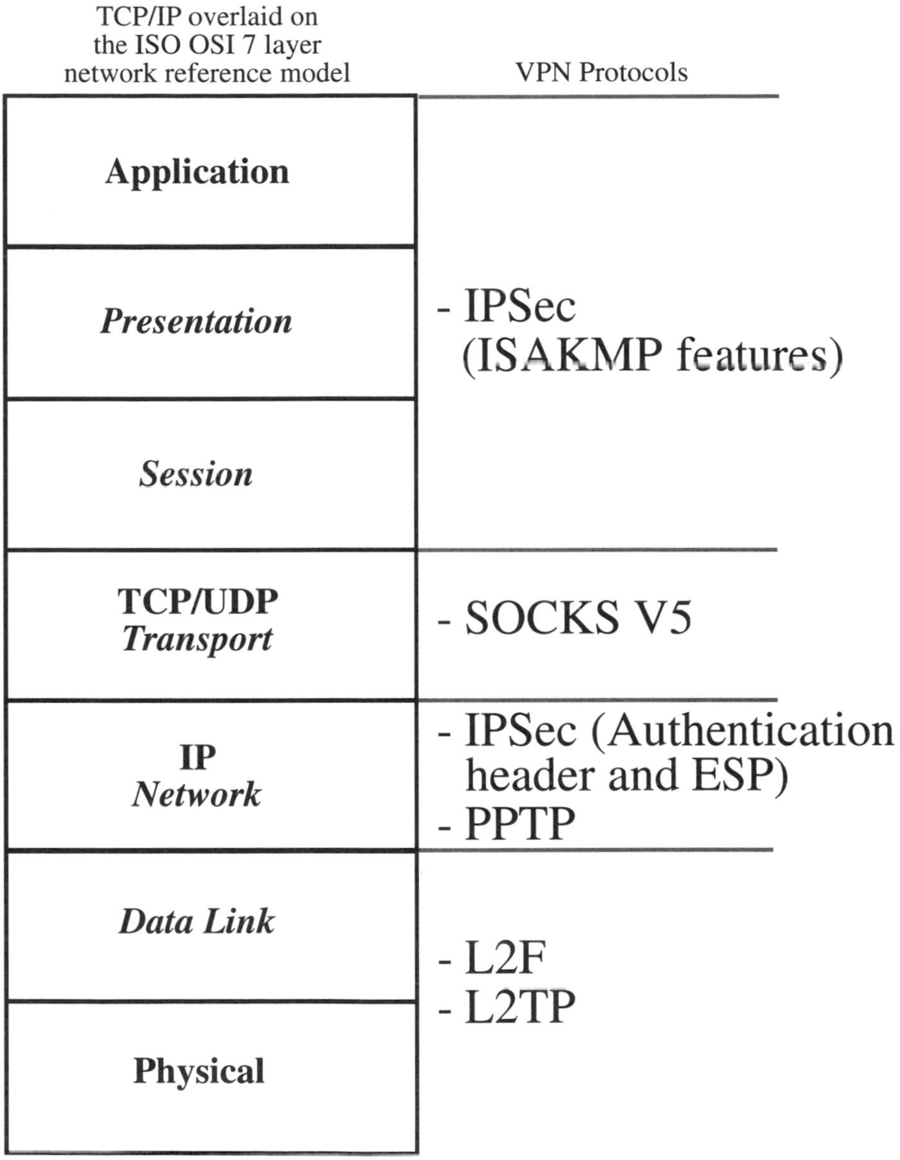

TCP/IP overlaid on
the ISO OSI 7 layer
network reference model   VPN Protocols

TCP/IP overlaid on the ISO OSI 7 layer network reference model	VPN Protocols
Application	
Presentation	- IPSec (ISAKMP features)
Session	
TCP/UDP *Transport*	- SOCKS V5
IP *Network*	- IPSec (Authentication header and ESP) - PPTP
Data Link	- L2F - L2TP
Physical	

Italic items represent the ISO Open Systems Interconnection 7 layer
network model. **Bold** text represents the four layers of the TCP/IP stack.

Figure 12-4. The IPSec RFC hierarchy.

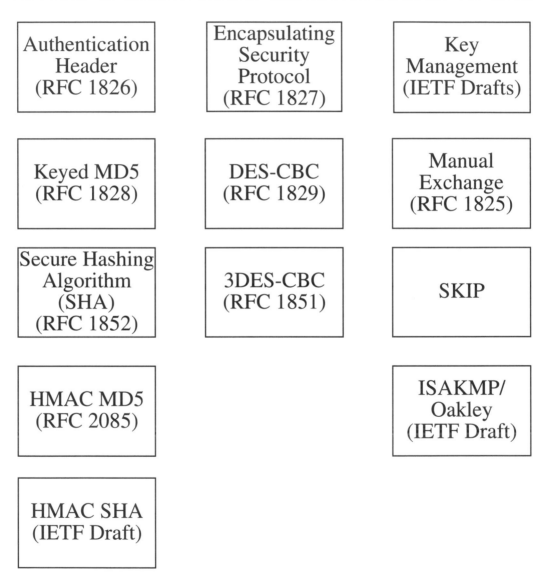

the security that an IPSec-compliant network already provides.

Recall that communication using computer networks can be deemed secure only when it meets three characteristics:

1. Sender authentication to prove that messages originate from their advertised source
2. Message integrity to assure that messages arrive intact and unaltered
3. Confidentiality to assure that only the intended receiver can successfully read private messages that are sent

IPSec meets these requirements using two security mechanisms: (1) Authentication Header (AH), and (2) Encapsulating Security Protocol (ESP).

Authentication Header (AH)

Authentication Header (AH) modifies IP datagrams by adding an additional field (attribute) that enables receivers to check the authenticity of the data within the datagram. AH provides connectionless data integrity, data authentication, and protection against replay attacks. The added block of data on IPSec packets is called an Integrity Value Check (IVC), which is generally used to carry a Message Authentication Code (MAC) or a digital signature (a message digest signed using sender's private key). Protection against replay attacks is provided by adding a sequence number to the packet to prevent reprocessing it if it's received multiple times. IPSec may be operated in one of two basic modes: transport mode or tunnel mode. Transport mode is useful when security is needed between two otherwise trusted hosts that use an untrusted network for communications. Tunnel mode is useful for all other forms of communication, including host-to-host, host-to-desktop, and desktop-to-desktop. Tunnel mode provides what's referred to as end-to-end security.

The AH format is illustrated in Figure 12-5. This IVC structure is added to IP datagrams to implement one of the security features of IPSec. Figure 12-6 illustrates how AH is used in IPSec transport mode. Figure 12-7 illustrates how AH is used in IPSec tunnel mode.

Figure 12-5. The Authentication Header format.

Next Header	Payload Length	Reserved
Security Parameters Index (SPI)		
Sequence Number Field		
Authentication Data (variable length)		

Figure 12-6. Using Authentication Header to transform IP packets to IPSec transport mode.

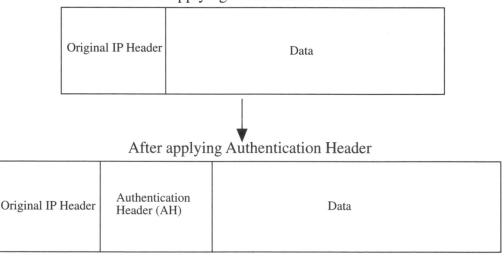

Before applying Authentication Header

Original IP Header	Data

After applying Authentication Header

Original IP Header	Authentication Header (AH)	Data

Authenticated Packet

Because IPSec defines the framework for using IP securely, it does not mandate specific cryptographic algorithms. Rather, it's written to permit the uses of a variety of cryptosystems for Message Authentication Code (MAC) and/or digital signatures.

Encapsulating Security Protocol (ESP)

The Encapsulating Security Protocol (ESP) is used to assure one or more of these security services:

- Confidentiality (in IPSec tunnel mode)
- Connectionless data integrity
- Data origin authentication
- Protection against replay attacks

Unlike AH, ESP operates under the principle of encapsulation: Encrypted data is sandwiched between an ESP header and an ESP trailer. The organization of ESP is shown in Figure 12-8. Figure 12-9 illustrates the position of ESP within IPSec packets under IPv4 transport mode. Figure 12-10 illustrates where ESP fits when operating under IPSec tunnel mode.

Again, IPSec does not mandate the use of any specific cryptosystem for confidentiality or sender authentication, but it supports the use of a number of cryptographic algorithms.

Security Associations

AH and ESP require a number of parameters that both senders and receivers must agree upon before communication can take place. To manage these parameters, IPSec uses the concept of a Security Association (SA). A Security Association is a one-way connection that provides security services to the traffic that it governs. You can think of an SA as the set of data that describes how a given communication is to be secured. When both AH and ESP are used for traffic, two or more SAs are created and are referred to as an SA Bundle. An SA is uniquely identified by the combination of these three fields:

(text continues on page 220)

Figure 12-7. Using Authentication Header to transform IP packets to IPSec tunnel mode.

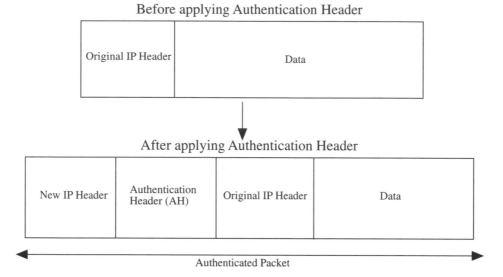

Figure 12-8. The Encapsulating Security Protocol format.

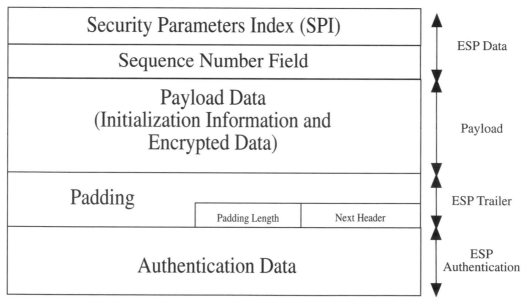

Figure 12-9. Encapsulating Security Protocol under IPSec transport mode.

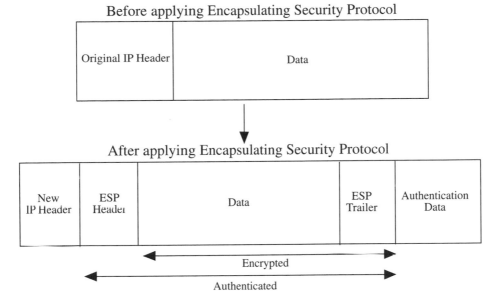

Figure 12-10. Encapsulating Security Protocol under IPSec tunnel mode.

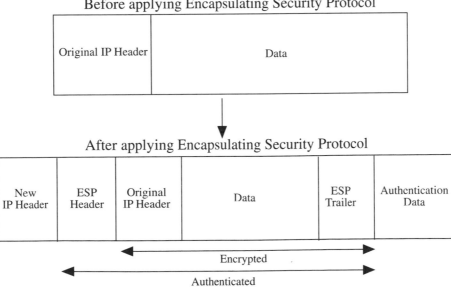

1. IP destination address
2. Security protocol identifier (AH or ESP)
3. Security Parameters Index (SPI)

IPSec stores these Security Associations in a database called the Security Association Database (SAD). It's used to store all the parameters used for a specific SA and is consulted each time a packet is sent or received.

SAs contain the actual keys used for encrypting data or signing Message Authentication Codes or message digests. Because key exchange is normally performed out-of-band to the communication that's reliant on previously exchanged keys, IPSec provides a separate protocol for exchanging Security Associations. Using this approach, IPSec decouples its key management mechanisms from other security mechanisms, enabling the substitution of key management methods without affecting the implementation of the security mechanism.

Internet Security Association and Key Management Protocol (ISAKMP)

The protocol to negotiate Security Associations under IPSec is called Internet Security Association and Key Management Protocol (ISAKMP). ISAKMP is not usable on its own since it defines a general framework that requires any number of key exchange protocols. To make ISAKMP useful, IPSec associates it with other session key exchange and establishment mechanisms. The Oakley Key Determination Protocol is one such mechanism. Together, ISAKMP and Oakley result in a new protocol called Internet Key Exchange (IKE). ISAKMP and Oakley are the two leading contenders for Internet Key Exchange being considered by the IPSec Working Group of the IETF.

Oakley uses a hybrid Diffie-Hellman key exchange protocol to exchange session keys on Internet hosts and routers. Oakley optionally provides the security property called Perfect Forward Secrecy (PFS). In addition to providing traditional key exchange under Diffie-Hellman, Oakley may be used to derive new keys from old keys or to distribute keys by encrypting them with a different shared secret key. Oakley consists of three components:

1. Cookies exchange for stateless connections (like the Internet)
2. Diffie-Hellman public key values exchange mechanism
3. Authentication mechanism with the options of anonymity, Perfect Forward Secrecy on the identities, and/or nonrepudiation

The Oakley Key Determination Protocol is defined in RFC 2412.

Security Policies

IPSec protects traffic based upon the policy choices defined in the Security Policy Database (SPD). The SPD is used for decision making, on each packet of traffic. Information in the SPD is consulted to determine whether or not a packet will undergo IPSec transformation, will be discarded, or will be allowed to bypass IPSec. The database contains an ordered list of rules that define which IP packets within the network will be affected by the rule and enforces the scrutiny or transformation by the IPSec gateway server(s). SPD rules correspond to Security Associations in the Security Association Database (SAD). The SPD is configured by the network administrator, is consulted with each receipt or transmission of IPSec (AH or ESP) packets, and refers to entries within the SAD. Figure 12-11 illustrates how all these components operate as a system.

IPSec Key Management

As you've seen, IPSec requires the generation and sharing of multiple keys to carry out its security features. The following are three of the most common methods used for key exchanges:

1. Manual key exchange
2. Simple Key Interchange Protocol (SKIP)
3. ISAKMP/Oakley

Figure 12-11. How all components of IPSec operate.

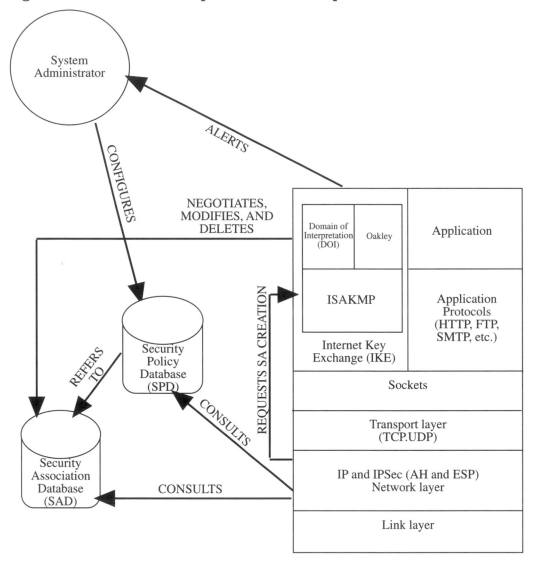

The simplest and most widely used method for key exchange is the manual key exchange, as defined in RFC 1825. Using the manual exchange, a person manually configures each system with its own keys and those needed to communicate with other Virtual Private Networks. Keys generated and managed under this approach are manually entered in the Security Association Database.

Simple Key Interchange Protocol (SKIP) is a key management standard proposed by Sun Microsystems. The IETF elected to use ISAKMP for IPv6 and skipped over SKIP. SKIP is based on the generation of a shared secret using Diffie-Hellman with already authenticated public key values. SKIP's only requirement is that those communicating already possess an authenticated Diffie-Hellman public key value to help prevent Man-in-the-Middle attacks.

ISAKMP was selected as the key management protocol for IPSec in September 1996. ISAKMP is used to negotiate Security Associations using the parameters (keys, protocols, etc.) related to any security mechanism. ISAKMP is needed to negotiate, establish, modify, and delete Security Associations and their corresponding data. A Domain of Interpretation (DOI) defines the negotiated parameters and conventions for using ISAKMP within a specified framework. The DOI identifier is needed to interpret ISAKMP messages. It is defined by RFC 2407.

ISAKMP operates using two phases that allow for the clear separation between ISAKMP traffic and SA negotiation for some given protocol. In the first phase, a set of security-related attributes are negotiated, the identities of the peers communicating is established, and some random keys are generated. These activities compose the first Security Association, called ISAKMP SA. Unlike IPSec, ISAKMP SAs are bidirectional and are used to secure all the subsequent ISAKMP message exchanges.

The second phase is needed to negotiate the security parameters related to a Security Association for a specific security mechanism (AH or ESP). The exchanges that take place in this phase are protected using the ISAKMP SA from the first phase.

THE FUTURE OF NETWORK TRANSPORT

As the use of the Internet continues to expand at an exponential rate, and as businesses continue to find solutions to supply chain inefficiencies through e-commerce applications, the demand for the secure transport of data across the Internet will garner more and more attention from industry experts. While other transport-layer native protocols, like Transport Layer Security (TLS), compete for attention, the uses of SSL and secure VPNs will become increasingly important to consumers and businesses alike that want assurances that the Internet is a safe place to do business.

13

Digital Signatures and PPK Cryptography

The anonymous nature of the public Internet is appealing in that it frees us to roam about without concern of someone peeking over our shoulders, watching our every move. This anonymity, however, instills high levels of distrust, especially where the transmission of private, sensitive, or confidential information occurs.

As described in previous chapters, efforts to add levels of trust include the use of secured access via IDs and passwords. Over the years, secured access to Internet sites proliferated, forcing the Internet community to collect—and remember—dozens of different IDs and passwords to instill the security that everyone demands. Besides the problems of remembering them, IDs and passwords are generally easy to guess or crack, with a resultant loss in their appeal of safety. Add to that the general lack of trust when we're not certain that the parties with whom we communicate are who they claim to be. Today, the lack of a complete Internet security solution jeopardizes the Internet's very existence.

DIGITAL CERTIFICATES

Digital certificates, or Digital IDs, behave in the online world the same way driver's licenses, passports, and other trusted documents behave in the offline world. Using basic Public-Private Key (PPK) cryptography principles, digital certificates offer the security that people are demanding for private communication and electronic commerce. The digital certificate standard, X.509, governs how certificates are constructed and used between communicating parties.

In 1988, X.509 became an International Telecommunications Union (ITU)–recommended standard and has since become a de facto industry standard for user authentication on open systems, such as the Internet. X.509 certificates are similar to notary seals in that they bind a person's identity to a pair of cryptographic keys. When used in signing electronic messages (creating digital signatures), the private key associated with the public key that's contained in the digital certificate creates an unforgeable fingerprint for the message. This fingerprint (1) proves to the recipient that the message could have originated only with the believed sender, and (2) proves that the message was not altered while en route.

For PPK's successful operation, the principles dictate that Public-Private Key-Pairs are obtained in a manner that's impervious to attack. The primary assumption is that a person's private key will always remain private. Digital certificates implement this principle. Certificates are issued by a trusted party operating a system called a Certificate Authority (CA). These CAs operate on behalf of those who wish to operate a Public Key Infrastructure (PKI) using X.509 recommended standards.

X.509 certificates typically contain:

- User name (public directory name, often found in X.500 directories)
- User organization
- Certificate effective date
- Certificate expiration date
- User public key (from the key-pair)
- Issuer CA name
- Issuer CA signature

Along with this information, certificates sometimes contain extensions that describe how the certificate may be used and under what conditions. In other words, a certificate used to access network resources cannot be used to access bank accounts. Each certificate is issued under specific uses and guidelines, as described in the certificate's extensions. The format of a typical X.509 digital certificate is shown in Figure 13-1.

CAs maintain a "tree of trust" that's checked each time a certificate is presented as proof of one's identity. Once the tree of trust is successfully traversed, proof of identity and proof of a person's right to use the key can be ascertained by the recipient.

Electronic commerce protocols, such as Secure Electronic Transaction (SET), use a robust set of digital certificates to authenticate cardholders, merchants, and operators of payment processors (gateways) to assure that all parties possess the rights needed to transact using payment cards over the Internet. Also, a corporation may issue digital certificates to its employees as an alternative to IDs and passwords for access to network services, mainframe applications, etc. These certificates are normally stored in software that resides on the user's PC within a Web browser. Certificates can also be stored on SmartCards (discussed later) to permit access to secured areas of the building, logins to network computers, and other specialized applications.

Using digital certificates, Internet users are offered high degrees of certainty along several dimensions of communication. Through their cryptography, anyone receiving a signed message, along with the public key in the sender's digital certificate, can be confident that the message came from the specific person (user authentication) and that the message itself arrived intact (integrity). By adding one more step to the message-sending process, the sender and receiver can also be sure that no one other than the receiver can read the message, adding the dimension of privacy too.

Digital certificates are cropping up wherever companies are pushing their customers to the Internet with the promise of security. Banks across the globe are issuing digital certificates to positively identify their online banking customers. ScotiaBank in Toronto signed up 32,000 customers as quickly as it opened its online banking service to the public. Bell South Telecommunications uses digital certificates to enable its employees to file and sign expense management reports via its internal network. Bell South

Figure 13-1. The format of a typical X.509 digital certificate.

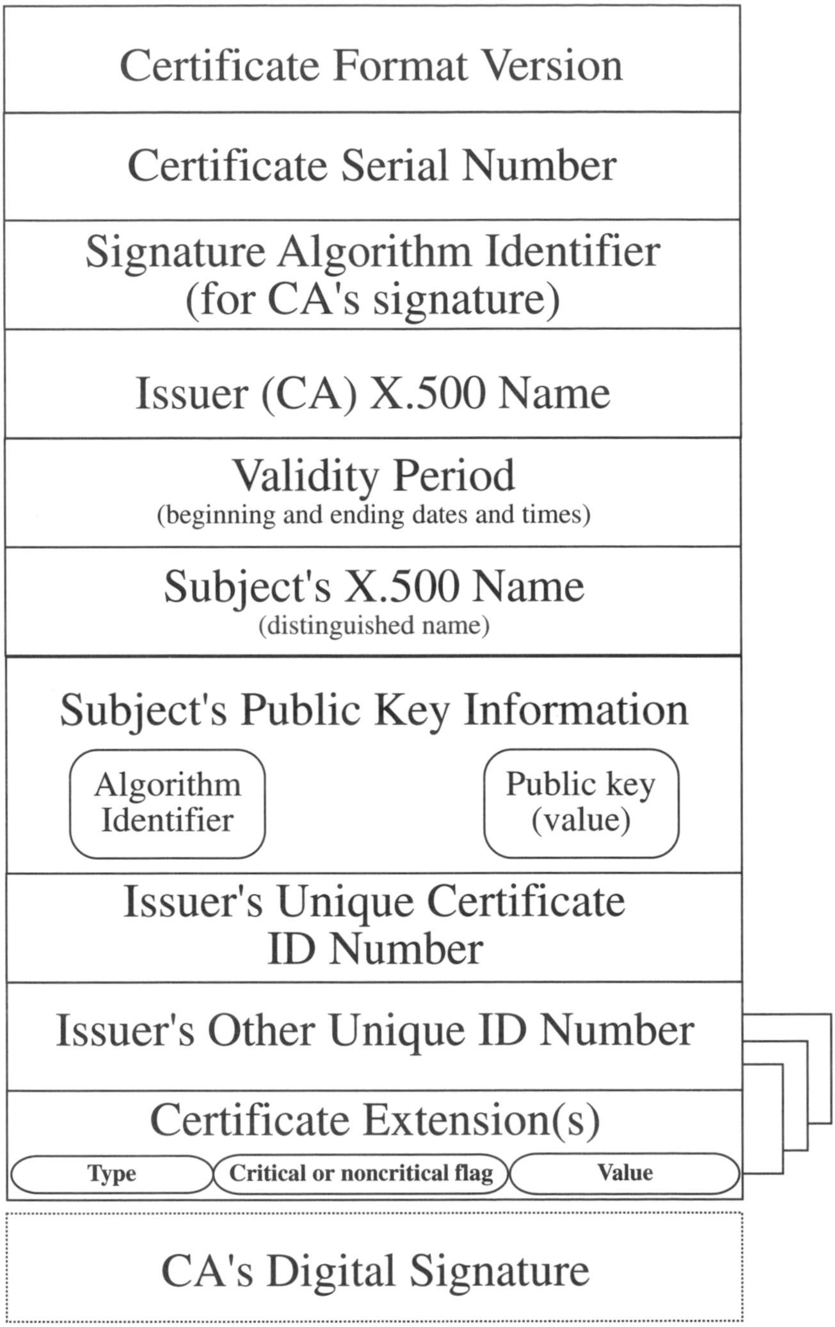

Certificate Format Version
Certificate Serial Number
Signature Algorithm Identifier (for CA's signature)
Issuer (CA) X.500 Name
Validity Period (beginning and ending dates and times)
Subject's X.500 Name (distinguished name)
Subject's Public Key Information — Algorithm Identifier — Public key (value)
Issuer's Unique Certificate ID Number
Issuer's Other Unique ID Number
Certificate Extension(s) — Type — Critical or noncritical flag — Value
CA's Digital Signature

expects to save over $5 million annually in process costs. United HealthCare Inc. uses digital certificates to share private information with its issuers and medical service providers via the Internet. Karl Kendall, vice president of computer operations and services at United HealthCare, claims, "For the first time, digital certificates are going to allow security to be a business enabler rather than a roadblock. Digital certificates are the only viable choice we have to provide safety to these 'new horizon' access methodologies."

Using Cryptography with Digital Certificates

Public-Private Key-Pairs

Cryptography can be performed under two basic approaches: shared keys and secret keys. Shared (symmetric) keys are used both to encrypt and decrypt messages. The problem is that the key must be delivered to the recipient prior to the beginning of communication under a process that prevents key theft along the way. This is no small feat.

Cryptography using asymmetric keys uses a pair of cryptography keys (public and private) to encrypt and decrypt communication. These keys are mathematically related but cannot be derived from each other. They operate such that messages encrypted using one key can be decrypted only with the other key, and vice versa. These keys are generated at the same time (when a certificate is requested), and the private key *never* leaves the machine upon which it was generated. The public key half of the key-pair is sent to the Certificate Authority to "wrap up" within a certificate. Certificates are meant to be shared with anyone the private keyholder desires to assure his privacy in communication. Before a session begins, the sharing of public key certificates must occur.

Message Signing

Using cryptography, a sender desiring private communication with another can *sign* or create a digital signature for her message by computing a special value, called a message digest. The algorithms that perform this computation are such that the chances of two messages having the same value are on the order of 1 in 1 X 1048, making drowning while water skiing in the Sahara Desert far more likely. Once computed, the message digest is encrypted with the sender's private key and attached to the message itself. These signatures are similar to fingerprints for the message: No two are ever alike.

Once the message is received, the receiver decrypts the message digest using the public key from the sender's digital certificate and computes his own message digest using the same algorithm the sender used. Next, the receiver compares the digest value he computed to the one just decrypted. If they match, the recipient is assured that the message must have come from whom he believes it came from (otherwise, the decryption step would fail), and he can be assured that the message was not altered en route (otherwise, the message digest would be different). The algorithms that are used in message digest computations are such that a change of a single byte in the message will change roughly half the bits in the message digest.

Furthermore, if the message and the digest together are encrypted using the receiver's public key (from his digital certificate), the sender can also be assured that only the receiver can read it. This process is known as creating a digital envelope for the message and is the last step prior to transmitting the private message. Using digital envelopes, the Internet becomes a Virtual Private Network (VPN) that tunnels communication between two parties, keeping it secure from prying eyes.

Storing Digital Certificates

Currently, Netscape Communicator and Microsoft Internet Explorer browsers support X.509 certificates through a certificate-store arrangement within the browser software. As Secure Electronic Transaction rolls out, consumers obtain an Electronic Wallet (E-wallet) that operates in conjunction with the browser (helper, plug-in, etc.). These E-wallets can also manage other X.509-based certificates.

Future means for storing digital certificates will include the use of SmartCards (described in Chapters 8 and 15). Today's typical SmartCards can store 16K-32K worth of data and application software, but as they mature further, their capacity for storage and processing will increase by orders of magnitude. With your SmartCard, you'll be able to positively identify yourself via the Internet; obtain electronic travel arrangements that are customized to the preferences stored on the chip; check in to hotels using a kiosk, based on preferences stored on the chip; or manage an electronic purse (e-purse) that you can replenish via the Internet or telephones equipped for the task.

BUILDING AN INFRASTRUCTURE FOR THE USE OF DIGITAL CERTIFICATES

We have already described how security is implemented as a series of layers, building upon the layers below and moving from the physical to the logical. Atop the highest layer, a Public Key Infrastructure (PKI) completes the security picture with a comprehensive solution that permeates all processing—person to person, person to resource, and resource to resource.

With the appropriate layers of security throughout the network, a PKI can put to rest the concerns of how to protect assets, freeing you to concentrate on adding value to your employees, your customers, and your business partners. It also helps you to shout out to the world that your site's security—and your customer's interests—are taken to heart.

What Are Public Key Infrastructures?

Using applied cryptography, PKIs govern the distribution and management of cryptograpic keys and digital certificates that allow you to take advantage of several fundamental features:

- *Confidentiality of information* assures users that their communications are safe and readable by only the intended recipients. Message encryption using digital certificates assures this confidentiality.

- *Integrity of data* guarantees that message contents are not altered during the transmission between the originator and the recipient. PKIs provide for digital signatures to ensure the integrity of all transmitted information.
- *User authentication* enables systems and applications to verify that a user is who she claims to be and has the authority to access the resource. PKIs use digital signatures and user certificates to assure the authentication of all end entities and system resources.
- *Nonrepudiation* prevents users of the PKI from denying that they've participated in a transaction or sent a message to another user or resource. With a legitimate digital signature in hand and the legitimate digital certificate that accompanies it, the chances that a message is forged or originated elsewhere approaches zero.
- *System interoperability*—due to strict standards compliance—enables a PKI's operation across a variety of hardware and software systems without concern for incompatibilities.

Effective PKIs are based on the Public Key Cryptographic Standards (PKCS), a family of standards that include:

- RSA encryption, for the construction of digital signatures and digital envelopes.
- Diffie-Hellman key agreements, which define how two people, with no prior arrangements, can agree on a shared secret key that's known only by them and used for future encrypted communications.
- Password-based encryption, which hides private keys when transferring them between computer systems, sometimes required under Public-Private Key (PPK) cryptography.
- Extended certificate syntax, which permits the addi-

tion of extensions to standard X.509 digital certificates. These extensions add information such as certificate usage policies and other identifying information.

- Cryptographic message syntax, which describes how to apply cryptography to related data, including digital signatures and digital envelopes.
- Private key information syntax, which describes how to include a private key along with algorithm information and a set of attributes to offer a simple way of establishing trust in information provided.
- Certification request syntax, which describes the rules and sets of attributes needed for a certificate request from a Certificate Authority (CA).

Recall that a digital certificate binds a previously authenticated private keyholder (a person) to the public key that accompanies it. This attestation, performed by a trusted party, creates a message containing the person's identification information, his public key, certificate usage rules, and other information. This message is then signed using the CA's private key and returned to the private keyholder. Public Key Infrastructure hierarchies of trust use this concept to manage the public keys for all users, internal and external. With a PKI in place, a tree of trust is formed to represent how Certificate Authorities control certain aspects of other Certificate Authorities in the branches below them. Constructing this tree is one of the first activities in developing a PKI. It is embodied in the Certificate Practice Statement (CPS), discussed later. For a view of one possible tree of trust, see Figure 13-2.

Work Performed by Certificate Authorities

Key and certificate management are not tasks to be taken lightly, nor are they for the faint-of-heart. Extremely tight security is an imperative to maintain the trust that PKIs require. At their essence, CAs provide three basic services to the entities (other CAs or end entities) directly below them on the tree:

1. Certificate issuance
2. Certificate renewal
3. Certificate revocation

The top of a tree of trust consists of a root CA from which all branches below form.

Figure 13-2. An example of a tree of trust for a large corporation.

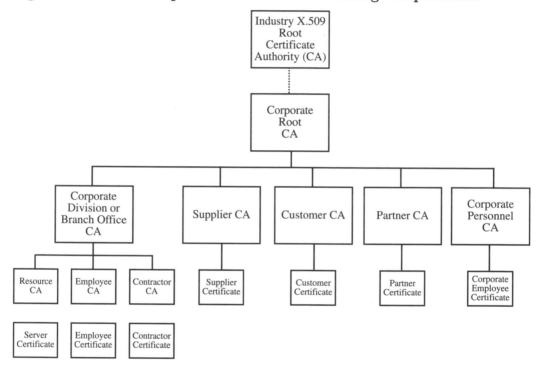

Root Certificate Authority

The highest level, or root, of the hierarchy of trust is the root Certificate Authority. It is normally maintained offline and accessed only when needed for signing purposes. Root CA responsibilities also include the generation and distribution of the Certificate Revocation List (CRL) in cases of any private key compromise in the branches directly below the root. Root certificates are self-signed. Their presence is required for validating a PKI certificate chain. Enterprise or specific corporate root certificates are normally imbedded in the Web browsers used by employees to access PKI-protected resources.

What Is a Certificate Revocation List (CRL)?

The purpose of a CRL is to stop the uses of any certificates that are tied to private keys that were compromised (stolen). If a thief gains a copy of a private key and possesses its accompanying certificate, he has essentially stolen the identity of the private keyholder. If the theft is not detected, the thief could use the key-pair (certificate and private key) either to: (1) masquerade as the legitimate keyholder without any suspicion, or (2) use the private key to sign forged certificates (if a CA system key was stolen). Once a theft or compromise is detected, it's critical that the CA system that signed the key-pair knows about it, places the certificate's serial number on the Certificate Revocation List immediately, and republishes the list.

CRLs are defined by the X.509 standard for publication and distribution of the identity of revoked, unexpired certificates. CRLs are composed of the serial numbers for all revoked certificates, with the CA system that signed those certificates responsible for its near real-time maintenance to prevent any fraud or abuses during compromised private keys.

PROTECTING PRIVATE KEYS

Protecting the private keys that are tied to a digital certificate's public key, especially those keys that are used to sign lower-level digital certificates, is very serious business under any PKI. Without this protection, the notion of any trust goes out the window, and the infrastructure will inevitably fail.

Stolen (copied) private keys from any end entity could be used to transact or communicate without any cause for suspicion. It's the same as a stolen identity, where a thief masquerades as the legitimate keyholder without any reasons for anyone to suspect wrongdoing. Similarly, if the keys for a Certificate Authority were compromised, the repercussions could be severe. With a stolen (copied) CA key in hand, a would-be forger could issue bogus certificates without any way to detect the forgery. Protection of all CA keys is absolutely critical to maintain the PKI's level of trust.

The more a private key is used to sign messages, the more instances a would-be attacker can obtain it for cryptanalysis. If these keys are changed often and regularly, stored under NORAD-like conditions (North American Air Defense Command), and managed well, they'll remain safe from all forms of attack.

PKI cryptographic key uses are extremely sophisticated to deter would-be cryptosystem attackers. Because of its robustness, it's not really worth the effort to try breaking the cryptography. Even with all the computers on the planet working in tandem, an attacker would still find a tough time determining a key through reverse-engineering or attempting brute-force methods (trying all possible combinations of a key). CAs normally guard against such attacks anyway by using extremely long keys. They also change their keys regularly and reissue new certificates whenever they do. Rather than try to discover the key, thieves are better off trying to steal the actual key from where it's stored, so extra precautions must be taken to assure that this can't happen. Because CAs clearly understand the value of the keys in their possession, they go out of their way to keep them safe from all possible attacks, physical and logical.

Every end entity under a PKI is responsible for the safety of its own keys and certificates. This is a central theme and cannot be overemphasized. A PKI's ability to guarantee assurances of authentication, message integrity, privacy, and security cannot be realized once keys get into the wrong hands. Private keys are valuable. Although some are considered more valuable than others, that doesn't lessen the degree of care required for all keys at all times.

CA systems can be the subject of attacks through several different ways. Besides hacker attacks from the outside, CA operations are vulnerable to collusion, sabotage, disgruntlement, or outright theft by employees from within.

External Attacks on the CA

External attacks attempt to steal private keys using computers located outside the physical CA system environment. They may arrive via the Internet, break-ins to private lines, or back-door methods through a local area network within the CA. The break-ins might attempt to foil Web page security, try to exploit known operating system flaws, or try and gain control of the server.

Internal Attacks on the CA

At least as great a threat to private keys lies with those employees responsible for operating and maintaining the CA system. CA private keys are an attractive target to those who work with them.

CAs can help lessen the keys' attractiveness to internal theft by limiting their access and ensuring that no one person has full knowledge of a complete key. Keys should be stored across several hardware devices (crypto-boxes), and the environment in which the hardware itself resides should be ultrasecure. Strict access control, electronic monitoring, and intruder-detection on each device should deter even the most tenacious would-be thieves.

What Can Be Done with Stolen Private Keys?

In the unlikely event of a private key compromise, the effects differ depending on which keys are stolen, who performed the theft, and what his motivation is. A user's private key could be stolen if the user's PC was stolen or was used by someone other than her. Electronic Wallets can also be vulnerable. Although E-wallets storing the keys and certificates are usually protected by a password, if a correct guess does open the E-wallet, the thief instantly assumes the identity of the authorized keyholder. If the theft is then not reported, message and transaction recipients are left with no choice other than to believe that the messages and transactions were performed in earnest. At certificate issuance time, users must be made aware of these consequences when they agree to the use policies before accepting their certificates.

Theft of a CA private key is a whole other matter. With the proper systems, a CA key thief could establish himself as a CA, ready to issue certificates. These forged certificates would be undetectable as forgeries and could be used without question.

CERTIFICATE PRACTICE STATEMENTS

Beyond the limits of physical and logical protection of keys used to sign certificates, CA policies and procedures are clearly spelled out in Certificate Practice Statements (CPSs). CPSs consist of detailed descriptions of certificate policies and how they're implemented by a particular CA. The American Bar Association defines a CPS as: "A statement of the practices which a certification authority employs in issuing certificates."

When CAs negotiate cross-certification services, they examine and compare the two services' CPSs. The liability that certificate issuers and end entities assume plays a role in the degrees of trust. X.509 certificates contain certificate policies that allow certificate holders to decide how much trust to place in their certificates. According to X.509 Version 3, a CPS is: "A named set of rules that indicates the applicability of a certificate to a particular community and/ or class of application with common security requirements."

DEVELOPING A PKI

You might be ready to embark down the PKI path if several of the following conditions are true:

- You've migrated your application interfaces to Web browser technology, including the access to mainframe and midrange system applications. This is a requirement to permit the use of directory services, like LDAP, to enable a single sign-on capability that not only identifies the requester but also determines her rights and provides for access.

- You've migrated to browser-based e-mail systems that support S/MIME and digital signing of messages.

- You've migrated to application software that can deal with signed documents and messages to eliminate the routing of paperwork for authority determination purposes.

- You're prepared for logical access controls via SmartCards or token devices that store private keys and digital certificates.

As you can see, developing PKI is far from trivial. More than a few companies have tried to build one on their own only to discover that trust is tenuous without the ultimate protection of CA private keys. Many have turned to outside companies that specialize in offering CA services to corporations around the world.

What to Look for in a CA

Obvious expectations for a CA include an ability to operate key management under NORAD-like conditions, especially where root keys and certificate-generation processing occurs. Attempting to build such a system is too daunting for most companies that don't normally operate the military-grade systems that are required for such work. Do yourself a favor: Find a CA service provider who specializes in security!

Another fundamental feature your CA should offer is a rich set of application program interfaces (APIs) into the CA operation that will enable you to easily integrate your legacy systems into the PKI. You'll need several interfaces from multiple systems, depending upon the application mix you elect for digital certificates. The APIs should permit seamless Registration Authority (RA) services within a fully interactive, fully batch, or combination operating environment. Anything less only begs for problems. RA services are typically performed by your employees who have access to the systems of record that store verification data and decide who is entitled to use digital certificates in your organization.

Your CA should offer digital certificates and access controls that are supportive of industry standards. Be very careful of proprietary implementation of directory services, public key cryptosystems, or private tunnels through the Internet known as "secure pipes" (as with Virtual Private Networks). Rather, be sure that their products comply with protocols such as LDAP, X.500, X.509, and IPSec. Without assurances of standards compliance, you could well lock yourself out from communicating with customers, other companies, and business partners.

Next, your CA should offer the highest forms of protection on key material and data that the RA needs for checking the credentials of certificate requesters. Although this is primarily under your control, the CA should provide for these activities under the tightest security.

CAs should be able to assist you with key escrow and recovery activity. You need these services if any of the digital certificate uses involve encrypting company-owned documents or messages. To realize why this is important, it's critical to understand the distinction between message signing and data encryption. Typically, digital certificates are used for one purpose or the other—not both. Each user possesses both a signing private key and an encryption private key. It's not important to recover a signing key since the accompanying certificate is used only to verify a digital signature. If the person leaves the organization, there's no need to further verify her electronic signature. However, she may leave behind documents that were encrypted using the public key from her digital certificate. The only way to decrypt these documents is with the private key that accompanies the encryption public key certificate. If you're unable to recover the key from her PC's hard drive, you need a way to recover it from your CA. The common solution here is to maintain a copy of the entire key-pair (private key and public key certificate) at the time of certificate generation. The CA should be responsible for this activity. One other factor also surfaces. It's better to issue people key-pairs that the CA system generates if they're used for data encryption, and it's better to permit people to generate their own key-pairs when they're used for message signing. This is especially important with the concept of nonrepudiation.

What Is Nonrepudiation?

Repudiation is the principle that permits someone to disavow that a particular transaction or activity occurred—a denial that he participated in some activity. Nonrepudiation is the principle where repudiation is not possible—where undeniable proof exists that they *must* have participated in the activity. Using digital cryptography, it operates as follows. If a person who possesses a private key has taken adequate precautions to protect access to his key, then messages signed using that key *could only have come from him.* In other words, if a digital signature is properly verified through the person's public key certificate, then *only* the private key could have been used to sign the message. This is especially important where digital signatures are accepted for financial transactions. Using credit cards as an example, if nonrepudiation is enforced within the PKI, then the card issuer can treat any electronic transactions *as though* the physical piece of plastic was used to make the transaction (credit card present versus credit card not present).

Another aspect of nonrepudiation involves the process of requiring the proper mix of credentials to prove one's existence or right to request a digital certificate. If the process is such that the data requested from one user could be easily spoofed by another user, nonrepudiation won't take. For example, suppose you ask for the following information in using your human resources systems to verify employee data prior to issuing a certificate for secure e-mail:

- Employee name
- Date of hire

- Social Security number
- Home address

That information is readily obtained in the offline world, so another employee could simply request a certificate that permits him to masquerade as the real employee. Rather, you want to request information that, with high likelihood, could *only* be known by the real employee. The following mix of attributes might be a better bet:

- Employee name
- Date of last merit increase
- Gross amount of last paycheck
- Emergency contact phone number

In the event of a full match of all these elements, you're far more assured that you're giving the certificate to the right person. In this case, because you've proved—beyond a reasonable doubt—that the keyholder *is indeed* the employee and no other, nonrepudiation can take root.

More CA Requirements

CA systems should, as best as possible, implement the feature of Certificate Revocation Lists (CRLs) to keep unexpired, revoked certificates out of day-to-day operations. This function requires tight coupling with RA (Registration Authority) functions and is needed at the time certificates are shared or requested from the directory service. Many implementations do not support CRLs, but finding one that does places you ahead of the game and adds security to the overall system. CRL update mechanisms should include an ability to alert the CA to a compromised or suspected compromise of a private key. The process should enable easy revocation and certificate replacement *without* undue efforts. In the absence of this ability, the PKI may become next to worthless with the first private key compromise. Remember: The PKI is based on trusting the security of private keys!

Last, you want to make sure your CA provides sufficient training for all levels of personnel working within the PKI. This includes people who operate the RA functions, system developers, and end-users. You also want help from the CA in developing internal certificate practices statements. operating procedures, key escrow and recovery procedures, and any other documentation to support the PKI project's development life cycle.

What a CA Expects of You

Any PKI worth its salt must be rooted in appropriate and judicious uses of digital certificates. You define what this means to you in how you use digital certificates within (and outside) your organization. To that end, you must specify—in exacting detail—for what purposes digital certificates arc to be used (secure e-mail, access control, document signing, etc.), who is authorized to request digital certificates, what information they must present to prove their identity or their rights, how long certificates will be valid, and a host of other variables.

Because you're the one who operates the systems that contain the data to be used to check credentials, you need resources that can hook in to CA systems to communicate approvals and decline decisions as the Registration Authority (RA). This activity alone is anything *but* trivial! In principle, you want certificate request and fulfillment processing to occur within a single session. Doing so assumes the presence of automated processing that can obtain credentials from requesters,' check them against legacy systems, and forward the results to the CA along with the data that you want contained in the certificate. If you choose to perform this work offline or in batch mode, certificate requests must operate under the following process:

1. Requester enters her request on the CA-supplied interface and terminates her secure session.
2. Credentials are forwarded to the RA for batch or offline verification.
3. RA verification results are returned to the CA system.

4. CA initiates postprocessing.
5. Requester of approved request receives an e-mail message from the CA instructing her on what to do.
6. Requester reestablishes a secure session with the CA.
7. Requester again proves her identity to satisfy the CA.
8. Requester downloads and stores her new certificate.

In the absence of online RA functionality, no other scenario is possible. This illustrates why the APIs into the CA systems are critical to PKI success. On small volumes, perhaps a manual RA function can work fine, but it will not scale up as certificate popularity increases. Furthermore, there's no shortcutting the process. Doing so requires relinquishing some control over your internal corporate data. Extra careful thought is required before you embark down that path.

CAs also expect you to provide a high degree of technical readiness for certificate uses. This often requires robust directory services like LDAP and interfaces to systems that support digital certificates as an alternative to user IDs and passwords. If you intend to use SmartCards, you further need capable devices on all PCs that support system access. Remember: What you're truly building here is an infrastructure from the ground up. Don't try to find shortcuts!

Successful PKIs, by definition, require secure environments throughout. If you're not prepared to provide such an environment, it may not be worth your efforts to try. Make certain you've obtained the required support—all the way up the ladder—to assure PKI success. And be prepared to spend significant time and effort doing it. A good night's sleep is never cheap!

14

Key Management Considerations

Cryptographic key management is needed to safeguard the integrity, authenticity, and confidentiality of critical data and processes, as well as to protect against losses from fraudulent duplication or repudiation of transactions. Key management is concerned with the entire life cycle of the cryptographic keys employed with a cryptographic-based security system, including:

- Generation
- Distribution
- Entry and use
- Storage
- Destruction
- Archiving

This chapter looks at the principles of secure cryptosystems, threats to systems rooted in cryptography, security requirements for key management systems and devices, and tamper-resistant hardware cryptographic modules (crypto-boxes).

PRINCIPLES OF SECURE CRYPTOSYSTEMS

Cryptography often plays an important role in key management. A hardware-based cryptographic module (also called a cryptomodule) not only has its own key management requirements but may play a part in the key management process for other cryptographic modules or cryptographic-based security systems.

One of the fundamental principles for protecting keys is the practice of split knowledge and dual control. The American National Standards (ANSI) X9.17-1985, Financial Institution Key Management (*www.ansi.org*), defines split knowledge as: "A condition under which two or more parties separately have key components which, individually, convey no knowledge of the resultant cryptographic key. The resultant key exists only within secure equipment." Dual control is defined in the standard as: "A process of utilizing two or more separate entities (usually persons), operating in concert, to protect sensitive functions or information."

Split knowledge and dual control may be used to protect centrally stored user secret or private keys and root private keys, secure the distribution of user tokens, and initialize all cryptomodules in the system to "authorize" their use in performing cryptographic functions within a system.

The security of cryptographic keys in an electronic or digital signature system is the foundation of a secure system. Users must maintain control of their keys at all costs. Each keyholder should be provided with a list of responsibilities and liabilities, and each user should sign a statement acknowledging these concerns before receiving her key (acceptable use policy or key request form). If different user types (e.g., security officer, regular user) are implemented in a system, they should be aware of their unique responsibilities, especially regarding the significance of key compromise or loss.

When keys are no longer needed for encryption or decryption, they should be destroyed. Even after a key is destroyed, the information that it protects often continues to be sensitive. It's best to assume that your ciphertext (at some point) has been exposed to unauthorized and untrusted people or systems. To safeguard against problems, make sure that the remains of any destroyed keys contain no information that could aid an adversary in the reconstruction of the original keys.

A cryptoperiod is the time during which a key can be used for signature verification or decryption. The period should extend beyond the lifetime of a key (where the lifetime is the time when a key may be used to generate a signature and/or perform encryption). Keys should be archived for a lengthy cryptoperiod (on the order of decades), so that they can be used to verify signatures and decrypt ciphertext during the entire cryptoperiod.

The key management aspects of a cryptography-based security system consist of the different types of cryptographic keys and their relationship, generation, use, distribution, storage, and validity. Decisions made in this area are critical to the security of the product as a whole. Damage to a system through the compromising of cryptographic keys can be reduced by limiting the use of each key. Many e-commerce systems contain different keys that provide access to different functions, such as payment and settlement functions.

E-commerce systems involve cryptographic keys that must be kept secret, or secure against unauthorized observation, in order to prevent unauthorized duplication or alteration of data. In the more secure systems, various security measures have been developed to safeguard keys in storage on devices and in transmission between devices. For software-based systems, in particular those that involve access to open computer networks, storage of cryptographic keys poses greater challenges, because the user's device isn't assumed to be secure with any degree of certainty.

WHAT THREATENS CRYPTOGRAPHIC SYSTEMS?

The electronic devices used in modern e-commerce systems provide the first line of defense against outside attacks. Systems using cryptography can be attacked by exploiting weaknesses in the algorithm, by stealing secret keys, or by testing all possible keys in turn (brute-force attacks). Bruce Schneier, CTO and founder of Counterpane Internet Security (www.counterpane.com), the foremost expert in cryptographic systems, and the author of *Applied Cryptography* and *Secrets and Lies: Digital Security in a Networked World*, points out the vast number of flaws that are introduced into implementations of cryptography:

Strong cryptography is very powerful when it is done right, but it is not a panacea. Focusing on the cryptographic algorithms while ignoring other aspects of security is like defending your house not by building a fence around it, but by putting an immense stake into the ground and hoping that the adversary runs right into it. Smart attackers will just go around the algorithms.

Counterpane consists of specialists who design, analyze, and break cryptographic systems. While their primary research is on cryptographic algorithms and protocols, they also examine actual products. They use every known (and unknown) trick in the book to break algorithms and exploit errors in design, errors in implementation, and errors in installation. Here are a few of the attack methods that Schneier uses, as explained in his paper "Security Pitfalls in Cryptography" (copyright 1998 Counterpane Systems). See *www.counterpane.com/pitfalls.html.*

Attacks against Cryptographic Designs

Cryptographic systems are only as strong as the encryption algorithms, digital signature algorithms, one-way hash functions, and message authentication techniques that are present in the system. Break any of them, and you've broken the system. While it's possible to build a weak structure using strong materials, it's also possible to build a weak cryptographic system using strong algorithms and protocols. According to Schneier:

> We often find systems that "void the warranty" of their cryptography by not using it properly: failing to check the size of values, reusing random parameters that should never be reused, and so on. Encryption algorithms don't necessarily provide data integrity. Key exchange protocols don't necessarily ensure that both parties receive the same key. In a recent research project, we found that some—not all—systems using related crypto-

graphic keys could be broken, even though each individual key was secure. Security is a lot more than plugging in an algorithm and expecting the system to work. Even good engineers, well-known companies, and lots of effort are no guarantee of robust implementation.

Attacks against Implementations

Schneier continues:

> Many systems fail because of mistakes in implementation. Some systems don't ensure that plaintext is destroyed after it's encrypted. Other systems use temporary files to protect against data loss during a system crash, or virtual memory to increase the available memory; these features can accidentally leave plaintext lying around on the hard drive. In extreme cases, the operating system can leave the keys on the hard drive. One product we've seen used a special window for password input. The password remained in the window's memory even after it was closed. It didn't matter how good that product's cryptography was; it was broken by the user interface.
>
> Other systems fall to more subtle problems. Sometimes the same data is encrypted with two different keys, one strong and one weak. Other systems use master keys and then onetime session keys. We've broken systems using partial information about the different keys. We've also seen systems that use inadequate protection mechanisms for the master keys, mistakenly relying on the security of the session keys. It's vital to secure all possible ways to learn a key, not just the most obvious ones.

Attacks against Hardware

Many of the Internet-based security systems rely on tamper-resistant hardware for security (SmartCards, etc.) as an important component. Counterpane automatically distrusts systems where the security relies on assumptions about tamper resistance. Schneier says: "We've rarely seen tamper resistance techniques that work, and tools for defeating tamper resistance are getting better all the time. When we design systems that use tamper resistance, we always build in complementary security mechanisms just in the case the tamper resistancc fails."

Some of the methods Counterpane uses to attack hardware include:

- Measuring power consumption
- Measuring radiation emissions or other "side channels"
- Fault analysis
- Deliberately introducing faults to determine the secret keys

Attacks against Trust Models

Many interesting attacks are launched against the underlying trust model of the system:

- Who or what in the system is trusted?
- In what way?
- To what extent?

According to Schneier:

- Simple systems, like hard-drive encryption programs or telephone privacy products, have simple trust models. Complex systems, like electronic-commerce systems or multiuser e-mail security programs, have complex (and subtle) trust models. An e-mail program might use uncrackable cryptography for the messages, but unless the keys are certified by a trusted source (and unless that certification can be verified), the system is still vulnerable. Some commerce systems can be broken by a merchant and a customer colluding, or by two different customers colluding. Other systems make implicit assumptions about security infrastructures, but don't bother to check that those assumptions are actually true. If the trust model isn't documented, then an engineer can unknowingly change it in product development, and compromise security. Many software systems make poor trust assumptions about the computers they run on; they assume the desktop is secure. These programs can often be broken by Trojan horse software that sniffs passwords, reads plaintext, or otherwise circumvents security measures. Systems working across computer networks have to worry about security flaws resulting from the network protocols. Computers that are attached to the Internet can also be vulnerable. Again, the cryptography may be irrelevant if it can be circumvented through network insecurity. And no software is secure against reverse-engineering. Often, a system will be designed with one trust model in mind, and implemented with another. Decisions made in the design process might be completely ignored when it comes time to sell it to customers. A system that is secure when the operators are trusted and the computers are completely under the control of the company using the system may not be secure when the operators are temps hired at just over minimum wage and the computers are untrusted. Good trust models work even if some of the trust assumptions turn out to be wrong.

Attacks on the Users

Even when systems are secure when they're used properly, users can subvert security by accident—especially if the system isn't designed very well. Schneier says:

> The classic example of this is the user who gives his password to his coworkers so they can fix some problems when he's out of the office. Users may not report missing SmartCards for a few

days, in case they are just misplaced. They may not carefully check the name on a digital certificate. They may reuse their secure passwords on other, insecure systems. They may not change their software's default weak security settings.

Attacks against Failure Recovery

Failure recovery describes a system's ability to maintain its security in the event of some component failure. Well-designed secure systems can prevent small security breaks from becoming big ones. Schneier notes:

> Recovering a key to one file shouldn't allow an attacker to read every file on a hard drive. A hacker who reverse-engineers a SmartCard should only learn the secrets in that SmartCard, not information that will help him break other SmartCards in the system. In a multiuser system, knowing one person's secrets shouldn't compromise everyone else's.

Some systems that Counterpane sees use a "default to insecure mode." If a security feature isn't working, most people just turn it off and move on. For example, if an on-line credit card verification system is down, merchants often default to a less-secure paper system. According to Schneier:

> For electronic commerce systems, which could have millions of users, this can be particularly damaging. Such systems should plan to respond to attacks, and to upgrade security without having to shut the system down. The phrase "and then the company is screwed" is never something you want to put in your business plan. Good system design considers what will happen when an attack occurs, and works out ways to contain the damage and recover from the attack.

Attacks against the Cryptography

Counterpane also finds that sometimes products even get cryptography wrong. They rely on proprietary encryption algorithms, which are often weak. In one system the company analyzed, the developers took the relatively strong design of S/MIME (an electronic-mail standard) and implemented it using a weak cryptographic algorithm. Says Schneier:

> We've seen many other cryptographic mistakes: implementations that repeat "unique" random values, digital signature algorithms that don't properly verify parameters, hash functions altered to defeat the very properties they're being used for. We've seen cryptographic protocols used in ways that were not intended by the protocols' designers, and protocols "optimized" in seemingly trivial ways that completely break their security.

Building Secure Cryptographic Systems

Schneier advises that good security products must defend themselves against every possible attack—even attacks that haven't been invented yet!

> Attackers only need to find one security flaw to defeat a system. And they cheat. They can collude, conspire, and wait for technology to give them additional tools. They can attack the system in ways the system designer never thought of. Building a secure cryptographic system is easy to do badly, and very difficult to do well. Unfortunately, most people can't tell the difference.

SECURITY REQUIREMENTS FOR CRYPTOMODULES

Commercial cryptographic modules should be validated to federal standards. The standard that covers cryptomodules, Federal Information Processing Standard 140 (or

FIPS 140), is binding on U.S. government agencies (unless otherwise exempted). Products sold to the U.S. government often must comply with one or more of the FIPS PUBS (Federal Information Processing Standards Publications) standards. Go to *www.itl.nist.gov/fipspubs.*

Because U.S. federal government requirements to protect unclassified data are similar to the needs of commercial businesses, it's in the best interests of manufacturers to comply with U.S. government–dictated standards to satisfy the market needs for both the commercial and government sectors. While FIPS PUBS (including FIPS 140-1) are not binding standards on individuals and organizations not associated with the U.S. government, there are many companies that do business with the U.S. government and adopt FIPS PUBS standards for their own use. This may be because of contractual requirements or government regulations or simply because the companies decide that certain FIPS PUBS have value as standards for internal use.

FIPS 140

The Federal Information Processing Standard 140 (FIPS 140, entitled "General Security Requirements for Equipment Using the Data Encryption Standard"), describes the security requirements for cryptographic modules, or cryptomodules. A cryptographic module is defined as hardware or software that encrypts and decrypts data or performs other cryptographic operations (such as creating or verifying digital signatures). FIPS 140 embodies the requirements for the proper design and implementation of products that do cryptography.

The FIPS 140-1 standard, which superseded FIPS 140, was created by the National Institute of Standards and Technology (NIST). Security requirements cover eleven areas related to the design and implementation of a cryptomodule. FIPS 140-1 is still the current version, but in November 1999, NIST released FIPS 140-2 for a nine-day comment period. The draft standard is intended to supersede FIPS 140-1. Deadline for comments was February 15, 2000. It is currently under review.

FIPS 140-1, entitled "Security Requirements for Cryptographic Modules," specifies security requirements that must be satisfied by a cryptographic module used within a security system protecting unclassified information. The FIPS 140-1 standard provides four increasing, qualitative levels of security—Levels 1 to 4—intended to cover the wide range of potential applications and environments in which cryptographic modules may be needed and used.

The security requirements of FIPS 140-1 cover areas related to the design and implementation of a cryptographic module. These areas include:

- Basic design and documentation
- Module interfaces
- Authorized roles and services
- Physical security
- Software security
- Operating system security
- Key management
- Cryptographic algorithms
- Self-testing

NIST has established a FIPS 140-1 validation program using the National Voluntary Laboratory Accreditation Program (NVLAP) to accredit laboratories to perform testing of cryptographic modules for conformance to FIPS 140-1. Under this process, NIST issues FIPS 140-1 validation certificates based on test reports produced by NVLAP-accredited laboratories.

NIST issues two types of certificates: FIPS 140-1 certificates, and algorithm-specific certificates. As part of cryptographic algorithm testing, the NVLAP-accredited laboratory issues a separate test report to NIST indicating that the algorithm conforms to specific NIST standards for that algorithm.

CHOOSING HARDWARE- OR SOFTWARE-BASED CRYPTOMODULES

E-commerce systems require tremendous processing power to handle the complexity of cryptography. While ten

SSL (Secure Sockets Layer) transactions per second can be processed on a 100 to 200 MHz Pentium server, that number drops to one or two per second for advanced uses of cryptosystems like SET (Secure Electronic Transaction) or other PKI (Public Key Infrastructure)–based systems, including access control systems.

Security-related calculations often absorb up to 95 percent of a server's processing capability, leaving little room for other work. These bottlenecks are responsible for server overloads, refused connections, and losses of business. Clearly, people won't wait forever for their charges to process or to login, and they certainly won't return if they're expected to.

E-commerce is highly dependent on robust encryption, and the challenge is to balance computing power, demand, and security. Depending on your site, your budget, your historical and predicted numbers of sales transactions, and your current Web server technology, you're going to need the appropriate processing power to handle the traffic or risk losing business. E-commerce–based systems often require continual access to cryptographic processing to implement security features. As an example, SET uses signaling, hashing, and certificate verification a minimum of fifteen times during a single purchase request message pair process.

Cryptography can be implemented through software routines (processor intensive) or hardware operations (processor assisting). Software toolkits offer routines and algorithms, invoked as calculations that are needed by programs. Hardware crypto-boxes appear as either add-on boards or separate computers that operate as servers for offloading the work in client-server fashion. Either approach yields complete transparency to the programs affected and to the users affected.

Major factors to help you decide whether hardware-only or software-only cryptography is appropriate include:

- Cost and available budgets for your site
- Performance requirements to serve your customers in a reasonable time

- Number of purchases per unit of time that require cryptographic processing

THE LAYERS OF CRYPTOGRAPHY

Robust payment systems typically require cryptographic calculations for every transaction needed to process charge requests and capture requests and for administrative or data-sharing (bulk encryption) purposes. Typically, the higher the volume of transactions, the higher the need for robust cryptographic processing, and the higher the cost in delivering that processing.

Merchants might rely upon software developer toolkits that integrate encryption libraries with existing merchant commerce servers. An example of this is RSA S/PAY (Secure Pay technology developed by RSA) toolkit. Programmers typically use off-the-shelf software in the form of application program interfaces (APIs) that may be invoked as required. End products ship with the requisite toolkits to bolt on to compatible commerce servers.

E-commerce cryptographic work can also be implemented via hardware through specially designed encryption components (crypto-boxes and cryptocards). Merchants can add security/encryption cards into the same servers that provide Web shopping access. The current array of encryption boards support most major computer operating systems. These add-on boards operate in a fashion similar to the math coprocessor boards that are present where high computational power is required.

To best understand how cryptography processing works, it's useful to see it as a series of abstract layers:

- Primitive cryptographic processing: computing a hash, generating random numbers, etc.
- Protocol-level cryptographic processing: SHA (Secure Hashing Algorithm)-1 hashes, DES (Data Encryption Standard) encrypt, PKCS (Public Key Cryptographic Standards) envelope creation, etc.

- Application software invocation of message-level cryptography

Each of these "layers" is delivered in the form of software called toolkits. These toolkits provide access to their services via application program interfaces (APIs) that are called by a higher-layer program (as viewed by moving up from primitive processing through application layer processing).

The Microsoft CryptoAPI is a general-purpose cryptography toolkit that developers can use instead of developing their own cryptography programs from scratch. Another toolkit is RSA's S/PAY, which enables the cryptographic processing that's specific to payment processing systems. With S/PAY, primitive cryptographic steps are transformed into those standard algorithms that a payment system requires (SHA-1, PKCS envelopes, DES encrypt, etc.). Finally, the application layer software uses S/PAY (or a similar toolkit) in the actual preparation and processing of protocol-specific message pairs.

Further, the operations performed by the lowest (primitive) layer can be implemented via software-only or software and firmware. This firmware consists of cryptographic algorithms in Programmable Read Only Memory (PROM) that operates at the speed of electricity. Because they're abstract layers, it makes no difference (from the system's point of view) whether you use software cryptography, hardware cryptography, or a combination of the two. Where it does indeed make a difference is how your actual implementation behaves and how well it's secured while it's operating.

Protocol Cryptography Toolkits

The lowest layer of cryptographic processing instructs hardware to perform some work (compute a hash, generate a random number, etc.). Developers of cryptography APIs include Microsoft (CryptoAPI), RSA, and others. Payment protocol toolkits, like RSA's S/PAY, are the next higher layer of software that use the primitive cryptography APIs as needed to perform security work. S/PAY knows how to carry out the work that a properly formatted payment message system needs without requiring the developer to specify each step to create a properly formed message. For example, with its API, a developer can simply supply the content and call a DES ENCRYPT operation. The result can be placed directly within a message while it's being constructed. These toolkits not only spare the developer from considerable effort but also help assure that cryptographic processing is consistent, removing any concerns of proprietary implementations.

Application-Layer Toolkits

Merchant applications—such as POS (Point of Sale) systems—are what most c-commerce operators actually purchase and install on their own systems. They typically rely on the two lower-level toolkits, adding specific business and processing rules. They also offer a series of APIs that you use to customize the installation for your business. These APIs provide flexibility to enable relatively simple programming to link in legacy system data sources, request in-process information from the system, etc. You can usually find prebuilt class-libraries that you can also use in your programs. These toolkit library functions can be modified or expanded to meet any of your specific needs. Additional functions can be added through programming language such as C, C++, Perl, or Java.

HARDWARE-ASSISTED CRYPTOGRAPHY

When encryption work is added to a server, processing times can slow from several hundred transactions per second to as little as a few transactions per second. Hardware specifically designed for encryption comes to the rescue when system processing begins grinding to a halt. Encryption hardware prices are dropping from several thousands dollars to a few hundred dollars, with even lower prices expected as more and newer products appear on the market. Encryption hardware is supplied as either stand-alone servers (security servers) or as add-on boards that are installed into open slots on the POS system server hardware itself.

Hardware encryption devices can also monitor the security of the data they process and alert system administrators when problems occur. They can also monitor the activity of private keys. If a security breach is detected, the data at risk may be zeroed-out, or zeroized. Encryption hardware reduces or eliminates the risk of private key theft by placing the keys inside the encryption hardware itself. One drawback of storing private keys in hardware is the relative difficulty in changing them, and, in some cases, the inability to change them at all. If hardware has been "stamped" by the manufacturer with a preassigned private key, you may need to exchange the board to obtain a different key. This may require that you keep a spare board on hand.

Add-On Boards

Cryptography add-on boards and servers function using the same layered approach that's used by software-only cryptography. Some board manufacturers provide toolkits that interface to the APIs used to control the device's operation. Hardware providers may supply their own libraries but often use the same toolkits that software cryptography uses. If you start out with software-based cryptography and eventually decide to move to hardware-assisted processing, it's best to look for the same toolkit support to minimize or eliminate the need to rewrite functions.

Cryptography APIs are stored into the memory (PROM) of add-on boards and servers, along with storage space for private keys. They typically contain their own RAM (random access memory) storage to speed up processing. By placing keys and certificates directly into hardware, you're assured that sensitive data is not vulnerable to outside attacks.

Security Servers

Security servers follow a client-server architecture model, with the merchant system acting as the client. Since these security servers contain their own processors, they provide an operator's console interface to control connectivity, key management, and certificate management services.

Hardware implementations are special-purpose devices that offer both physical and logical security. Hardware Cryptography Modules (HCMs) are connected to other server platforms through a physical I/O (input/output) connection (direct or via the network). They use their own databases to store the keys that are not within the hardware itself. An API, similar to software APIs, permits multiple applications to access the device's services.

15

Multifactor Access Controls Using Cryptography

Using the principles and practices you've learned throughout this section of the book, we can begin to integrate this information into systems and services that perform useful work. Today's modern access control mechanisms are increasingly reliant on multifactor authentication that mixes what a person knows, with what a person owns, with what a person is. Chapter 8 touched upon some of the uses of cryptographic access controls (SmartCards, biometrics, etc.) as a means of controlling physical access. These same tools and techniques are just as useful for logical access control as well. This chapter drills down deeper into these emerging technologies to illustrate how you can use them to help batten down the hatches to prevent unwanted access to your systems. We start with another look at Smart-Card technologies.

SMARTCARDS

As we meander into the 21st century, experts are predicting that over 8 billion SmartCards will be in people's wallets across the globe by 2004, serving a variety of purposes. As access controls find their way to imbedded SmartCard chips, proliferating IDs and passwords will be relegated to history.

SmartCards change the mechanics of accessing electronic-based services from what a person knows to what a person physically possesses. SmartCards resemble plastic credit cards, but they contain an imbedded processor, random access memory (typically 16–32K or more), and cryptographic processing capabilities.

Physical Classification of SmartCards

SmartCards are essentially working computers with infinite possible uses. On the physical level, SmartCards are classified as contact, contactless, or a combination of the two. Contact SmartCards require a reader (and/or writer) in which the card is inserted when it's needed. Contactless cards contain an antenna that can be read by remote receivers. Combination cards can be used both ways, depending on the applications they're intended for.

For e-commerce purposes, you'll likely find contact cards as the most prevalent, especially as the newer desktop computer systems—which come equipped with readers/writers either bulll-lii lu the keyboard or the computer chassis—become ubiquitous. An example of an external SmartCard reader from Gemplus Corporation is shown in Figure 15-1.

Contactless cards are most often found where transaction speed is critical, as with mass-transit toll payment and replenishment and physical access controls. These cards are similar to transponder units that have a variety of other uses where metered applications are present.

Logical Classifications of SmartCards

At the logical level, SmartCards are classified in three different ways:

1. Memory cards
2. Protected memory cards
3. Microprocessor cards

Memory Cards

Memory cards (the simplest form) are used to store value for future uses. The most common example of a memory

Figure 15-1. An external SmartCard reader from Gemplus Corporation.

card is a prepaid phone card that is redeemable through the bright-yellow reader slot found on modern pay phones. Other common uses are electronic purse (e-purse) applications that eliminate the need to carry cash, ID systems that are used in place of medical identification bracelets to store vital information in the event of a medical emergency (name, blood type, allergies, medical conditions, etc.), or any other applications that can benefit from stored, portable data.

Protected Memory Cards

Protected memory cards require the entry of a secret code, or PIN (personal identification number), before a stream of data can be sent to or received from the chip. The holder of the PIN may be the card user herself or the card issuer that needs the PIN to replenish value on the card (as with e-purse applications) or to modify information that it specifically maintains.

Microprocessor Cards

Microprocessor cards contain a semiconductor chip to hold microcode that defines command structures, data file structures, and security structures. These cards are needed when more "intelligence" or storage of dynamic information is present, and they are often found used in multiapplication products and services.

Costs and Uses

The cost of blank (uninitialized, unpersonalized) Smart-Cards varies widely, depending on card type and functionality. Memory cards run from $2 to $5 per card, protected memory cards run from $1 to $4.50 per card, and microprocessor cards run anywhere from $3.50 to $16 per card.

Personalization costs may be the deciding factor in offering SmartCards since they can quickly become exorbitant as the functionality desired for the card increases. With added functions and benefits, data sources become diverse, disparate, and distributed across several possible participating companies—adding tremendous costs to card preparation and chip updating. Certain uses of the Internet should aid in the updates to chip information and may help to reduce some of these costs and complexities.

SmartCards differ from traditional magnetic strip credit cards in that they maintain state information that can change with each use or encounter. The uses of Smart-Cards range from the simple to the very complex. With a multiapplication card, users can combine controlled access (as with badge readers), credit or charge card privileges, traveler profile information, frequent-stayer program information, loyalty programs, car rental programs, electronic purse applications, and logical access control to computing services—all on a single device.

At the Memorial University of Newfoundland in Canada, the University of Michigan, and various other universities, SmartCards are being issued in lieu of student ID cards to replace separate ID, library, and student services cards. These SmartCards also contain an application for calling cards and an e-purse application for copiers, vending machines, and other coin-operated services.

With X.509 digital certificates (see Chapter 13) added to SmartCards, colleges can offer cost-effective student identification that also supports a host of other applications:

- *Portable Identity:* Authenticate user identity, store user preferences, and access online applications from anywhere at any time
- *Secure Access:* Control access to buildings, information, and university networks
- *Class Registration:* Online class registration with real-time class availability
- *Secure E-Mail:* Security for intercampus communications with nonrepudiation
- *Electronic Purse:* Electronic storage of money for use at campus cafeterias, student bookstores, and point-of-sale terminals, such as vending machines, laundry machines, and parking meters

Combining corporate purchasing or procurement SmartCards with Open Buying on the Internet (OBI) digital certificates (see Chapter 10), along with payment-system–based digital certificates (like Secure Electronic Transaction, or SET), can help drive down the costs of business-to-business e-commerce even further than OBI or SET alone. This synergy not only enables both authentication of parties for purchasing purposes and for payment purposes; it also enables purchase order creation from any Internet-connected device anywhere in the world—not just from the user's regular desktop computer. Other combinations of technologies still not dreamed of yet could bring about computing environments totally unimaginable today.

Barriers to SmartCard Acceptance

While SmartCards themselves are a proven technology that may well improve our lives, they still have a way to go before they're part of the everyday fabric of living. The lack of a common Point-of-Sale (POS) infrastructure in the United States and in other parts of the world is probably the largest barrier in place today. Until SmartCard-ready POS terminals become affordable enough to make the decision to replace the traditional magnetic-stripe POS readers a no-brainer, SmartCards may be left wanting.

Another current barrier is that the standards that govern how SmartCard applications will behave in the imbedded chip are still under development or are waiting to be shaken out by other competing standards. The activity occurring on this front is furious, and time will be the final judge as to which standards will prevail.

Some critics of SmartCards complain that they're yet another vehicle with which to invade privacy and personal liberties and that they'll only serve as a tool for "Big Brother." On the other hand, people who gain a good understanding of SmartCards today can help to eliminate some of these criticisms and can aid in envisioning Smart-Card potential.

BIOMETRICS

As you saw in Chapter 13, digital cryptography is useful to authenticate people, secure their communications, and assure the integrity of their messages upon arrival. Biometrics, as a complementary technology, offers even higher levels of user authentication. Someday you may find yourself staring into a camera or slipping your finger into a reader before you're able to complete an online sales transaction using a credit card. Biometrics—the measurement of human traits—is rapidly becoming both more reliable and less expensive. As the quest for better ways to identify people continues, biometrics, in combination with cryptography, offers a more complete solution than either approach alone.

The Use of Fingerprints

Based on the premise that certain human characteristics are both random (they do not occur often within a population) and stable (they do not change over time), it's natural to pursue their uses rather than rely on easily forgotten passwords, IDs, or external devices, such as tokens or SmartCards. Fingerprints, for example, offer an image that can be transformed into a digital representation that's unique but consistently regenerated when the same fingerprint is encountered. Recognition software transforms data about the coordinates where ridges terminate or where loops converge, which scientists call minutiae. These minutiae may contain up to seven characteristics that are found to be unique. Human fingers contain about seventy minutiae points, making it possible to arrive at 490 data elements that can be recorded. Some recognition systems combine minutiae points with other information (e.g., the distance between points, the direction). Once captured, this digitized information is stored for later comparison purposes, often in template forms using 1K or so of memory.

Instead of using pseudorandom number generators to

create Public-Private Key (PPK) pairs, it's possible to use fingerprint information as the basis for private keys. This is appealing since the images can't be shared, stolen, or easily forged. You never have to rely on your memory, your browser, or your Electronic Wallet to protect your private key again!

Future applications of biometrics are combining the security of SmartCards for storing your public key (contained in your digital certificates) along with the information that's needed to match your fingerprint to assure the highest form of identity matching and help to assure the appropriate levels of security needed for e-commerce.

Fingerprint Readers

One fingerprint recognition device, called U.are.U, comes from Digital Persona. The U.are.U sensor offers touch-activated fingerprint capture and automatic correction for latent prints. It comes with a secured interface that uses challenges and responses for image encryption, works with Universal Serial Bus interfaces, provides verification in under a second, and costs less than $200. Software is available for Windows 95 and Windows 98. Digital Persona also provides a software developer's kit (SDK) that enables integrating the system into custom-developed applications for corporate or e-commerce uses. The U.are.U sensor is shown in Figure 15-2.

Other fingerprint recognition systems are also available. The BioMouse from American Biometrics Corporation is a combination fingerprint and SmartCard reader that works under Windows 95, Windows 98, NT, DOS, Solaris, Linux, IRIX, and HP-UX.

National Registry Inc., the developers of the Human Authentication Application Program Interface (HA-API), offers Secure Authentication Facility (SAF) products for various computer platforms. You can also find biometrics devices from Identix Corporation and Biometric Access Corp. (BAC), as well as several others.

Using Your Head

Although hands are the most commonly used body part, biometrics are possible on other human attributes too.

- A voice verification system is used to speed up travel between Montana and Canada for those who cross the border frequently.
- Inmates at Cook County Jail in Illinois are subject to retinal scans as they come and go to court appearances.
- Finger image matching is used for welfare recipients in Connecticut and Pennsylvania.
- Coca-Cola uses a hand geometry scanner to prevent employees from punching someone else's time card.

Figure 15-2. The U.are.U sensor from Digital Persona.

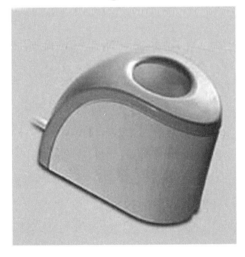

Written signatures may be used for dual purposes, especially with financial transactions or other applications where signatures are needed to identify someone. Over one hundred patents have been issued for signature recognition systems. Facial recognition and vein recognition are two other biometrics that have caught the attention of security experts since they represent viable alternatives to fingerprint recognition systems alone. Keystroke systems are yet another biometrics that could serve as a means to personal identification. Researchers have found that people's typing habits are unique enough to capture information about them that's suitable for identification uses.

The Biometrics Consortium

Critics charge that biometrics are nothing more than another invasion of privacy. In 1998, the religious broadcaster Pat Robertson apprised viewers of the *700 Club* that biometrics signal the coming of the Apocalypse. "The Bible says the time is going to come that you cannot buy or sell except with a mark placed on your hand or on your forehead. . . . It is happening, ladies and gentlemen, exactly according to the Book of Revelations," claimed Robertson on his Christian Broadcasting Network in a segment entitled "Biometrics: Chipping Away Your Rights?"

Perhaps he's right, but supporters of biometrics are forging ahead, with the U.S. government leading the way. The Biometrics Consortium, a working group within the National Security Agency (NSA), promotes the science and performance of biometrics for the U.S. government. The consortium serves as a forum for researchers to exchange information and results about their developments in the field. Some of the planned uses and those generating interest include:

- The Electronic Benefits Transfer Task Force, for disbursement of federal benefits (retirement, Social Security, welfare, etc.) through ATMs (Automatic Teller Machines) and POS systems
- The National Crime Information Center 2000 (NCIC 2000), to equip police patrol cars with devices that capture faces and fingerprints in the field and relay them to central computers that check for wants and warrants
- Department of State passport issuance processing
- Department of Defense network security enhancements
- Federal Aviation Administration airport security applications

Although they're not ready yet for prime time, it won't be too long before biometrics devices are as common as ATMs. As standards for interfaces, software, and storage technologies are being developed and promulgated, e-commerce via the Internet stands to gain the most. Once fearful consumers understand that biometrics can provide unassailable proof of identity, they'll naturally gravitate to on-line shopping. The future of buying will soon be as close as your fingertips!

16

Minding the Store for the Long Run

Hacking has become commonplace, and new vulnerabilities and new ways to exploit old vulnerabilities arrive daily. What's considered a safe practice today may become useless or even dangerous tomorrow. But with the timeless security consciousness that you're building and fortifying by reading and applying this book, you become a member of a much larger community that takes computer security *very* seriously and is quick to react in an ever-changing environment.

In Chapter 16, you'll find software and resources to help you effectively stand guard over your systems and networks. Thanks to efforts throughout the security community, you can sleep better at night, knowing you've done all that you can to keep yourself protected.

GOVERNMENT RESOURCES

Computer Emergency Response Team (CERT)

The Software Engineering Institute (SEI) is a federally funded research and development center sponsored by the U.S. Department of Defense. SEI is operated at Carnegie Mellon University *(www.cmu.edu)* and is staffed by technical and administrative professionals from government, industry, and academia. One of SEI's primary projects is the Computer Emergency Response Team (CERT) Coordination Center, which serves as the authoritative source for networked systems vulnerabilities and threats, and falls under the umbrella of the Defense Advanced Research Project Agency (DARPA).

The CERT Coordination Center team (as described on its Web site at *www.cert.org*) helps system administrators who:

- Are on a networked host and have the practical responsibility for the security of their site's computing systems.
- Would like to share information with colleagues at other sites.
- Could use technical and administrative recommendations to advance their system security.
- Want to take advantage of fixes to enhance the security of products on which they rely.
- Are facing a computer security emergency.
- Need help with a security breach that has already happened.

The center, which has experts on call for emergencies twenty-four hours a day, has the following characteristics:

- It is a twenty-four-hour single point of contact for emergencies.
- It has the capability to facilitate communications among experts working to solve problems.
- It is a central point for the identification and correction of security vulnerabilities.
- It is a secure repository of computer incident information.

As an operator of highly secure facilities, you certainly want to keep CERT's Web site handy at all times.

CERT also is involved in the Networked Systems Survivability Program, based on the experience of CERT to counter intrusions into computer systems connected to the Internet. On the basis of this experience, the Software Engineering Institute develops and distributes a security management process, security practices, and an information security evaluation method to enable organizations to protect their systems against current and emerging threats.

Federal Computer Incident Response Capability Program (FedCIRC)

Another important U.S. federal government security advisory and incident response initiative is the Federal Computer Incident Response Capability (FedCIRC) Program. This was initiated by the National Institute of Standards and Technology (NIST) in answer to the need for a U.S. governmentwide incident response capability to assist federal *civilian* agencies. FedCIRC assists federal civilian agencies in their incident handling efforts by providing proactive and reactive computer security–related services.

The mission of FedCIRC is to develop a self-sustaining incident response capability that meets the needs of the federal civilian agencies. FedCIRC combines the experience and expertise of NIST's Computer Security Division, the Defense Advanced Research Project Agency's CERT Coordination Center (discussed above), and the Department of Energy's Computer Incident Advisory Capability (CIAC, discussed below) to provide agencies with direct technical assistance and incident handling support.

Operations

Each organization (NIST, CERT Coordination Center, and CIAC) has primary roles and responsibilities. NIST subcontracts the operational incident handling capability to the CERT Coordination Center and CIAC. NIST is responsible for operational management and for facilitating the development of incident handling standards and guidelines by utilizing the threat and vulnerability data collected by FedCIRC. The vulnerability information is also used in the analysis and testing of software and other products.

Services and Activities

FedCIRC provides six primary services to federal civilian agencies. These services are:

1. Incident handling information
2. Incident response and hotline support

3. Annual FedCIRC incident handling conference
4. Semiannual "state of the threat" subscriber meetings
5. Information security evaluation
6. Assistance in establishing an on-site incident response capability

Activities offered through the FedCIRC incident response team include:

- *Problem Analysis:* Analyze the problem, determine the magnitude of the threat, and provide technical assistance in identifying and closing vulnerabilities.
- *Technical Advice:* Issue advisories to the agencies warning of the problem and describing countermeasures, and provide guidelines on implementing vulnerability patches and other security controls.
- *Technical Assistance:* Facilitate the interaction of victims and relevant law enforcement agencies in reporting security incidents involving violations of the law, coordinate with other security organizations, and work with vendors to provide critical security patches and work-arounds.
- *Vulnerability Analysis:* Perform vulnerability analysis to identify a vulnerability's root cause to mitigate or prevent potential problems before they occur.

The FedCIRC Web site can be found at *csrc.nist.gov/fedcirc.*

Computer Incident Advisory Capability (CIAC)

The Computer Incident Advisory Capability (CIAC), another advisory board for government and civilian uses, is the Department of Energy's computer security incident response team. CIAC handles computer security incidents through damage assessment, software "patches" when necessary, and advice to site personnel on recovery procedures. CIAC also provides training and education and acts as a center of excellence on computer security matters, carefully tracking the latest technology trends, products, and system network security threats and vulnerabilities.

Dozens of other computer security advisories also exist, filling in niche needs as required. Several of these are listed in Appendix B.

REPORTING INTERNET-RELATED CRIME

Understanding that there is no such thing as absolute security, you may still fall victim to an attack despite your best efforts. Recognizing that computer crimes are at least as serious as violent crimes, the following bulletin from the U.S. Department of Justice Computer Crime and Intellectual Property Section (CCIPS) should help you determine whom to contact in the event of a suspected breach of your networks.

Internet-related crime, like any other crime, should be reported to appropriate law enforcement investigative authorities at the local, state, federal, or international levels, depending on the scope of the crime. Citizens who are aware of federal crimes should report them to local offices of federal law enforcement.

Some federal law enforcement agencies that investigate domestic crime on the Internet include the Federal Bureau of Investigation (FBI), the United States Secret Service, the United States Customs Service, and the Bureau of Alcohol, Tobacco, and Firearms (ATF). Each of these agencies has offices, located in every state, to which crimes can be reported. (Contact information for these local offices can be found in local telephone directories.) In general, federal crimes can be reported to the local office of an appropriate law enforcement agency by a telephone call and by requesting the "duty compliance agent."

Each law enforcement agency also has a headquarters (HQ) in Washington, D.C., which has agents who specialize in particular areas. For example, the FBI and the Secret Service both have headquarters-based specialists in computer intrusion (i.e., computer hacker) cases. In fact, the FBI HQ hosts an interagency center, the National Infrastructure Protection Center (NIPC), created just to support investigations of computer intrusions. The NIPC's general number for criminal investigations is 202-324-0303. The Secret Service's Electronic Crimes Branch can be reached at 202-435-5850. The FBI and the Customs Service also have specialists in intellectual property crimes (i.e., copyright, software, movie, or recording piracy; trademark counterfeiting). The Customs Service has a nationwide toll-free hotline for reporting at 800-BE-ALERT (800-232-2538).

The FBI investigates general violations of federal criminal law. Certain law enforcement agencies focus on particular kinds of crime. Other federal agencies with investigative authority are the Federal Trade Commission (FTC) and the U.S. Securities and Exchange Commission (SEC).

To determine some of the federal investigative law enforcement agencies that may be appropriate for reporting certain kinds of crime, see Table 16-1.

SECURITY VULNERABILITY SCANNING

Computer security is not one of those disciplines where you can *set it and forget it.* Because of fast-flying changes in both the business and security environments, you need vigilance through ongoing security testing, monitoring, and maintenance. These activities alone are usually enough to provide work that keeps several people busy full-time. To help you in standing sentry over your installation, an entire class of programs, called vulnerability assessment tools, can continuously scan your network for problems and test your security policies' effectiveness.

This section looks at several of the proactive measures you can take to help assure that you're the first to find and fix potential and perceived problems on your e-commerce systems specifically and your corporate networks in general.

Security Administrator Tool for Analyzing Networks (SATAN)

In Chapter 5, you were introduced to the Security Administrator Tool for Analyzing Networks (SATAN), which hackers

Table 16-1. Federal agencies to which to report Internet-related crimes.

Type of Crime	Appropriate Federal Investigative Law Enforcement Agencies
Computer intrusion (i.e., hacking)	FBI local office; NIPC (202-324-0303); U.S. Secret Service local office
Password trafficking	FBI local office; NIPC (202-324-0303); U.S. Secret Service local office
Copyright (software, movie, sound recording) piracy	FBI local office; if imported: U.S. Customs Service local office (800-BE-ALERT, 800-232-2538)
Theft of trade secrets	FBI local office
Trademark counterfeiting	FBI local office; if imported: U.S. Customs Service local office (800-BE-ALERT, 800-232-2538)
Counterfeiting of currency	U.S. Secret Service local office; FBI local office
Child pornography or exploitation (specifically on the Internet)	FBI local office; if imported: U.S. Customs Service local office (800-BE-ALERT, 800-232-2538)
Internet fraud	FBI local office; FTC; if securities fraud: SEC
Internet harassment	FBI local office
Internet bomb threats	FBI local office; ATF local office
Trafficking in explosive or incendiary devices or firearms over the Internet	FBI local office; ATF local office

might use to scan your systems for weaknesses. Realizing that tools like SATAN are double-edged swords that can be used for good *and* evil purposes, you can beat intruders to the punch by stepping into their shoes and using the software for your own scanning purposes.

Recall that SATAN is a tool to help systems administrators. It recognizes several common networking-related security problems and reports the problems without actually exploiting them. SATAN collects information that is available to everyone with access to the network. With a properly configured firewall in place, that should be near-zero information for outsiders.

For each type or problem SATAN finds, it offers a tutorial that explains the problem and what its impact could be. The tutorial also explains what can be done about the problem:

- Correct an error in a configuration file.
- Install a bug fix or patch from the vendor.
- Use other means to restrict access.
- Disable the service.

Experts conducting research with SATAN find that in networks consisting of more than a few dozen systems, SATAN inevitably finds problems. Here are some of the problems typically found.

- NFS (Network File System) file systems reported to arbitrary hosts.
- NFS file systems reported to unprivileged programs.
- NFS file systems exported via the portmapper.
- NIS (Network Information Service) password file access from arbitrary hosts.
- Old (i.e., before 8.6.10) Sendmail versions.
- REXD access from arbitrary hosts (REXD daemon executes programs for a remote when a client issues a request to execute a program on a remote machine).
- X server access control disabled.
- Arbitrary files accessible via TFTP (Trivial File Transfer Protocol)
- Remote shell access from arbitrary hosts.
- Writable anonymous FTP (File Transfer Protocol) home directory.

Many of these are well-known problems contained in advisories from CERT, CIAC, or other groups. They are also described extensively in other books on Internet security (see Appendix D).

Adaptive Security Management

The Adaptive Security Management Model from Internet Security Systems, Inc. (ISS) expects to redefine network security. To support the model, ISS has bolstered its SAFESuite™ product family, calling it a complete adaptive security management system for the enterprise.

Adaptive Security Management is described as the capability to automatically monitor, detect, and respond to threats and vulnerabilities found on computer networks. According to Tom Noonan, the president and CEO of ISS (see *www.iss.net*):

> An organization is only as secure as its weakest link. Attackers often access sensitive information through less significant network devices that are all too often insecure. Firewalls and other security services, although critical to a successful security program, are not providing the full protection needed in today's complex and dynamic network environment. ISS's new Adaptive Security Management process is the first method that fills in the remaining, critical security gaps and provides automatic management of network security risks.

The Adaptive Security Management process defines four essential steps:

1. *Ongoing and Comprehensive Detection of Security Vulnerabilities.* Frequent, automated network security scanning to detect security weaknesses.
2. *Automatic Response to Security Weaknesses.* User-defined responses such as alarms, automatic correction, and dynamic reconfiguration of network devices.
3. *Around-the-Clock Intrusion Detection of Security Threats.* Real-time monitoring and intrusion detection of misuse of internal network resources and external network attacks.
4. *Automatic Response to Security Threats.* User-defined responses such as alarms that actively terminate the connection and log the activity based on detected threats.

ISS's SAFESuite includes both proactive and reactive products, such as the Internet Scanner, to detect and correct vulnerabilities on the network, and the System Scanner, which does the same at the server level. In addition, RealSecure handles intrusion detection and responds to threats on the network. It sits either in front of or behind a firewall.

SAFESuite also includes a central security policy management system to actively enforce the security policy across the network, dynamically reconfigure network devices and services such as firewalls and routers, and provide automatic updates and corrections to operating systems, network services, and applications through traditional network management vendors such as IBM's Tivoli Systems.

NetSonar Security Vulnerability Scanner and Network Mapping System

Cisco Systems's NetSonar automates the process of auditing a network's security posture through its comprehensive vulnerability scanning and network mapping capabilities. NetSonar's vulnerability scanner and network mapping systems incorporate security assessment expertise into a software tool that's designed for network administrators and network security consultants. NetSonar can quickly analyze the security posture of an entire enterprise network, compile an electronic inventory of the network, and create meaningful reports to effectively communicate potential security risks.

NetSonar's services are as follows:

- *Network Mapping:* Compile an electronic inventory of the systems and services on a network.
- *Security Vulnerability Assessment:* Identify potential security holes by probing for and confirming vulnerabilities.
- *Risk Management:* Allows for effective management of vulnerability data.
- *Data Browsing and Viewing:* Navigate through vul-

nerability information and view it from a variety of perspectives and levels of detail.

- *Decision Support:* Communicate results through comprehensive reports and charts, and make effective decisions to improve your security posture.
- *Data Management and Presentation:* Navigate through vulnerability data, and interpret and present this information in meaningful ways to management or technical audiences. Details of each vulnerability, why it is important, how to fix it, and the potential for exploitation are all available to the user.

NetSonar also enables you to build your own vulnerability *rules* for custom, user-specific applications and run these new rules against archived data from previous scans to generate trend analyses.

Sniffer Total Network Visibility (TNV)

Network Associates (*www.nai.com*) offers the Sniffer Total Network Visiblity (TNV) as another set of network monitoring and analysis tools. Mirage Resorts, a leading developer and operator of casino-based resorts, uses the TNV 3.0 Suite to help assure network availability and performance. Network Associates's system consists of Sniffer Pro, DSS/RMON, and Network Informant products, offering visibility into the entire high-speed switched network, with analysis and alert mechanisms to identify and correct problems before they affect users. The Mirage high-speed switched network connects hundreds of Windows NT Servers and approximately 13,000 network nodes, including about 7,000 desktop PCs. Each Mirage operation runs nearly one hundred applications from various vendors, including hotel and restaurant applications, financial packages, and a host of other systems used to help manage its hospitality and leisure enterprise.

The remote monitoring capabilities of TNV enable a Mirage system administrator at a central site to gain a complete view of network performance across all hotel properties. Administrators can also see traffic flow and data volume passing through the network switches. Database transaction times are measured against predetermined performance thresholds, with analysis that provides guidance on likely causes and remedies. If a network traffic or performance threshold is breached, DSS/RMON beeps a warning or sends an e-mail to the administrator with a description of the problem and suggestions for resolution.

REINFORCING NETWORK SECURITY RESPONSIBILITIES

Failing to consider security as part of the ongoing support and operations of computer systems is often the Achilles' heel of many organizations. It's easy to locate examples where organizations undermine expensive security measures because of poor documentation, old user accounts, conflicting software, or poor control of maintenance accounts.

The following section, adapted from a NIST publication on computer security, offers a final big-picture view of ongoing responsibilities to maintain a secure installation. Included here are these considerations:

- Software support
- Configuration management
- Backups
- Media controls
- Documentation
- Maintenance
- Interdependencies

Software Support

Software is the heart of an organization's computer operations, regardless of the size and complexity of the system. As such, it's essential that software functions correctly and is protected from corruption. Several elements of control are needed for software support.

The first controls what software is used on what systems. If your users or systems personnel can load and execute any software on any system, these systems become more vulnerable to viruses, to unexpected software interactions, and to software that may subvert or bypass security controls. One method of controlling software is to inspect or test it before it is loaded (e.g., to determine compatibility with custom applications or identify other unforeseen interactions). This applies to new software packages, upgrades, off-the-shelf products, or custom software. In addition to controlling the loading and execution of new software, organizations should be cautious with off-the-shelf or downloaded system utilities. Some of the system utilities are designed to compromise the integrity of operating systems or breach logical access controls.

Another element of software support is to assure that software is not modified without proper authorizations. This involves protecting all software and backup copies. This is often accomplished using a combination of logical and physical access controls.

Many organizations also include on their agendas a program to help assure that software is properly licensed, as required. For example, an organization can audit systems for illegal copies of copyrighted software. This problem is primarily associated with PCs and LANs (local area networks) but can apply to any type of system.

Configuration Management

Closely related to software support is configuration management—the process of keeping track of changes to the system and, if needed, approving them. Configuration management normally addresses hardware, software, networking, and other changes; it can be formal or informal. The primary security goal of configuration management is ensuring that changes to the system do not unintentionally or unknowingly diminish security. Some of the methods discussed under software support, such as inspecting and testing software changes, can be used.

For networked systems, configuration management should include external connections. Is the computer system connected? To what other systems? In turn, to what systems are these systems and organizations connected? Note that the security goal is to know what changes occur—not to prevent security from being changed. There may be circumstances when security will be reduced. However, the decrease in security should be the result of a decision based on all appropriate factors.

A second security goal of configuration management is ensuring that changes to the system are reflected in other documentation, such as the contingency plan. If the change is major, it may be necessary to reanalyze some or all of the security of the system.

Backups

Support and operations personnel—and sometimes users—back up software and data. This function is critical to contingency planning. The frequency of backups depends upon how often data changes and how important those changes are. Also, as a safety measure, it is useful to test that backup copies are actually usable. Finally, backups should be stored securely, as appropriate.

Users of smaller systems are often responsible for their own backups. However, in reality, they do not always perform backups regularly. In some organizations, support personnel are charged with making backups periodically for smaller systems, either automatically (through server software) or manually (by visiting each machine).

Media Controls

Media controls include a variety of measures to provide physical and environmental protection and accountability for tapes, diskettes, CDs, Zip disks, printouts, and other media. From a security perspective, media controls should be designed to prevent the loss of confidentiality, integrity, or availability of information, including data or software, when stored outside the system. This can include storage of information before it is input to the system and after it is output.

The extent of media control depends upon many factors, including the type of data, the quantity of media, and the nature of the user environment. Physical and environmental protection is used to prevent unauthorized individuals from accessing the media. It also protects against such factors as heat, cold, or harmful magnetic fields. When necessary, logging the use of individual media (e.g., a tape cartridge) provides detailed accountability to hold authorized people responsible for their actions.

Marking or Labeling

Controlling media may require some form of physical labeling. The labels can be used to identify media with special handling instructions, to locate needed information, or to log media (e.g., with serial/control numbers or bar codes) to support accountability. Identification is often by colored labels on diskettes or tapes or banner pages on printouts.

If labeling is used for special handling instructions, it is critical that people are appropriately trained. The marking of PC input and output is generally the responsibility of the user, not the system support staff. Marking backup diskettes can help prevent them from being accidentally overwritten.

Logging

The logging of media is used to support accountability. Logs can include control numbers (or other tracking data), times and dates of transfers, names and signatures of individuals involved, and other relevant information. Periodic spot checks or audits can be conducted to determine that no controlled items have been lost and that all are in the custody of the individuals named in control logs. Automated media tracking systems can be helpful for maintaining inventories of tape and disk libraries.

Integrity Verification

When electronically stored information is read into a computer system, it may be necessary to determine whether it has been read correctly or has been subject to any modification. The integrity of electronic information can be verified using error detection and correction or, if intentional modifications are a threat, cryptographic-based technologies.

Physical Access Protection

Media can be stolen, destroyed, replaced with a lookalike copy, or lost. Physical access controls to limit these problems include locked doors, desks, file cabinets, or safes. If the media requires protection at all times, it may be necessary to actually output data to the media in a secure location (e.g., printing to a printer in a locked room instead of to a general-purpose printer in a common area).

Physical protection of media should be extended to backup copies stored off-site. They generally should be accorded an equivalent level of protection to media containing the same information stored on-site. (Equivalent protection does not mean that the security measures need to be exactly the same. The controls at the off-site location are quite likely to be different from the controls at the regular site.)

Environmental Protection

Magnetic media, such as diskettes or magnetic tape, require environmental protection since they are sensitive to temperature, liquids, magnetism, smoke, and dust. Other media (e.g., paper and optical storage) may have different sensitivities to environmental factors.

Transmittal

Media control can be transferred both within the organization and to outside elements. Possibilities for securing such transmittal include sealed and marked envelopes, authorized messenger or courier, or U.S. certified or registered mail.

Disposition

When media is disposed of, it may be important to ensure that information is not improperly disclosed. This applies both to media that is external to a computer system (such as a diskette) and to media inside a computer system (such as a hard disk). The process of removing information from media is called sanitization. Three techniques are commonly used for media sanitization:

1. Overwriting
2. Degaussing
3. Destruction

Overwriting is an effective method for clearing data from magnetic media. As the name implies, overwriting uses a program to write (1s, 0s, or a combination) onto the media. The common practice is to overwrite the media three times. Overwriting should not be confused with merely deleting the pointer to a file (which typically happens when a delete command is used). Overwriting requires that the media be in working order. *Degaussing* is a method to magnetically erase data from magnetic media. Two types of degaussers exist: (1) strong permanent magnets and (2) electric degaussers. The final method of sanitization is *destruction* of the media by shredding or burning.

Why is sanitization so important? People often throw away old diskettes, believing that erasing the files on the diskettes has made the data unretrievable. In reality, however, erasing a file simply removes the pointer to that file. The pointer tells the computer where the file is physically stored; without this pointer, the files do not appear on a directory listing. But this does not mean that the file was removed. Commonly available utility programs can easily retrieve information that is presumed deleted.

Documentation

Although it's the bane of most developers and IT professionals, documentation of all aspects of computer support and operations is important to ensure continuity and consistency. Formalizing operational practices and procedures with sufficient detail helps to eliminate security lapses and oversights, gives new personnel sufficiently detailed instructions, and provides a quality assurance function to help ensure that operations are performed correctly and efficiently.

The security of a system also needs to be documented. This includes many types of documentation, such as security plans, contingency plans, risk analyses, and security policies and procedures. Much of this information, particularly risk and threat analyses, has to be protected against unauthorized disclosure. Security documentation also needs to be both current and accessible. Accessibility should take special factors into account (such as the need to find the contingency plan during a disaster).

Security documentation should be designed to fulfill the needs of the different types of people who use it. A security procedures manual should be written to inform various system users how to do their jobs securely. Such a manual may address a wide variety of technical and operational concerns in considerable detail for system operations and support staff.

Maintenance

System maintenance requires either physical or logical access to the system. Support and operations staff, hardware or software vendors, or third-party service providers may maintain a system. Maintenance can be performed on-site, or it may be necessary to move equipment to a repair site. Maintenance can also be performed remotely via communications connections. If someone who does not normally have access to the system performs maintenance, then a security vulnerability is introduced.

In some circumstances, it may be necessary to take additional precautions, such as conducting background investigations of service personnel. Supervision of maintenance personnel can prevent some problems, such as "snooping around" the physical area. However, once someone has access to the system, it is very difficult for supervision to prevent damage done through the maintenance process.

Many computer systems provide maintenance accounts. These special login accounts are normally preconfigured at the factory with preset, widely known passwords. One of the most common methods hackers use to break into systems is through maintenance accounts that still have factory-set or easily guessed passwords. It is critical to change these passwords or otherwise disable the accounts until they are needed. Procedures should be developed to ensure that only authorized maintenance personnel can use these accounts. If the account is to be used remotely, authentication of the maintenance provider can be performed using callback confirmation. This helps ensure that remote diagnostic activities actually originate from an established telephone number at the vendor's site. Other techniques can also help, including encryption and decryption of diagnostic communications; strong identification and authentication techniques, such as tokens; and remote disconnect verification.

Larger systems may have diagnostic ports. In addition, manufacturers of larger systems and third-party providers may offer more diagnostic and support services. It is critical to ensure that these ports are used only by authorized personnel and cannot be accessed by hackers.

Interdependencies

Support and operations components coexist in most computer security controls:

- *Personnel.* Most support and operations staff have special access to the system. Some organizations conduct background checks on individuals filling these positions to screen out possibly untrustworthy individuals.

- *Incident Handling.* Support and operations may include an organization's incident handling staff. Even if they are separate organizations, they need to work together to recognize and respond to incidents.

- *Contingency Planning.* Support and operations staff normally provide technical input to contingency planning and carry out the activities of making backups, updating documentation, and practicing responding to contingencies.

- *Security Awareness, Training, and Education.* Support and operations staff should be trained in security procedures and should be aware of the importance of security. In addition, they provide technical expertise needed to teach users how to secure their systems.

- *Physical and Environmental Aspects.* Support and operations staff often control the immediate physical area around the computer system.

- *Technical Controls.* The technical controls are installed, maintained, and used by support and operations staff. They create the user accounts, add users to access control lists, review audit logs for unusual activity, control bulk encryption over telecommunications links, and perform the countless operational tasks needed to use technical controls effectively. In addition, support and operations staff provide needed input to the selection of controls based on the staff members' knowledge of system capabilities and operational constraints.

- *Assurance.* Support and operations staff ensure that changes to a system do not introduce security vulnerabilities by using assurance methods to evaluate or test the changes and their effect on the system. Operational assurance is normally performed by support and operations staff.

CONCLUSION

From the start, you've seen the folly and dangers of connecting unsecured private networks to the Internet, but along the way you discovered how to avoid most of the pernicious problems. Beyond the principles, tools, and techniques offered to help you secure your Internet-attached networks and e-commerce sites, we hope you've also begun to shift your thinking toward a security consciousness that will keep you secure as long as you choose to remain a member of the Global Village. By adequately securing your little corner of cyberspace, you'll instill—and maintain— the right levels of trustworthiness that your customers both demand and deserve.

You have seen throughout this book that computer security requires a holistic approach. It is as much a set of behaviors as it is a bundle of software tools and network sniffers that by themselves might leave you with a false sense of security. Analogies abound in our everyday lives. We buy expensive alarm systems for our homes, move into gated communities, opt for a German shepherd or a Doberman pinscher instead of a golden retriever, and yet we know that these are only partial solutions.

As this chapter has pointed out, true security requires that you educate your staff, develop manageable security policies and procedures, and create a security organization (whether it be one or many employees) that enforces those policies. It requires that you properly configure your network *for your organization* without assuming that off-the-shelf configurations are right for you. It also means investing in the tools and expertise that you deem necessary to evaluate and monitor your network in order to detect intrusions before they happen, as well as to develop a clear strategy for dealing with an intrusion when it inevitably occurs. Finally, a secure network calls for constant vigilance. This means keeping up with the technological changes around you by reading trade journals and periodicals, joining user groups that discuss security issues and disseminate the latest security information, attending conferences and seminars, and undergoing any relevant training that will keep you abreast of evolving security needs.

Our objective in this book has been to give you the information that we feel is fundamental to a good night's sleep. We hope that you take the importance of security to heart and respond to the challenge not with trepidation but with the confidence of informed security experts.

Appendix A

A Sample Internet Security Policy

Appendix A is presented as an example of the type of network-specific Internet security policy that should be developed for each major Internet user community. As noted in the main body of the policy, it is recommended that all agencies/organizations involved in the use of the Internet establish a policy statement appropriate to the agency/organization, its Internet activities, and its relationships to other agencies or organizations.

The example given here is a security policy written specifically for the National Research and Education Network (NREN). It was developed by Dr. Dennis Branstad, Dr. Arthur Oldehoff, Dr. Robert Aiken, and others based on an Internet RFC (Request for Comments) written by Richard Pethia. While written for the specific Internet community, it contains basic elements that should be part of other policy statements. NREN is an Internet-based collaboration environment used by educators and researchers at universities across the United States.

SECURITY POLICY FOR USE OF THE NREN

1. Objectives

This security policy has the following objectives:

A. Establish a high-level policy for protection of the National Research and Education Network (NREN).
B. Establish a basis for further refinement of the high-level policy.

    C. Establish a common foundation for the development and use of security services and mechanisms to be used in the NREN.

    D. Establish the responsibility for security among the users, managers, administrators, vendors, service providers, and overseers of the NREN.

    E. Inform NREN users, managers, administrators, vendors, service providers, and overseers of their security responsibility.

2. Scope

This security policy covers protecting the confidentiality, integrity, and availability of all sensitive information and information-processing resources of the NREN.

3. Applicability

This security policy is applicable to all users, managers, administrators, vendors, service providers, and overseers of the NREN.

4. Threats and Vulnerabilities

This security policy defines various security responsibilities and seeks to counter threats and reduce vulnerabilities in the NREN. This is termed Risk Management and should be understood to encompass only cost-effective means to reduce, but not remove, residual risks. This policy specifically informs users and overseers that all threats and vulnerabilities *will not* be removed. No guarantees or warranties for confidentiality, integrity, and availability will be explicitly or implicitly given through this policy.

5. Principles

The following principles should be followed in using this policy:

    A. *Personal Accountability:* Individuals are responsible for understanding, respecting, and following the security policies of the systems (computers and transmission facilities) they are using and are personally accountable for their behavior and actions.

B. *Authorized Use:* Authorized use of the NREN is defined as those activities authorized to be performed by an individual in accordance with the NREN Acceptable Use Policy. Unauthorized use includes any activity that is illegal, disrupts authorized use, compromises privacy of other users, or destroys the integrity of information or processing capability.

C. *Reasonable and Prudent Precautions:* Each person using or supporting use of the NREN shall take reasonable and prudent precautions to assure the availability and integrity of its resources and the confidentiality of information known, or assumed, to be sensitive to disclosure to unauthorized persons.

D. *Cooperative Protection:* All persons using or supporting use of the NREN shall cooperate in providing and using appropriate protection of its resources and information.

6. Responsibilities

This section defines basic responsibilities for security by those groups of organizations and individuals as identified in the scope of this policy. The responsibilities are general and are not based on existing or planned protection technologies or practices.

A. Users

Authorized users of the NREN are responsible for:

U1. Knowing and complying with relevant federal and state laws, NREN policies, organizational codes of ethics, and acceptable security practices for the systems they use

U2. Employing available security mechanisms for protecting the confidentiality and integrity of their own information when required

U3. Advising others to follow U1 and U2

U4. Notifying a system administrator or management if a security violation or failure is observed, detected, or suspected

U5. Not exploiting security vulnerabilities

U6. Supplying correct and complete identification as required by authentication or access control processes in the network

U7. Using the network only for authorized purposes in a cooperative, legal, ethical, and responsible manner

U8. Using standard security mechanisms to promote interoperability when available and to the maximum extent possible

B. Management (Multiuser Hosts and Facilities)

Multiuser host computer and facility managers are responsible for:

M1. Implementing cost-effective risk management procedures, security mechanisms, and protection features for the hosts and facilities they manage

M2. Providing trusted personnel to support the security specified in M1

M3. Implementing management directives and awareness programs for the administrators and users of their hosts and facilities

C. System Administrators

System administrators (or their designated personnel) are responsible for:

S1. Applying, monitoring, and auditing the security procedures, mechanisms, and features available on the hosts or facilities under their control

S2. Advising management on the workability of existing policies and technical provisions of the system, including recommending improvements for security purposes

S3. Securing computer systems and subnetworks within the facility/site and the interfaces to outside networks

S4. Responding to emergency events that are or may be affecting their hosts or subnetworks in a timely and effective manner

S5. Employing available and approved monitoring and auditing tools to aid in the detection of security violations and actively participating in educating and counseling users who violate security

S6. Remaining cognizant of NREN security policies and recommended practices and, when appropriate, informing local users and advising local management of changes or new developments

S7. Communicating and cooperating with administrators of other sites connecting to the NREN and with emergency response centers for the purposes of information exchange and responses to perceived threats, increasing vulnerabilities, or observed security violations

S8. Judiciously exercising the powers and privileges inherent in their duties, appropriately considering the security of the NREN and the privacy of the individuals using it

D. Federal Networking Council

The Federal Networking Council (FNC), serving as the principal body coordinating the activities of federal research and education network organizations, is responsible for:

N1. Developing, approving, maintaining, and promulgating an NREN security policy

N2. Recommending, approving, and promulgating standards for interoperable security services, mechanisms, and procedures for the NREN

N3. Establishing rules for accepted and authorized use for selected (e.g., federal) portions of the NREN

N4. Coordinating with federal agencies, educational institutions, private organizations, and special interest groups (service providers, vendors, system developers, emergency response centers) regarding security of the NREN

N5. Interacting with appropriate national and international standards organizations developing security standards that may be relevant to the NREN

N6. Preparing reports or input to reports to executive organizations and congressional committees responsible for oversight of the NREN

E. Vendors and System Developers

Vendors and system developers are responsible for:

V1. Employing sound development and distribution methodologies for implementing or providing secure systems, subnetworks, and networks as specified in procurement or management documents supporting the NREN

V2. Seeking technical improvements to security of their products and services appropriate to the policies and specifications of the NREN

V3. Correcting security flaws discovered in existing products and making the system administrators aware of the availability of product improvements

F. Computer Network and Service Providers

Computer network and service providers are responsible for:

P1. Providing network security services and mechanisms as specified in procurement or management documents and making information available to managers, administrators, and users on how to administer and use these security provisions

P2. Seeking technical improvements to the security of

the NREN that is within their areas of responsibility

P3. Cooperating with the FNC in providing appropriate network availability and integrity assurance capability

Internet Bookmarks to Security-Related Sites

ATALLA SECURITY PRODUCTS HOME PAGE

http://www.tandem.com/iBase.asp?PAGE=iAtalla

Compaq's Atalla Network and Internet Security Processor products provide a complete range of hardware security processors for banking, Internet, and enterprise security applications. These products use encryption technology embedded in hardware to safeguard sensitive data, such as financial transactions over private and public networks, and to offload all security processing from the server.

CERTCO INC. HOME PAGE

http://www.certco.com/

CertCo is a leading online risk assurance authority, providing secure e-business technology and systems. Its business solutions provide corporations and trust institutions with the capability to safely conduct global high-value transactions over open networks. CertCo's integrated product suites feature electronic authentication and assurance systems based on PKI (Public Key Infrastructure) technologies. Products include CertAuthority™, CertValidator™, and Professional Services.

THE COAST HOME PAGE

http://www.cerias.purdue.edu/coast/

COAST—Computer Operations, Audit, and Security Technology—is a multiple-project, multiple-investigator laboratory in computer security research at the Computer Sciences Department at Purdue University. It functions with close ties to researchers and engineers in major companies and government agencies. Research is focused on real-world needs and limitations, with a special focus on security for legacy computing systems.

COMMON CRITERIA PROJECT

http://csrc.nist.gov/cc/

On this site is found the latest information about the Common Criteria (CC) for IT Security Evaluation, plus CC-related documents made available for information and public comment. Other documents that bear on the development of internationally accepted standards for IT security functional and assurance requirements and evaluation are also posted or linked from time to time.

COMMON VULNERABILITIES AND EXPOSURES (CVE) HOME PAGE

http://www.cve.mitre.org/

The Common Vulnerabilities and Exposures (CVE) List (as discussed in Chapter 7):

- Standardizes the names for all publicly known vulnerabilities and security exposures.
- Makes it easier to share data across separate vulnerability databases and security tools.

THE COMPUTER SECURITY DIVISION (DIVISION 893) OF THE NATIONAL INSTITUTE OF STANDARDS AND TECHNOLOGY'S INFORMATION TECHNOLOGY LABORATORY (ITL)

http://www.itl.nist.gov/div893/index.html

This site provides information-related security standards–setting activities, security assurance criteria, and testing of security products for U.S. government users.

COMPUTER SECURITY EVALUATION FAQ

http://www.radium.ncsc.mil/tpep/process/faq.html

These Frequently Asked Questions are designed to answer common questions about the evaluation of trusted products. It is simultaneously posted to *comp.security.misc, comp.security.unix, comp.answers,* and *news.answers.*

COMPUTERWORLD MAGAZINE ONLINE

http://www.computerworld.com

Computerworld is an information services company for the IT industry, providing print and online publications, books, conferences, and research services. Members of the IT community can use this daily resource to interact with their peers and to keep abreast of the issues, trends, and specific technologies that affect their jobs. The site complements the print edition of *Computerworld* with a continuous feed of technology news and analysis, as well as research and other services.

eEYE DIGITAL SECURITY HOME PAGE

http://www.eeye.com/html/

eEye provides consulting and security services to help companies secure their networks and the vital corporate data that reside on their servers.

FEDERATION OF AMERICAN SCIENTISTS HOME PAGE

http://www.fas.org

The Federation of American Scientists (FAS) is engaged in analysis and advocacy on science, technology, and public policy concerning global security. A privately funded nonprofit policy organization whose board of sponsors includes over fifty-five American Nobel laureates, FAS was founded as the Federation of Atomic Scientists in 1945 by members of the Manhattan Project, who produced the first atomic bomb.

GEMPLUS HOME PAGE

http://www.gemplus.com/
Gemplus is a leading provider of plastic and Smart-Card-based solutions, with sales offices and production facilities throughout the world.

GTE CYBERTRUST

http://www.cybertrust.gte.com/cybertrust/index.html
CyberTrust is a leading enabler of secure extranets and e-commerce for companies extending their high-value relationships to the Web. CyberTrust's Secure Extranet Method is for certificate-enabled extranets that support privilege-based user access, data confidentiality, audit trails, and digitally signed, binding transactions. CyberTrust offers a suite of PKI-based products, outsourced services, and consulting.

ICSA.NET WEB SITE AND LIBRARY

http://www.icsa.net/library/
ICSA.net is a leader in security assurance services for Internet-connected companies. ICSA.net's services can help reduce risk and improve the quality of Internet security implementations, enabling the safe deployment of new Internet technologies and applications.

INFORMATION SECURITY MAGAZINE HOME PAGE

http://www.infosecuritymag.com/
This is the online edition of the popular *Information Security Magazine* for security professionals and practitioners.

INTERNET ENGINEERING TASK FORCE (IETF) HOME PAGE

http://www.ietf.org/
The Internet Engineering Task Force is a loosely self-organized group of people who make technical and other

contributions to the engineering and evolution of the Internet and its technologies. It is the principal body engaged in the development of new Internet standard specifications. Its mission includes: (1) identifying and proposing solutions to pressing operational and technical problems on the Internet; (2) specifying the development or use of protocols and the near-term architecture to solve such technical problems for the Internet; (3) making recommendations to the Internet Engineering Steering Group (IESG) regarding the standardization of protocols and protocol use on the Internet; (4) facilitating technology transfer from the Internet Research Task Force (IRTF) to the wider Internet community; and (5) providing a forum for the exchange of information within the Internet commmunity among vendors, users, researchers, agency contractors, and network managers.

THE MAN-IN-THE-MIDDLE ATTACK (INVINCIBLE DATA SYSTEMS)

http://www.incrypt.com/mitma.html
Description of a Man-in-the-Middle (MITM) attack to steal cryptographic keys, described by Invincible Data Systems, Inc.

NATIONAL SECURITY AGENCY (NSA) HOME PAGE

http://www.nsa.gov:8080/
The National Security Agency is the U.S. government's cryptologic organization. It coordinates, directs, and performs highly specialized activities to protect U.S. information systems and produce foreign intelligence information. A high-technology organization, NSA is on the frontiers of communications and data processing. It is also one of the most important centers of foreign language analysis and research within the government.

NATIONAL SECURITY INSTITUTE SECURITY RESOURCE NET

http://www.nsi.org/

The National Security Institute's Web site features industry and product news, computer alerts, travel advisories, a calendar of events, a directory of products and services, and access to an extensive virtual security library.

NETWORK COMPUTING SECURITY GUIDE

http://www.networkcomputing.com/core/core8.html

The Network Computing security guide covers firewalls, Certificate Authorities, authentication, encryption, Virtual Private Networks, and antivirus technologies.

NIST IPSEC PROJECT

http://csrc.nist.gov/ipsec/

The NIST (National Institute of Standards and Technology) IPSec Project is concerned with providing authentication, integrity, and confidentiality security services at the Internet Protocol (IP) layer, for both the current IP protocol (IPv4) and the next generation IP protocol (IPv6). Current efforts are concentrated on IPv4 because of the high level of interest in fielding Internet security technology as rapidly as possible. Implementing IPSec requires modifications to the system's communications routines and a new systems process that conducts secret key negotiations.

NT BUGTRAQ WEB SITE

http://ntbugtraq.ntadvice.com/

NT Bugtraq is a mailing list for the discussion of security exploits and security bugs in Windows NT and related applications.

THE PKI GURU HOME PAGE

http://www.pkiguru.com/
A complete online resource for information related to Public Key Infrastructures.

PRIVACY RIGHTS CLEARINGHOUSE WEB SITE

http://www.privacyrights.org/FS/fs12-ih2.htm
This site includes Fact Sheet #12: Responsible Information-Handling Practices, which is a checklist that provides an overview of key points to consider when preparing information-handling policies and conducting privacy audits within your organization. The checklist can be used by private, public, and not-for-profit organizations alike.

RAINBOW SERIES LIBRARY

http://www.radium.ncsc.mil/tpep/library/rainbow/
This is the U.S. Department of Defense collection of security assurance criteria guidelines.

RAINBOW TECHNOLOGIES HOME PAGE

http://isg.rainbow.com/
Rainbow Technologies offers hardware performance solutions for Virtual Private Networks (VPNs), secure Web servers, and e-commerce servers. It also offers public key cryptography supporting IPSec, SSL (Secure Sockets Layer), and SET (Secure Electronic Transaction) protocols.

THE RISKS DIGEST

http://catless.ncl.ac.uk/Risks
This is a forum on risks to the public in computers and related systems.

ROOTSHELL

http://www.rootshell.com
The Rootshell Web site combines advisory information from a variety of sources, listing attacks that succeeded, new threats that have been discovered, and a search engine for information related to specific exploits.

SANS INSTITUTE ONLINE

http://www.sans.org/newlook/home.htm
The SANS (System Administration, Networking, and Security) Institute is a cooperative research and education organization through which more than 62,000 system administrators, security professionals, and network administrators share the lessons they are learning and find solutions for challenges they face. As a part of this effort, SANS offers a series of educational conferences featuring up to eight days of in-depth courses and multitrack technical conferences focusing on user experiences and problem solving. SANS also produces a series of cooperative research reports, electronic digests, posters of authoritative answers to current questions, and cooperatively created software.

SECURE ELECTRONIC TRANSACTIONS, LLC (SETCO)

http://www.setco.org/
This site provides information about SET's governing body and certification programs. SETCo (Secure Electronic Transactions, LLC) manages the SET specification, promoting and supporting the use of SET Secure Electronic Transaction on the Internet.

THE SECURITY SEARCH ENGINE—FIREWALLS, ANTIVIRUS, INTRUSION DETECTION, VULNERABILITIES, ADVISORIES, AND AUDITING SOFTWARE

http://www.securitysearch.net/
Security Search is a search engine designed to provide Internet users with links to IT security information and re-

sources. It was developed as a free service by Shake Communications Pty Ltd.

THE SPARTAN HORSE

http://www.thetopoftheworld.com/spartan/

There has been a lot of attention in the news recently regarding the potential threat of Trojan horse attacks on the Internet. However, most of these attacks involve the user having to inadvertently run the Trojan horse program once it has been transferred to his computer. Now, a new breed of Trojan horse exists, one that is much less complicated yet just as effective. This new attack method (dubbed Spartan horse) makes use of the blurring boundary between the operating system and Internet software.

SPYRUS HOME PAGE

http://www.spyrus.com/

SPYRUS provides cryptographic hardware and software products to corporations, OEMs (Original Equipment Manufacturers), and governments worldwide. These products enable encryption, digital signatures, access control, and metering solutions for corporate information systems, Internet, and intranet applications, as well as commerce and government applications.

VERISIGN CORPORATION HOME PAGE

http://www.verisign.com/

VeriSign, Inc., provides Public Key Infrastructure (PKI) and digital certificate solutions used by enterprises, Web sites, and consumers to conduct secure communications and transactions over the Internet and private networks.

Appendix C

Security and Security-Testing Specialists

In Chapter 6, you learned about the importance of product and system testing by qualified personnel to enable you to make more informed decisions when selecting security products. You also learned that security testing is unlike all other kinds of testing and requires expertise that's not commonly found on the streets. Throughout this book, you've been advised to locate a reputable security consulting company to conduct testing on your behalf. Listed below are several security consulting, security testing, and professional services organizations you may wish to contact. Inclusion on this list does not constitute an endorsement; rather, the list is intended for informational purposes to illustrate the depth and breadth of available computer security services.

COUNTERPANE SYSTEMS

Counterpane Systems is a cryptography and computer security consulting company based in Minneapolis. Bruce Schneier, who is mentioned a number of times in this book, is a principal of Counterpane Internet Security, Inc. The company provides consulting services in these areas:

- Design and analysis of commercial cryptographic systems and system designs.
- Implementation and testing of cryptographic systems using its homegrown and industry standard designs, such as SET (Secure Electronic Transaction), the electronic-mail standard S/MIME, and

SSL (Secure Sockets Layer). Counterpane also performs security testing and verification of software implementations and products.

- Threat modeling using attack tree analysis. Counterpane provides a comprehensive threat analysis of systems and products, which can determine a system's vulnerability and the avenues of attack most likely to succeed.

- Product research and forecasting to assess potential product ideas and offer opinions on their viability in the marketplace. Counterpane also publishes reports on different areas of commercial cryptography—electronic commerce, Internet security, PKI (Public Key Infrastructure), and secure tokens.

- Classes and training, ranging from daylong classes on the basics of computer security to weeklong classes on the mathematics of cryptography or the philosophy of secure system design. Other classes include advanced protocol design and analysis, Internet security protocols, PKI, and electronic commerce security.

- Intellectual property opinions on patentability and prior art on cryptographic systems, and help in finding ways to implement systems that avoid infringing on existing patents. Counterpane maintains a database of over 1,000 cryptography-related patents.

- Export consulting to help you through the process of receiving Commodity Jurisdictions (rights to export) from the U.S. Department of State, and getting U.S. Department of Commerce approval for products for export.

URL: *www.counterpane.com*

DELOITTE AND TOUCHE'S SECURE e-BUSINESS

Deloitte and Touche is one of the Big Six accounting and consulting groups in the United States. Deloitte and

Touche's Secure e-Business practice helps you to identify risks and opportunities, implement e-business solutions, and manage the system(s). The firm assists companies in the following ways:

- Developing e-business strategies and communities
- Implementing secure applications
- Implementing a secure infrastructure
- Security management
- Security testing and assurance
- Privacy and regulatory compliance
- Product evaluations
- Research and development

URL: *www.dttus.com/Risk/ebusiness/services.htm*

ERNST & YOUNG'S eSECURITY SOLUTIONS

Ernst & Young (E&Y) is another of the Big Six accounting and consulting firms. Ernst & Young's eSecurity Solutions practice consists of three major sections:

1. Security Profiling Services helps you to create a "blueprint" of vulnerabilities within your company and provides you with detailed technical, procedural, and strategic recommendations to reduce the exposures found. Top-to-bottom assessments of external and internal access are also performed to test the effectiveness of your current position in addressing security risks and exposures.
2. Security Architecture Services helps you to determine the systemic causes of the vulnerabilities identified, and helps you to develop risk-based strategic plans and solutions to assure that security risks are addressed. Security architectures developed can then be implemented by you or by E&Y's specialized security practitioners.

3. Security Implementation Services helps you to manage and control your network through the implementation of security solutions that you select.

URL: *www.ey.com*

INFOSEC LABS INC.

InfoSec Labs (formerly Miora Systems Consulting) helps you to protect your information by providing expertise in the areas of Internet and information security, electronic commerce, and related areas. InfoSec Labs serves a wide variety of industries, including financial services, manufacturing, warehousing and distribution, retail, and service companies. Some of the assistance that InfoSec Labs offers includes:

- Security assessment to protect you against losses caused by invaders to your system from the outside or from within. Assessments are composed of a threat analysis, vulnerability and risk assessment, countermeasure development, and recommendations.
- Virus assessments to help you locate, eradicate, and strengthen your levels of protection against computer viruses.
- Security policy development to create the policies that you need to protect your company against unintentional actions that could lead to liabilities and vulnerabilities.
- Disaster recovery assessments to help you examine your current procedures and operations to determine if critical operations can continue in the face of a disaster.
- Disaster recovery planning to help you to bridge the gap between disaster and rapid hot site recovery. Included are disaster recovery plans and procedures.
- Firewall verification to simulate attacks launched from within by trusted personnel and externally by hackers and crackers. These tests help ensure that

firewall rule bases are simple and appropriate to minimize vulnerabilities. Another goal of the entire testing process is to determine the organizational ability to detect and react to potential attacks.

- PBX (Private Branch Exchange) and war-dialing attacks to scan company telephone exchanges to catalog modem and fax connections. As modem connections are discovered, attempts to exploit the modems are carried out to see the extent of their vulnerability.
- Ongoing evaluations and readiness testing, which consists of biannual evaluations and disaster recovery exercises to help prevent the degradation in plans and procedures that occurs over time when they fail to correspond to system evolution and growth.
- User education and awareness programs to keep your employees aware of risks and threats. InfoSec Labs offers online courses via the Internet and in-house seminars to help raise and maintain security awareness.
- Security education to help system administrators, help desk personnel, and others learn effective security practices on specific platforms and systems.

URL: *www.miora.com*

LOpht HEAVY INDUSTRIES

LOpht Heavy Industries is a unique group of hackers turned consultants. They have developed a reputation placing them among the leading security specialists. Some of the services they offer to commercial businesses include:

- Consulting on security audits (penetration testing), cryptographic research, establishing a corporate security effort, and review of company security business plans.
- Source code security review to locate and identify se-

curity vulnerabilities (such as buffer overflows or the use of insecure libraries) on customer-developed computer programs to catch problems before production uses.

- Product assessment on equipment and software loaned to LOpht Heavy Industries for security reviews of the system or product.

URL: *www.LOpht.com/*

NETWORK ASSOCIATES GLOBAL PROFESSIONAL SERVICES

Network Associates Global Professional Services consists of three service groups:

1. Professional Consulting assists businesses with network development and security from the planning phase through ongoing management of the network. They specialize in NT network architecture design and implementation, managed security, and custom consulting.
2. Educational Services includes Sniffer University, Trusted Information Systems consulting services, McAfee University, and Magic University for customer training in network protocol analysis and troubleshooting, security, help desk, and network management.
3. Product Support offers FTP (File Transfer Protocol) and Web-based support including downloadable fixes to security and virus threats, technical documents, and twenty-four-hour customer service.

URL: *www.nai.com/asp_set/about_nai/products_ services/global_professional_services.asp*

NETWORK SECURITY LABORATORIES, INC. (NSLI)

Network Security Laboratories, Inc. (NSLI) is a consulting firm specializing in information systems security. It was founded in 1991 and is headquartered in metropolitan Washington, D.C. Areas of expertise include:

- Operating system, network, and DBMS (Data Base Management System) security: Orange Book, TNI, TDI
- Federal infosec standards: FIPS (Federal Information Processing Standard) publications and regulations
- Internet firewalls, advanced authentication, encryption, VPN (Virtual Private Network), SmartCards
- Public key cryptography—PKI (Public Key Infrastructure)—and electronic commerce security
- Formal modeling of secure systems and cryptographic protocols
- UNIX kernel, TCP/IP (Transmission Control Protocol/Internet Protocol), and DBMS internals
- Commercial software product internals development

Among typical projects are:

- Design of secure systems and intranets
- Integration of security products: firewalls, Kerberos, authentication services
- Risk analysis, security plans, vulnerability studies, and penetration testing
- Certification and accreditation of networks and Web sites
- Secure operation and disaster recovery
- Data integrity and assurance: antivirus, Y2K
- NCSC (National Computer Security Center), TCSEC (Trusted Computer Security Evaluation Criteria), and ITSEC (Information Technology Security Evaluation Criteria)
- UNIX-based product internals engineering
- Secure systems integration, management, and proposal support
- Custom software development

- Parser, compiler, and interpreter development: yacc, lex
- "Expert witness" litigation support

URL: *www.nsli.com/*

SECURE COMPUTING CORPORATION

Secure Computing Corporation is headquartered in San Jose, California, and is a provider of network perimeter security to the U.S. federal government. It is the second largest provider of identification and authentication solutions and the third largest provider of firewalls. Secure Computing's SecureZone firewalls are the first of the next generation of firewalls that use role-based access control and policy management. Among Secure Computing's network security solutions are:

- Firewalls
- Identification
- Authentication
- Authorization
- Web productivity
- Extranet Web access and authorization

URL: *www.securecomputing.com*

SecureIT

SecureIT, a subsidiary of VeriSign, focuses on Internet and enterprise security. It provides a wide range of services and products to help companies with designing, implementing, and assessing security solutions. Some of the services offered by SecureIT include:

- Security policy creation and maintenance
- Network and firewall architecture and design
- Securing a compromised network following an attack

- PKI (Public Key Infrastructure) development and training
- VPN (Virtual Private Network) implementation and testing
- Certified training for Check Point FireWall-1

URL: *www.secureit.com/*

TRIDENT DATA SYSTEMS

Trident was founded in 1975 and offers a wide variety of comprehensive network security services to the U.S. government, intelligence communities, and commercial organizations. Trident's knowledge gained from the government sector provides commercial customers with a comprehensive suite of secure technology solutions. Trident has offices in Los Angeles, metropolitan Washington, D.C., Texas, Colorado, and Florida. It offers a range of professional consulting and support services to help companies to communicate and use their computer systems securely. Trident helps organizations with:

- Implementation of network security measures and technologies
- Firewall implementation and training
- Risk management
- Security policy development
- Systems security integration

URL: *www.tds.com*

Appendix D

Suggested Readings

The following list of books is offered to help you build a complete library on information security, which no single book could possibly provide.

Applied Cryptography: Protocols, Algorithms, and Source Code in C, 2nd ed. by Bruce Schneier (New York: John Wiley & Sons, 1995)

Bruce Schneier's *Applied Cryptography: Protocols, Algorithms, and Source Code in C* offers an authoritative introduction to the field of cryptography, suitable for both the specialist and the general reader. The book adopts an encyclopedic approach to cryptographic systems throughout history, from ciphers to public key cryptography. Schneier also outlines cryptographic protocols—the steps required for secure encryption—with the precision of a chess master.

Readable, instructive, and truly exhaustive, this text is a must for anyone wanting a solid introduction to the field in a single volume. *Applied Cryptography* presents the source code for most algorithms and other procedures in C rather than using pure math. The book also includes source code for the Data Encryption Standard (DES) and other algorithms, but readers don't need to know programming to benefit from this text. With a truly comprehensive bibliography of over 1,600 entries, *Applied Cryptography* provides the reader with plenty of sources for more information.

At Large: The Strange Case of the World's Biggest Internet Invasion by David H. Freedman and Charles C. Mann (New York: Simon & Schuster, 1977)

This story centers on the exploits of a young hacker, known as both phantomd and Infomaster, and the terror he inflicts on computer systems worldwide. The essential question raised by Freedman and Mann is: If phantomd, who is both physically and mentally handicapped, can penetrate into university, corporation, and military systems through sheer tenacity, what will stop the legions of better equipped, more intelligent cybercriminals from doing far worse? Their conclusion is not pretty.

Building Internet Firewalls by D. Brent Chapman, Elizabeth D. Zwicky, and Deborah Russell (editor) (Cambridge, Mass.: O'Reilly & Associates, 1995)

 Building Internet Firewalls is a practical guide to building firewalls on the Internet. If your site is connected to the Internet, or if you're considering getting connected, you need this book. It describes a variety of firewall approaches and architectures and discusses how you can build packet filtering and proxying solutions at your site. It also contains a full discussion of how to configure Internet services—e.g., FTP (File Transfer Protocol), SMTP (Simple Mail Transport Protocol), Telnet—to work with a firewall. The book also includes a complete list of resources, including the location of many publicly available firewall construction tools.

Building SET Applications for Secure Transactions by Mark S. Merkow, James Breithaupt, and Ken Wheeler (New York: John Wiley & Sons, 1998)

 The authors of *Building SET Applications for Secure Transactions* show you why the Secure Electronic Transaction (SET) standard makes secure e-commerce a reality. This wide-ranging text informs information systems (IS) managers what SET is, how it works, and how to implement a secure commerce system on their Web sites. The book's strength is its wide-ranging perspective on e-commerce and how it fits into traditional business systems. Several chapters provide checklists for the IS manager considering the move toward the Web for commerce. Analyzing and designing, planning for security, and testing are just some of the issues that must be faced when implementing a successful e-business. Clearly, SET is not a magic bullet against fraud, but the authors show why the future of electronic commerce is bright.

Client/Server Survival Guide, 3rd ed. by Robert Orfali, Dan Harkey, and Jeri Edwards (New York: John Wiley & Sons, 1999)

 With this new edition, Orfali, Harkey, and Edwards fully update their classic book with information on the many new technologies that have emerged in the last two years that are reshaping the client/server industry. The book includes coverage of JavaBeans, Dynamic HTML (HyperText Markup Language), XML (eXtensible Markup Language), Windows NT 5.0, and Object Transaction Monitors.

The Code Book: The Evolution of Secrecy from Mary, Queen of Scots to Quantum Cryptography by Simon Singh (New York: Doubleday Books, 1999)

People love secrets, and ever since the first word was written, humans have written coded messages to each other. In *The Code Book*, Simon Singh, author of the best-selling *Fermat's Enigma*, offers a peek into the world of cryptography and codes, from ancient texts through computer encryption. Singh's compelling history is woven through with stories of how codes and ciphers have played a vital role in warfare, politics, and royal intrigue. The major theme of *The Code Book* is what Singh calls "the ongoing evolutionary battle between codemakers and codebreakers," never more clear than in the chapters devoted to World War II. Cryptography came of age during that conflict, as secret communications became critical to either side's success.

In the information age, the fear that drives cryptographic improvements is both capitalistic and libertarian—corporations need competitors and regulators, and ordinary people need encryption to keep their everyday communications private in a free society. Similarly, the battles for greater decryption power come from said competitors and governments wary of insurrection. *The Code Book* is an excellent primer for those wishing to understand how the human need for privacy has manifested itself through cryptography. Singh's accessible style and clear explanations of complex algorithms cut through the arcane mathematical details without oversimplifying.

Computer Communications Security: Principles, Standard Protocols and Techniques by Warwick Ford (New York: Prentice-Hall, 1994)

This book identifies and explains all the modern standardized methods of achieving network security in both TCP/IP (Transmission Control Protocol/Internet Protocol) and OSI (Open Systems Interconnection) environments, with a focus on intersystem, as opposed to intrasystem, security functions. Part I is a technical tutorial introduction to computer network security; Part II describes security standards, protocols, and techniques. The book covers such topics as cryptography, authentication, access control, and nonrepudiation; describes a wide range of standard security protocols and techniques, drawn from international, national, government, and Internet standards; and considers areas such as network and transport layer security, local area network security, security management, and security for applications such as electronic mail, directory services, EDI (Electronic Data Interchange), and banking.

Computer Networks: Protocols, Standards and Interface by Uyless D. Black (New York: Prentice-Hall, 1993)

This book offers a succinct tutorial on the major types of networks in use today for anyone involved in programming or purchasing. Each chapter describes a major computer network technology and covers the latest developments and specific protocols. This is written for a wide audience; an electronic engineering or math background is not necessary.

The Cuckoo's Egg: Tracking a Spy through the Maze of Computer Espionage by Clifford Stoll (New York: Pocket Books, 1995)

A sentimental favorite, *The Cuckoo's Egg* seems to have inspired a whole category of books exploring the quest to capture computer criminals. Still, even several years after its initial publication and after much imitation, the book remains a good read with an engaging story line and a critical outlook, as Stoll becomes, almost unwillingly, a one-man security force trying to track down faceless criminals who've invaded the university computer lab he stewards. What first appears as a 75-cent accounting error in a computer log is eventually revealed to be a ring of industrial espionage, primarily thanks to Stoll's persistence and intellectual tenacity.

Cyberpunk: Outlaws and Hackers on the Computer Frontier by Katie Hafner and John Markoff (Carmichael, Calif.: Touchstone Books, 1995)

A classic look into cracker subculture, *Cyberpunk* tells the stories of notorious hackers Kevin Mitnick, Robert T. Morris, and the Chaos Computer Club. Like *Where Wizards Stay Up Late*, the book Hafner cowrote on the origins of the Internet, *Cyberpunk* is informative, well-written, and entertaining. The story of Morris, who became infamous for unleashing a crippling worm that brought the Internet to a grinding standstill, is still as relevant and ominous today as it was at the time. The space devoted to Mitnick is a must-read companion to either of the books *Takedown* or *The Fugitive Game*. Many of the stories surrounding the Dark Side Hacker, such as the story of his NORAD (North American Air Defense Command) break-in, are called into question in *Cyberpunk*, making this book a good launching pad for many different accounts of the Mitnick legend. The portrait of the two members of the Chaos Computer Club is a memorable look into the minds of the younger generation of computer hackers.

Digital Cash: Commerce on the Net, 2nd ed. by Peter Wayner (San Francisco: Morgan Kaufmann Publishers, 1997)

This second edition of the highly acclaimed *Digital Cash* is an updated and comprehensive guide to exchanging money over the Net. The changes in this new edition are based on the excellent user feedback received and encompass dozens of new topics and expansion of chapters from the first edition. The enclosed DOS disk contains CGI (Common Gateway Interface) scripts and demos of digital cash software.

E-Commerce Security: Weak Links, Best Defenses by Anup K. Ghosh (New York: John Wiley & Sons, 1998)

Online security investigator and research scientist Anup Ghosh takes a realistic look at the state of security for electronic commerce. He is neither a Pollyanna believing that all is fine nor a doomsayer predicting catastrophe for transactions lacking virtual plate armor. In fact, he feels that some levels of security are excessive. But he emphasizes that any security system is only as strong as its weakest point. If you're going to trust your money to online transactions, you need to know where your weaknesses lie and how to correct them.

To that end, Ghosh discusses real-life security failures, how they occurred, and how recurrences can be prevented. He then takes a systematic look at the areas of risk. One chapter deals with potential problems in active Web content, such as Java applets, ActiveX controls, and push technology. He examines data protocols to secure transactions with the warning that the data can be vulnerable before and after the secure transmission. The weaknesses of server hardware and software come under scrutiny as well. Ghosh calls for greater attention to security as software is being developed and looks at what advances are likely to be coming down the road.

Fermat's Enigma: The Epic Quest to Solve the World's Greatest Mathematical Problem by Simon Singh and John Lynch (New York: Bantam Books, 1998)

$$x^n + y^n = z^n, \text{ where n represents } 3,4,5, \ldots \text{ no solution}$$

"I have discovered a truly marvelous demonstration of this proposition which this margin is too narrow to contain." With these words, the 17th-century French mathematician Pierre de Fermat threw down the gauntlet to future generations. What came to be known as Fermat's Last Theorem looked simple; proving it, however, became the Holy Grail of mathematics, baffling its finest minds for more than 350 years. In *Fermat's Enigma*—based on the author's award-winning documentary film, which aired on PBS's *Nova*—Simon Singh tells the astonishingly entertaining story of the pursuit of that Grail, and the lives that were devoted to, sacrificed for, and saved by it. Here is a mesmerizing tale of heartbreak and mastery that will forever change your feelings about mathematics.

Hackers: Crime in the Digital Sublime by Paul A. Taylor (New York: Routledge, 1999)

The practice of computer hacking is increasingly being viewed as a major security dilemma in Western societies, by governments and security experts alike. Using material taken from interviews with a wide range of interested parties, such as computer scientists, security experts, and hackers themselves, Paul Taylor provides a revealing and richly sourced account of the debates that surround this controversial practice. By doing so, he reveals the dangers inherent in the extremes of conciliation and antagonism with which society reacts to hacking and argues that a new middle way must be found if we are to make the most of society's high-tech meddlers.

Hacking Exposed: Network Security Secrets and Solutions by Stuart Mc-Clure, Joel Scambray, and George Kurtz (Berkeley, Calif.: Computing McGraw-Hill, 1999)

Whenever Hollywood does a movie in which someone breaks into a computer, the hacking scenes are completely laughable to anyone who knows the first thing about computer security. Think of *Hacking Exposed: Network Security Secrets and Solutions* as a computer thriller for people with a clue. Certainly, this is a technical book—URLs (Uniform Resource Locators), procedures, and bits of advice take the place of plot and characters—but the information about hackers' tools will leave you wondering exactly how vulnerable your system is. More to the point, the explicit instructions for stealing supposedly secure information (a Windows NT machine's Security Access Manager file, for example) will leave you absolutely certain that your computers have gaping holes in their armor.

The book describes the security characteristics of several computer-industry pillars, including Windows NT, UNIX, Novell NetWare, and certain firewalls. It also explains what sorts of attacks against these systems are feasible, which are popular, and what tools exist to make them easier. The authors walk the reader through numerous attacks, explaining exactly what attackers want, how they defeat the relevant security features, and what they do once they've achieved their goal. In what might be called after-action reports, countermeasures that can help steer "bad boys" toward less well-defended prey are explained.

ICSA Guide to Cryptography by Randall K. Nichols (New York: McGraw-Hill Text, 1998)

This book provides a survey of the principles and practice of cryptography with respect to business applications and, more specifically, commercial computer systems. The business value gained from implementation of cryptographic countermeasures is discussed. Other issues covered include processes, protocols, key management, implementation mistakes, and product certification. An enclosed CD-ROM contains a variety of papers and materials regarding cryptography and cryptographic products.

Intrusion Detection: Network Security Beyond the Firewall by Terry Escamilla (New York: John Wiley & Sons, 1998)

This superior text on computer security is extremely rich in information, based on experience, and a pleasure to read. In addition, the author is donating part of his royalties from this book to various charities—initially, a foundation that fights child abuse.

Escamilla begins by exploring intrusion prevention systems—firewalls, user authentication routines, and access controls—and telling how to set up such systems properly. He then describes mechanisms that identify and minimize damage caused by electronic break-ins once they occur. The author covers both system-level and network-level intrusion/detection systems, describing tools that attempt to catch not only outsiders who have broken in but also legitimate system users who are up to no good. Escamilla details several anti-intruder tools, including packet sniffers and vulnerability scanners. He describes a lot of UNIX hacks and tells what you can do to prevent them from taking place on your systems. Other chapters focus on intrusions in Windows NT environments and what to do when your system is under attack. Escamilla closes with references to other sources.

Maximum Security: A Hacker's Guide to Protecting Your Internet Site and Network by Anonymous (Indianapolis: Sams Publishing, 1998)

This book is written for system administrators who need to know how to keep their systems secure from unauthorized use. The anonymous author takes a hacker's view of various systems, focusing on how the system can be cracked and how you can secure the vulnerable areas.

The book makes it clear from the outset that you cannot rely on commercial software for security. Some of it is flawed, and even the best of it has to be used correctly to provide even the most basic security measures. The author scrutinizes such operating systems as Microsoft Windows, UNIX, Novell, and Macintosh. He details many of the tools crackers use to attack the system, including several that have legitimate uses for system administration. Rather than merely cataloging areas of risk and showing how various flaws can be exploited, the author makes every effort to show how security holes can be avoided and remedied. *Maximum Security* tells you which software to avoid and then details which security tools are invaluable, providing the URLs (Uniform Resource Locators) necessary to acquire them. An enclosed CD-ROM provides links to many of the tools and resources discussed in the book. The CD-ROM also leads you to several online documents where you can learn more about Internet security in general and specifics for securing your own site.

The Privacy Rights Handbook: How to Take Control of Your Personal Information by Beth Givens (New York: Avon Books, 1997)

The Privacy Rights Handbook gives you all the information you need to be aware of threats to your privacy and to be assertive about safeguarding it. You'll learn how to find out what's in your credit and medical reports (and correct damaging mistakes); put an end to junk mail and telemarketing calls; reduce the chances that someone will "steal" your identity; keep your online activities safe from prying eyes; question requests for unnecessarily detailed information from business or government; and much more. Givens is founder and director of the Privacy Rights Clearinghouse, a nonprofit program based in San Diego.

Security Issues for the Internet and the World Wide Web by Debra Cameron (Charleston, S.C.: Computer Technology Research Corporation, 1996)

This is a report designed to assist management in deciding how to address the issue of Internet security and to determine what security approaches are appropriate for a given organization. An executive summary is followed by chapters addressing Internet security risks, encryption technology, digital signatures and authentication, creating a shield for corporate systems (firewalls), security scanners and other approaches, transaction security for electronic commerce, security for the Web and other information services, and developing security policies and procedures. It includes several appendices, including Internet resources for security administrators and a CERT (Computer Emergency Response Team) incident report form, a bibliography, and an extensive glossary of terms.

Virtual Private Networks for Dummies by Mark Merkow (Indianapolis: IDG Books Worldwide, 1999)

Virtual Private Networks let you create a secure business network over the Internet and avoid the expense of dedicated access lines. This friendly guide walks you through this complex technology and leads you to a VPN solution that's just right for your business.

Appendix E

Glossary of Terms

The following glossary of terms is excerpted and adapted from a computer security glossary prepared by the U.S. National Security Agency (NSA). In April 1998, the NSA completed this glossary for use in computer security and intrusion detection activities. The work, done primarily by Greg Stocksdale of the NSA Information Systems Security Organization, is comprehensive, accurate, and useful.

Because of the value of a comprehensive security glossary, the System Administration, Networking, and Security (SANS) Institute is operating a communitywide program to expand and update the glossary on a continuing basis. A copy of the complete database is available in MS Access with built-in queries. For an updated copy of this glossary, visit SANS at: *www.sans.org/netlook/resources/glossary.htm.*

active attack   An attack that results in an unauthorized state change, such as the manipulation of files or the adding of unauthorized files.

administrative security   The management constraints and supplemental controls established to provide an acceptable level of protection for data. Also called *procedural security.*

AIS   Automated information system, any equipment within an interconnected system or subsystems of equipment that is used in the automatic acquisition, storage, manipulation, control, display, transmission, or reception of data. This includes software, firmware, and hardware.

alert   A formulated message describing a circumstance relevant to network security. Alerts are often derived from critical audit events.

ankle-biter   A person who aspires to be a hacker/cracker but has very limited knowledge or skills related to AISs. Usually associated with young teens who collect and use simple malicious programs obtained from the Internet.

anomaly detection model   A model where intrusions are detected by looking for activity that is different from the user's or system's normal behavior.

application-level gateway   A firewall system in which service is provided by processes that maintain complete TCP connection state and sequencing. Application-level gateways often readdress traffic so that outgoing traffic appears to have originated from the firewall, rather than the internal host.

ASIM Automated Security Incident Measurement, software that monitors network traffic and collects information on targeted unit networks by detecting unauthorized network activity.

assessment Surveys and inspections done to provide an analysis of the vulnerabilities of an AIS. The information acquisition and review process designed to assist a customer to determine how best to use resources to protect information in systems.

assurance A measure of confidence that the security features and architecture of an AIS accurately mediate and enforce the security policy.

attack An attempt to bypass security controls on a computer. The attack may alter, release, or deny data. Whether an attack succeeds depends on the vulnerability of the computer system and the effectiveness of existing countermeasures.

audit The independent examination of records and activities to ensure compliance with established controls, policy, and operational procedures, and to recommend any indicated changes in controls, policy, or procedures.

audit trail In computer security systems, a chronological record of system resource usage. This includes user login, file access, various other activities, and whether any actual or attempted security violations occurred, legitimate and/or unauthorized.

authenticate To establish the validity of a claimed user or object.

authentication To positively verify the identity of a user, device, or other entity in a computer system, often as a prerequisite to allowing access to resources in a system.

Authentication Header (AH) A field that immediately follows the IP (Internet Protocol) header in an IP datagram and provides authentication and integrity checking for the datagram.

automated information system See AIS.

automated security monitoring All security features needed to provide an acceptable level of protection for hardware, software, and classified, sensitive, unclassified, or critical data, material, or processes in the system.

availability The assurance that information and communications services will be ready for use when expected.

back door   A hole in the security of a computer system deliberately left in place by designers or maintainers; a hidden software or hardware mechanism used to circumvent security controls. Synonymous with *trap door.*

bomb   A general synonym for crash, normally said of software or operating system failures.

breach   The successful defeat of security controls that could result in a penetration of the system. A violation of controls of a particular information system such that information assets or system components are unduly exposed.

buffer overflow   What happens when more data is put into a buffer or holding area than the buffer can handle. This occurs because of a mismatch in processing rates between the producing and consuming processes. It can result in system crashes or the creation of a back door leading to system access.

bug   An unwanted and unintended property of a program or piece of hardware, especially one that causes it to malfunction.

Certificate Authority (CA)   Trusted parties who operate on the behalf of the corporation to manage the distribution and currency of X.509 digital certificates. Each layer in a tree of trust is represented by a well-defined certificate authority.

Certification Revocation List (CRL)   A mechanism that X.509 Public Key Infrastructures use to ensure that revoked certificates cannot be used for access or transacting. CRLs contain revoked certificate serial numbers, their date of revocation, the date the CRL was generated, its expiration date, issuer name, and serial number of the CA certificate used to sign it.

CGI   Common Gateway Interface, the method that Web servers use to allow interaction between servers and programs.

CGI scripts   Allow for the creation of dynamic and interactive Web pages. They tend to be the most vulnerable part of a Web server (besides the underlying host security).

Chernobyl packet   A network packet that induces a broadcast storm and network meltdown. Typically an IP (Internet Protocol) Ethernet datagram that passes through a gateway, with both the source and destination Ethernet and IP address set as the respective broadcast addresses for the subnetworks being gated between.

circuit level gateway   One form of a firewall. Validates TCP and UDP (User Datagram Protocol) sessions before opening a connection. It creates a handshake, and once that takes place, passes everything through until the session is ended.

cleartext   See plaintext.

Clipper chip   A tamper-resistant Very Large Scale Integration (VLSI) chip designed by the National Security Agency for encrypting voice communications. It conforms to the Escrow Encryption Standard (EES) and implements the Skipjack encryption algorithm.

COAST   Computer Operations, Audit, and Security Technology, a computer security research institute at the Computer Sciences Department at Purdue University. Its research focuses on real-world needs with a special focus on security for computing systems.

common criteria   A collective set of international information systems security requirements, expressed in terms of evaluation assurance levels (EALs) needed to ascertain a security product's ability to protect a computer-based information system. Also known as ISO 15408.

Common Gateway Interface (CGI)   A standard method of invoking a program that runs on a Web server through the uses of Web-based forms.

Common Vulnerabilities and Exposures list (CVE)   An initiative led by MITRE Corporation to define a common taxonomy for known Internet- and TCP/IP-based problems and exploits.

compromise   An intrusion into a computer system where unauthorized disclosure, modification, or destruction of sensitive information may have occurred.

computer abuse   The willful or negligent unauthorized activity that affects the availability, confidentiality, or integrity of computer resources. It includes fraud, embezzlement, theft, malicious damage, unauthorized use, denial of service, and misappropriation.

computer fraud   Computer-related crimes involving deliberate misrepresentation or alteration of data in order to obtain something of value.

Computer Network Attack (CNA)   Operations to disrupt, deny, degrade, or destroy information resident in computers and computer networks, or such operations directed at the computers and networks themselves.

computer security   Technological and managerial procedures applied to computer systems to ensure the availability, integrity, and confidentiality of information managed by the computer system.

computer security incident   Any intrusion or attempted intrusion into an AIS. Incidents can include probes of multiple computer systems.

computer security intrusion Any event of unauthorized access or penetration to an AIS.

confidentiality The assurance that information will be kept secret, with access limited to appropriate persons.

COTS software Commercial off-the-shelf software, sold through a commercial vendor. This software is a standard product, not developed by a vendor for a particular project or business.

countermeasure An action, device, procedure, technique, or other measure that reduces the vulnerability of an AIS. Countermeasures that are aimed at specific threats and vulnerabilities involve more sophisticated techniques as well as activities traditionally perceived as security.

Crack A popular hacking tool used to decode encrypted passwords. System administrators also use Crack to assess weak passwords by novice users in order to enhance the security of an AIS.

cracker One who breaks security on an AIS.

cracking The act of breaking into a computer system.

crash A sudden, usually drastic failure of a computer system.

cryptanalysis (1) The analysis of a cryptographic system and/or its inputs and outputs to derive confidential variables and/or sensitive data including cleartext. (2) Operations performed in converting encrypted messages to plaintext without initial knowledge of the crypto-algorithm and/or key employed in the encryption.

Cryptographic Hash Function A process that computes a value (referred to as a *hashword*) from a particular data unit in a manner such that, when the hashword is protected, manipulation of the data is detectable.

cryptography The art or science concerning the principles, means, and methods for rendering plaintext unintelligible and for converting encrypted messages into intelligible form.

cryptology The science that deals with hidden, disguised, or encrypted communications.

cyberspace The world of connected computers and the society that gathers around them. Commonly known as the Internet.

daemon A *helper* program, typically associated with the UNIX operating system, that serves a special service on a specified open network port.

Dark-side hacker A criminal or malicious hacker.

DARPA   Defense Advanced Research Projects Agency, responsible for overseeing the developoment of what has become today's Internet.

data driven attack   A form of attack that is encoded in innocuous-seeming data, which is executed by a user or a process to implement an attack. A data driven attack is a concern for firewalls, since it may get through the firewall in data form and launch an attack against a system behind the firewall.

Data Encryption Standard (DES)   (1) An unclassified crypto-algorithm adopted by the National Bureau of Standards for public use. (2) A cryptographic algorithm for the protection of unclassified data, published in Federal Information Processing Standard (FIPS) 46. The DES, which was approved by the National Institute of Standards and Technology (NIST), is intended for public and government use.

demon dialer   A program that repeatedly calls the same telephone number. This is benign and legitimate for access to a BBS (bulletin board system), or malicious when used as a denial of service attack.

denial of service   An action that prevents any part of an AIS from functioning in accordance with its intended purpose.

derf   The act of exploiting a terminal that someone else has absent-mindedly left logged-on.

digital certificate   A certificate of authentication using Public-Private Key (PPK) cryptography to identify people, privileges, and relationships.

DNS spoofing   Assuming the DNS (Domain Name Service) name of another system by either corrupting the name service cache of a victim system, or by compromising a domain name server for a valid domain.

Encapsulating Security Protocol (ESP)   A mechanism to provide confidentiality and integrity protection to IP (Internet Protocol) datagrams.

Ethernet   The mostly widely implemented local area network (LAN) technology, originally developed by Xerox Corporation, DEC, and Intel in 1976.

Ethernet sniffing   Listening with software to the Ethernet interface for packets that interest the user. When the software sees a packet that fits certain criteria, it logs it to a file. The most common criteria for an interesting packet is one that contains words like *login* or *password.*

false negative   What occurs when an actual intrusive action has occurred but the system allows it to pass as nonintrusive behavior.

false positive   What occurs when the system classifies an action as anomalous (a possible intrusion) when it is a legitimate action.

fault tolerance   The ability of a system or component to continue normal operation despite the presence of hardware or software faults.

firewall   A system or combination of systems that enforces a boundary between two or more networks; a gateway that limits access between networks in accordance with local security policy. The typical firewall is an inexpensive micro-based UNIX box kept clean of critical data, with many modems and public network ports on it, but just one carefully watched connection back to the rest of the cluster.

fishbowl   To contain, isolate, and monitor an unauthorized user within a system in order to gain information about the user.

fork bomb   Code that can be written in one line of code on any UNIX system. Used to recursively spawn copies of itself, it "explodes," eventually eating all the process table entries and effectively locking up the system. Also known as a *logic bomb.*

GUI   Graphical User Interface. It includes elements such as windows, pull-down menus, buttons, scroll bars, iconic images, wizards, the mouse, etc., which, along with a computer's input devices, is sometimes referred to as its "look-and-feel."

gateway   A hardware device that serves to bridge subnetworks or to translate protocols between networks.

gray hat hacker   A hacker who works on both sides of the law, identifying problems and sharing information about them with both professionals and malicious users.

hacker   A person who enjoys exploring the details of computers and programming systems and how to stretch their capabilities, as opposed to most users, who prefer to learn only the minimum necessary. Often a malicious or inquisitive meddler who tries to discover information by poking around.

hacking   Unauthorized use, or attempts to circumvent or bypass the security mechanisms of an information system or network.

hacking run   A hack session extended long outside normal working times, especially one longer than twelve hours.

host   A single computer or workstation. It can be connected to a network.

host based   Information, such as audit data from a single host, that may be used to detect intrusions.

HTML Hyper Text Markup Language, an elaborate protocol used by the Internet to control the appearance of Web pages.

HTTP Hyper Text Transfer Protocol. A "request-response" type protocol, which specifies that a client will open a connection to a server, then send a request using a very specific format. Used to access and retrieve URL-named resources.

IDEA International Data Encryption Algorithm, a private key encryption-decryption algorithm that uses a key that is twice the length of a DES (Data Encryption Standard) key.

IDIOT Intrusion Detection in Our Time, a system that detects intrusions using pattern-matching.

Information Assurance (IA) Information Operations that protect and defend information and information systems by ensuring their availability, integrity, authentication, confidentiality, and nonrepudiation. This includes providing for restoration of information systems by incorporating protection, detection, and reaction capabilities.

Information Operations (IO) Actions taken to affect adversary information and information systems while defending one's own information and information systems.

information security The result of any system of policies and/or procedures for identifying, controlling, and protecting from unauthorized disclosure any information whose protection is authorized by executive order or statute. Sometimes referred to as infosec.

information superiority The capability to collect, process, and disseminate an uninterrupted flow of information while exploiting or denying an adversary's ability to do the same.

integrity The assurance that information will not be accidentally or maliciously altered or destroyed.

Internet An international computer network connecting government agencies, universities, research institutions, businesses, and (most recently) individuals not affiliated with any of the above. The Internet started as a Defense Department research project to encourage communications between a few large university research computers, but it has grown to become a maze of millions of interconnected computer networks.

Internet Engineering Task Force (IETF) A loosely knit group of professionals from multiple disciplines who develop industry standards for the Internet and associated systems.

Internet Protocol (IP) Part of the Transmission Control Protocol/Internet Protocol (TCP/IP) suite of programs that implements open and standard network connectivity.

intranet Private uses of IP-based services (Web servers, etc.) without a connection to the public Internet.

intrusion Any set of actions that attempt to compromise the integrity, confidentiality, or availability of a resource.

intrusion detection Techniques that attempt to detect intrusion into a computer or network by observation of actions, security logs, or audit data. Detection of break-ins or attempts either manually or via software expert systems that operate on logs or other information available on the network.

IP Security (IPSec) A standard method, defined for IP Version 6, for building secure pipes using cryptography over public networks like the Internet. See VPN.

IP splicing/hijacking An action whereby an active, established session is intercepted and coopted by an unauthorized user. IP (Internet Protocol) splicing attacks can occur after an authentication has been made, permitting the attacker to assume the role of an already authorized user. Primary protections against IP splicing rely on encryption at the session or network layer.

IP spoofing An attack whereby a system attempts to illicitly impersonate another system by using the IP (Internet Protocol) network address.

key A symbol or sequence of symbols (or electrical or mechanical correlates of symbols) applied to text in order to encrypt or decrypt.

key escrow The system of giving a piece of a key to each of a certain number of trustees such that the entire key can be recovered with the collaboration of all the trustees.

keystroke monitoring A specialized form of audit trail software, or a specially designed device, that records every key struck by a user and every character of the response that the AIS returns to the user.

LAN Local area network, a computer communications system limited to no more than a few miles and using high-speed connections (2 to 100 megabits per second). A short-haul communications system that connects DP (data processing) devices in a building or group of buildings within a few square kilometers, including workstations, front-end processors, controllers, switches, and gateways.

leapfrog attack Use of user ID and password information obtained illicitly from one host to compromise another host. The act of Telneting through one or more hosts in order to preclude a trace (a standard cracker procedure). Also called *network weaving.*

letterbomb   A piece of e-mail containing live data intended to do malicious things to the recipient's machine or terminal. Under UNIX, a letterbomb can also try to get part of its contents interpreted as a shell command to the mailer. The results of this could range from silly to denial of service.

logic bomb   A resident computer program that, when executed, checks for a particular condition or particular state of the system; when satisfed, it triggers the perpretation of an unauthorized act. Also known as a *fork bomb.*

mailbomb   The mail sent to urge others to send massive amounts of e-mail to a single system or person, with the intent to crash the recipient's system. Mailbombing is widely regarded as a serious offense.

malicious code   Hardware, software, or firmware that is intentionally included in a system for an unauthorized purpose, e.g., a Trojan horse.

metric   A random variable x representing a quantitative measure accumulated over a period.

mimicking   See *Spoofing.*

Misuse Detection   A system that detects intrusions by looking for activity that corresponds to known intrusion techniques or system vulnerabilities. Also known as *Rules Based Detection.*

mockingbird   A computer program or process that mimics the legitimate behavior of a normal system feature (or other apparently useful function) but performs malicious activities once invoked by the user.

multihost based auditing   Using audit data from multiple hosts to detect intrusions.

Nak Attack   Negative Acknowledgment, a penetration technique that capitalizes on a potential weakness in an operating system that does not handle asynchronous interrupts properly and thus leaves the system in an unprotected state during such interrupts.

National Computer Security Center (NCSC)   A center that is responsible for encouraging the widespread availability of trusted computer systems throughout the federal government. Originally named the DoD (Department of Defense) Computer Security Center.

National Information Infrastructure (NII)   The nationwide interconnection of communications networks, computers, databases, and consumer electronics that make vast amounts of information available to users. The NII encompasses a wide range of equipment, including cameras, scanners, keyboards, fax machines, computers, switches, compact disks, videotape, audiotape, cable, wire, satellites, fiber-optic transmission lines, networks of all types, monitors, and printers. Both the friendly and adversary personnel who make decisions and handle the transmitted information constitute a critical component of the NII.

network Two or more machines interconnected for communications.

network based Network traffic data along with audit data from the hosts used to detect intrusions.

network level firewall A firewall in which traffic is examined at the network protocol (IP, or Internet Protocol) packet level.

network security The protection of networks and their services from unauthorized modification, destruction, or disclosure, and the provision of assurance that the network performs its critical functions correctly and there are no harmful side effects. Network security includes providing for data integrity.

network security officer The individual formally appointed by a desig nated approving authority to ensure that the provisions of all applicable directives are implemented throughout the life cycle of an AIS network.

network weaving See *leapfrog attack.*

nonrepudiation The method by which the sender of data is provided with proof of delivery and the recipient is assured of the sender's identity, so that neither can later deny having processed the data.

Open Buying on the Internet (OBI) A protocol that specifies the roles of participants who engage in business-to-business procurement via the Internet.

open security An environment that does not provide sufficient assurance that applications and equipment are protected against the introduction of malicious logic prior to or during the operation of a system.

open systems security Provision of tools for the secure internetworking of open systems.

Open Users Recommended Solutions (OURS) A Chicago-based committee of corporate users and computer vendors working to solve problems associated with large commercial computer installations.

operational data security The protection of data from accidental, unauthorized, or intentional modification, destruction, or disclosure during input, processing, or output operations.

Orange Book See *Trusted Computer Systems Evaluation Criteria.*

OSI Open Systems Interconnection, a set of internationally accepted and openly developed standards that meet the needs of network resource administration and integrated network utility.

packet A block of data sent over a network transmitting the identities of the sending and receiving stations, error-control information, and message.

packet filter A device that inspects each packet for user-defined content, such as an IP (Internet Protocol) address, but does not track the state of sessions. This is one of the least secure types of firewall.

packet filtering A feature incorporated into routers and bridges to limit the flow of information based on predetermined communications such as source, destination, or type of service being provided by the network. Packet filters let the administrator limit protocol-specific traffic to one network segment, isolate e-mail domains, and perform many other traffic control functions.

packet sniffer A device or program that monitors the data traveling between computers on a network.

passive attack An attack that does not result in an unauthorized state change, such as an attack that only monitors and/or records data.

passive threat The threat of unauthorized disclosure of information without changing the state of the system. A type of threat that involves the interception, not the alteration, of information.

PEM Privacy Enhanced Mail, an IETF (Internet Engineering Task Force) standard for secure electronic mail exchange.

penetration The successful unauthorized access to an automated system.

penetration signature The description of a situation or set of conditions in which a penetration could occur, of of system events that in conjunction can indicate the occurrence of a penetration in progress.

penetration testing The portion of security testing in which the evaluators attempt to circumvent the security features of a system. The evaluators can be assumed to use all system design and implementation documentation, which may include listings of system source code, manuals, and circuit diagrams. The evaluators work under the same constraints applied to ordinary users.

perimeter based security The technique of securing a network by controlling access to all entry and exit points of the network. Usually associated with firewalls and/or filters.

perpetrator The entity from the external environment that is taken to be the cause of a risk. An entity in the external environment that performs an attack, i.e., a hacker.

personnel security The procedures established to ensure that all personnel who have access to any classified information have the required authorizations as well as the appropriate clearances.

PGP Pretty Good Privacy, a freeware program primarily for secure electronic mail.

phage A program that modifies other programs or databases in unauthorized ways, especially one that propagates a virus Trojan horse.

PHF A phone book file demonstration program that hackers use to gain access to a computer system and potentially read and capture password files.

PHF hack A well-known and vulnerable CGI script that does not filter out special characters (such as a new line) input by a user.

phracker An individual who combines phone phreaking with computer hacking.

phreak(er) An individual fascinated by the telephone system. Commonly, an individual who uses his or her knowledge of the telephone system to make calls at the expense of another.

phreaking The art and science of cracking the phone network.

physical security The measures used to provide physical protection of resources against deliberate and accidental threats.

Ping of Death The use of ping with a packet size higher than 65,507. This will cause a denial of service. Ping is an ICMP command for testing the presence of a given IP address on a TCP/IP-based network.

piggy back The gaining of unauthorized access to a system via another user's legitimate connection.

plaintext Unencrypted data.

Private Key Cryptography An encryption methodology in which the encryptor and decryptor use the same key, which must be kept secret. This methodology is usually used only by a small group.

probe Any effort to gather information about a machine or its users for the apparent purpose of gaining unauthorized access to the system at a later date.

procedural security See *administrative security.*

profiles Patterns of a user's activity that can detect changes in normal routines.

promiscuous mode A mode that, when in use with an Ethernet inface, causes the interface to read all information (sniffer), regardless of its destination. Normally an Ethernet interface reads all address information and accepts follow-on packets only destined for itself.

protocol Agreed-upon methods of communications used by computers. A specification that describes the rules and procedures that products should follow to perform activities on a network, such as transmitting data. If they use the same protocols, products from different vendors should be able to communicate on the same network.

prowler A daemon that is run periodically to seek out and erase core files, truncate administrative log files, erase lost + found directories, and otherwise clean up network file systems.

proxy A firewall mechanism that replaces the IP (Internet Protocol) address of a host on the internal (protected) network with its own IP address for all traffic passing through it. A software agent that acts on behalf of a user, a typical proxy accepts a connection from a user, makes a decision as to whether or not the user or client IP address is permitted to use the proxy, perhaps does additional authentication, and then completes a connection on behalf of the user to a remote destination.

Public Key Cryptography A type of cryptography in which the encryption process is publicly available and unprotected, but in which a part of the decryption key is protected so that only a party with knowledge of both parts of the decryption process can decrypt the cipher text.

Public Key Cryptography Standards (PKCS) A family of public-key cryptography standards, which includes:

- Certification request syntax describing the rules and sets of attributes needed for a certificate request from a certificate authority.
- Cryptographic message syntax describing how to apply cryptography to data, including digital signatures and digital envelopes.
- Diffie-Hellman key agreements that define how two people, with no prior arrangements, can agree on a shared secret key that's known only between them and used for future encrypted communications.
- Extended certificate syntax permitting the addition of extensions to standard X.509 digital certificates. These extensions add information such as certificate usage policies, other identifying information, etc.
- Password-based encryption, which hides private keys when trans-

ferring them between computer systems, sometimes required under Public-Private Key Cryptography.

- Private-key information syntax describing how to include a private key along with algorithm information and a set of attributes offering a simple way of establishing trust in information provided,
- RSA encryption for the construction of digital signatures and digital envelopes.

Public Key Infrastructure (PKI) A policy and corresponding system that defines the uses of public key encryption for a specific organization. It describes the format of certificates and the functions of CAs in both the public and private sectors.

Public-Private Key (PPK) cryptography A scheme that uses a pair of asymmetric keys to encrypt and decrypt private messages.

RA Registration Authorities. Often a department within a corporation, which approves or rejects requests for digital certificates using systems and records of the corporation to determine rights and privileges.

RADIUS Remote Access Dial-In User Services. An authentication server that can be modified to different kinds of networks. It is popular because of the ease with which it interfaces with networks that have large modem pools.

Red Book See *Trusted Network Interpretation.*

replicator Any program that acts to produce copies of itself; examples include a program, a worm, a fork bomb, or a virus.

retro-virus A virus that waits until all possible backup media are infected too, so that it is not possible to restore the system to an uninfected state.

REXD A UNIX command that is the Sun RPC (Remote Procedure Call) server for remote program execution. This daemon is started by inetd (INternET Daemon) whenever a remote execution request is made.

risk assessment A study of vulnerabilities, threats, likelihood, loss, impact, and theoretical effectiveness of security measures. The process of evaluating threats and vulnerabilities, known and postulated, to determine expected loss and establish the degree of acceptability to system operations.

risk management The total process used to identify, control, and minimize the impact of uncertain events.

rootkit A hacker security tool that captures passwords and message traffic to and from a computer. A collection of tools that allows a hacker to provide a back door into a system, collect information on other systems on the network, mask the fact that the system is compromised, and much more. Rootkit is a classic example of Trojan horse software. It is available for a wide range of operating systems.

router   An interconnection device that is similar to a bridge but serves packets or frames containing certain protocols. Routers link LANs at the network layer.

routing control   The application of rules during the process of routing so as to choose or avoid specific networks, links, or relays.

RSA algorithm   A public key cryptographic algorithm that hinges on the assumption that the factoring of the product of two large primes is difficult. RSA stands for Rivest-Shamir-Aldeman, its inventors.

Rules Based Detection   The intrusion detection system that detects intrusions by looking for activity that corresponds to known intrusion techniques (signatures) or system vulnerabilities. Also known as *Misuse Detection.*

samurai   A hacker who hires out for legal cracking jobs, such as snooping for factions in corporate political fights, lawyers pursuing privacy rights and First Amendment cases, and other parties with legitimate reasons to need an electronic locksmith.

SATAN   Security Administrator Tool for Analyzing Networks, a tool for remotely probing and identifying the vulnerabilities of systems on IP (Internet Protocol) networks. A powerful freeware program that helps to identify system security weaknesses.

secure network server   A device that acts as a gateway between a protected enclave and the outside world.

secure shell   A completely encrypted shell connection between two machines protected by a super long pass-phrase.

security   A condition that results from the establishment and maintenance of protective measures that ensure a state of inviolability from hostile acts or influences.

security architecture   A detailed description of all aspects of a system that relate to security, along with a set of principles to guide the design. A security architecture describes how a system is put together to satisfy the security requirements.

security audit   A search through a computer system for security problems and vulnerabilities.

security countermeasures   Countermeasures that are aimed at specific threats and vulnerabilities or involve more active techniques as well as activities traditionally perceived as security.

security domains   The sets of objects that a subject has the ability to access.

security features   The security-relevant functions, mechanisms, and characteristics of AIS hardware and software.

security incident   Any act or circumstance that involves classified information that deviates from the requirements of governing security publications. Examples are compromise, possible compromise, inadvertent disclosure, and deviation.

security kernel   The hardware, firmware, and software elements of a Trusted Computing Base (TCB) that implement the reference monitor concept. It must mediate all accesses, be protected from modification, and be verifiable as correct.

security label   A piece of information that represents the sensitivity of a subject or object, such as its hierarchical classification (CONFIDENTIAL, SECRET, TOP SECRET), together with any applicable nonhierarchical security categories (e.g., sensitive compartmented information, critical nuclear weapon design information).

security level   The combination of a hierarchical classification and a set of nonhierarchical categories that represents the sensitivity of information.

security officer   The ADP (automated data processing) official having the designated responsibility for the security of an ADP system.

security perimeter   The boundary where security controls are in effect to protect assets.

security policies   The set of laws, rules, and practices that regulate how an organization manages, protects, and distributes sensitive information.

security policy model   A formal presentation of the security policy enforced by the system. It must identify the set of rules and practices that regulate how a system manages, protects, and distributes sensitive information.

security requirements   The types and levels of protection necessary for equipment, data, information, applications, and facilities.

security service   A service, provided by a layer of communicating open systems, that ensures adequate security of the systems or of data transfers.

security violation   An instance in which a user or other person circumvents or defeats the controls of a system to obtain unauthorized access to information contained therein or to system resources.

server A system that provides network service such as disk storage and file transfer, or a program that provides such a service. A kind of daemon that performs a service for the requester, which often runs on a computer other than the one which the server runs.

SET Secure Electronic Transactions. A specification developed jointly by Visa and Mastercard to ensure the security of electronic payments on the Internet.

Simple Network Management Protocol (SNMP) Software used to control network communications devices using TCP/IP.

SmartCard Closely resembles a regular plastic payment card, but also contains a semiconductor chip with logic and nonvolatile memory. It is used for a variety of purposes such as a stored value card.

Skipjack An encryption algorithm for the Clipper chip developed by the National Security Agency. The details of the algorithm are unpublished.

smurfing A denial of service attack in which an attacker spoofs the source address of an echo-request ICMP (Internet Control Message Protocol–ping) packet to the broadcast address for a network, causing the machines in the network to respond en masse to the victim, thereby clogging its network.

snarf To grap a large document or file for the purpose of using it, with or without the author's permission.

sneaker An individual hired to break into places in order to test their security. Analogous to *tiger team.*

sniffer A program to capture data across a computer network, used by hackers to capture user ID names and passwords. A software tool that audits and identifies network traffic packets. It is also used legitimately by network operations and maintenance personnel to troubleshoot network problems.

spam To crash a program by overrunning a fixed-size buffer with excessively large input data. Also, to cause a person or newsgroup to be flooded with irrelevant or inappropriate messages.

Spartan horse Similar to a Trojan horse, a Spartan horse program is intended to fool a user into surrendering access control information in order to hijack their identity, often for illicit uses.

spoofing Pretending to be someone else. The deliberate inducement of a user or a resource to take an incorrect action. An attempt to gain access to an AIS by pretending to be an authorized user. Impersonating, masquerading, and mimicking are forms of spoofing.

SSL Secure Sockets Layer, a session-layer protocol that provides authentication and confidentiality to applications.

subversion When an intruder modifies the operation of the intrusion detector to force false negatives to occur.

SYN flood A flooding of the SYN synchornize request queue, with the result that no new connection can be opened.

TCP/IP Transmission Control Protocol/Internet Protocol, the suite of protocols the Internet is based on.

tcpwrapper A software tool for security that provides additional network logging and restricts service access to authorized hosts by service.

Telnet A standard application that enables remote terminal connections via the network from user workstations.

terminal hijacking A method that allows an attacker, on a certain machine, to control any terminal session that is in progress. An attack hacker can send and receive terminal I/O (input/output) while a user is on the terminal.

threat The means through which the ability or intent of a threat agent to adversely affect an automated system, facility, or operation can be manifest. A potential violation of security.

threat agents Methods and things used to exploit a vulnerability in an information system, operation, or facility, such as fire or a natural disaster.

threat assessment The process of formally evaluating the degree of threat to an information system and describing the nature of the threat.

tiger A software tool that scans for system weaknesses.

tiger team Government- and industry-sponsored teams of computer experts who attempt to break down the defenses of computer systems in an effort to uncover and eventually patch security holes. Analogous to *sneaker.*

Tinkerbell program A monitoring program used to scan incoming network connections and generate alerts when calls are received from particular sites, or when logins are attempted using certain IDs.

topology The map or plan of a network. The physical topology describes how the wires or cables are laid out, and the logical or electrical topology describes how the information flows.

trace packet In a packet-switching network, a unique packet that causes a report of each stage of its progress to be sent to the network control center from each visited system element.

traceroute An operation of sending trace packets for determining information; it traces the route of UDP (User Datagram Protocol) packets from the local host to a remote host. Normally, a traceroute displays the time and location of the route taken to reach its destination computer.

trap door See back door.

tripwire A software tool for security. It works with a database that maintains information about the byte count of files. If the byte count has changed, it will identify it to the system security manager.

Trojan horse An apparently useful and innocent program containing additional hidden code that allows the unauthorized collection, exploitation, falsification, or destruction of data.

Trusted Computer Systems Evaluation Criteria (TCSEC) A system that employs sufficient hardware and software assurance measures to allow its use for simultaneous processing of a range of sensitive or classified information. Also called the Orange Book.

Trusted Computing Base (TCB) The totality of protection mechanisms within a computer system including hardware, firmware, and software, the combination of which are responsible for enforcing a security policy. A TCB consists of one or more components that together enforce a unified security policy over a product or system.

Trusted Network Interpretation The specific security features, the assurance requirements, and the rating structure of the Orange Book as extended to networks of computers ranging from isolated LANs to WANs. Also called the *Red Book*.

TTY watcher A hacker tool that allows hackers with even a small amount of skill to hijack terminals using a GUI (Graphical User Interface).

Vaccine A program that injects itself into an executable program to perform a signature check and warns if there have been any changes.

virus A program that can "infect" other programs by modifying them to include a possibly evolved copy of itself.

VPN Virtual Private Network. A connection that has the appearance and many of the advantages of a dedicated link, but occurs over a shared network. Using a technique called "tunneling," data packets are transmitted across a public routed network, such as the Internet or other commercially available network, in a private "tunnel," which simulates a point-to-point connection.

vulnerability   Hardware, firmware, or software flow that leaves an AIS open for potential exploitation. A weakness in automated system security procedures, administrative controls, physical layout, internal controls, and so forth, that could be exploited by a threat to gain unauthorized access to information or disrupt critical processing.

vulnerability analysis   The systematic examination of an AIS or product to determine the adequacy of security measures, identify security deficiencies, provide data from which to predict the effectiveness of proposed security measures, and confirm the adequacy of such measures after implementation.

WAIS   Wide Area Information Service, an Internet service that allows you to search a large number of specially indexed databases.

WAN   Wide area network, a physical or logical network that provides capabilities for a number of independent devices to communicate with each other over a common transmission-interconnected topology in geographic areas larger than those served by local area networks.

war-dialer   A program that dials a given list or range of numbers and records those that answer with handshake tones, which might be entry points to computer or telecommunications systems.

White Hat hacker   A hacker or professional security specialist who works to thwart the illegal efforts of Gray and Black Hat hackers.

worm   An independent program that replicates from machine to machine across network connections, often clogging networks and information systems as it spreads.

XML   eXtended Markup Language. Indicates structured information that is useful for identifying elements and data within a document.

Index